Self and Space
in the Theater
of Susan Glaspell

NOELIA HERNANDO-REAL

McFarland & Company, Inc., Publishers
Jefferson, North Carolina, and London

LIBRARY OF CONGRESS CATALOGUING-IN-PUBLICATION DATA

Hernando-Real, Noelia, 1977–
    Self and space in the theater of Susan Glaspell / Noelia
Hernando-Real.
        p.   cm.
    Includes bibliographical references and index.

    ISBN 978-0-7864-6394-7
    softcover : 50# alkaline paper ∞

    1. Glaspell, Susan, 1876–1948 — Criticism and interpretation.
2. Self in literature.   3. Space in literature.   I. Title.
PS3513.L35Z685 2011
812'.52—dc23   2011030560

BRITISH LIBRARY CATALOGUING DATA ARE AVAILABLE

On the cover: Ruth Everett as Nora Powers and Charles Daish as
Leon Whittaker in Glaspell's *Chains of Dew*, Orange Tree Theatre
production, 2008 (directed by Kate Saxon); photograph © Robert
Day); background image © 2011 Shutterstock

Manufactured in the United States of America

McFarland & Company, Inc., Publishers
  Box 611, Jefferson, North Carolina 28640
  www.mcfarlandpub.com

To Alejandro Hernando and Chany Real,
who taught me the importance of
having a voice and a place of one's own.
To Ana and Petra.

Table of Contents

Acknowledgments

I am very grateful to many people and institutions that throughout the years provided me with support, time and funds to work on this project. I am indebted to Antonia Rodríguez Gago, for her personal and intellectual support and guidance at the early stages of my research when I was a doctoral student at the Universidad Autónoma de Madrid (Spain). I wish to thank especially Bárbara Ozieblo, for sharing her enthusiasm, for her tireless commitment to Glaspell scholarship, and for her ready help with material from the start. I am also indebted to other members of the Susan Glaspell Society for their inspiring conversations on Glaspell, especially Martha C. Carpentier, Cheryl Black, J. Ellen Gainor, Linda Ben-Zvi, Sharon Friedman and Drew Eisenhauer. And to Sherry Engle, for her contagious energy and for offering me a home in New York City. I also thank Valentina Cook at the Glaspell Estate for her permission to quote from copyrighted material as well as from unpublished fragments and typescripts, and Peter Matson for his permission to quote from *The Comic Artist.*

My research could not have been possible without the financial support of the Spanish Ministry of Education (FPU Program, and Research Projects HUM 2004–00515 and FFI2009–2221), which financed the core four years of my research, and which throughout the years has sponsored my traveling to the many places Susan Glaspell takes me. These projects supported financially my research trips to Dublin, London, Delphi, New York and to several conferences, which contributed enormously to the development of this book. This research took me to many libraries, and the present work could not have been possible without the help I received along the way. I am particularly grateful to the librarians of the Biblioteca de Humanidades of the Universidad Autónoma de Madrid, Teresa Domingo and Mabel Redondo. Special thanks also to Stephen Crook and Philip Militto, librarians of the Henry W. and Albert A. Berg Collection of English and American Literature at the New York Public Library; to Dr. Isaac Gewirtz, curator of the Berg Collection;

and to the librarians of the British Library and the Theatre Museum Library, Blythe House Archive in London.

Several theaters must be mentioned here as well. Alex Roe, artistic director of the Metropolitan Playhouse, Alice Reagan, director of Performance Lab 115, and Sam Walters and Meg Dobson, director and press agent respectively of the Orange Tree Theatre. Their productions of Glaspell's plays were a force pushing me to pursue this project, and their efforts to help me gather all the permissions to reproduce photographs of their productions deserve my gratitude. I am grateful to Michelle DeBlasi, Sue Kessler and Robert Day for giving their permission to reproduce the photos from recent productions of Glaspell's plays.

Last but not least, thanks to all those who provided personal support and encouragement, especially my family, my friends and Félix, who probably know more about Susan Glaspell than they could ever have imagined.

Introduction

Susan Glaspell's appeal is first to the mind, and when she reaches the heart she does so completely and in a way not to be lightly forgotten by those who have yielded to its power [Royde-Smith 1926: 25].

Susan Glaspell (1876–1948), who today is still timidly acknowledged as the mother of modern America drama, was once "the great American thinker in dramatic form. She is the spirit and the mind and the soul of the real America of today, expressed in literature" (Rohe 1921: 18). Her plays were usually compared to those of master playwrights, such as Chekhov, Ibsen, Maeterlinck or Shaw. Indeed, her work alone was enough for a critic to justify the existence of the Provincetown Players, the little theatre group that she co-founded and that revolutionized the American stage in the second decade of the 20th century: "If the Provincetown Players had done nothing more than to give us the delicately humorous and sensitive plays of Susan Glaspell, they would have amply justified their existence" (Corbin 1919: np). But it was not only her plays that gave sense to the existence of the Provincetown Players, for Glaspell also constituted a galvanizing force behind the great writers of the group, such as Eugene O'Neill. An early friend of Glaspell described her as "my first heroine in the flesh, a glamorous presence of poetry and romance who fired one's imagination and made all glorious things seem possible. Her personality was a flame in the life of the student body, or at any rate in the group that felt themselves the social and literary leaders" (Fowler 1928: np).

Fortunately, although a lot of work is still to be done to relocate Glaspell for good in the place in American theater she once occupied but was banished from,[1] theater scholars recognize her merit, even if only for her acclaimed one-act *Trifles* (1916). Some of her plays (*Trifles*, *The Outside*, *Inheritors* and *The Verge*) were published in an anthology C. W. E. Bigsby edited in 1987, and which certainly encouraged critical works on Glaspell. But as Linda Ben-Zvi has asserted, after Glaspell's resuscitation in the late 1970s and early 1980s

1

through the groundbreaking works of Annette Kolodny (1986) and Judith
Fetterley (1986), "Glaspell criticism has moved to a second stage — assessing
the work of this important writer, no longer arguing her case" (1995a: 131).
Several works have appeared with the aim of assessing the work of Susan
Glaspell from different perspectives. After Veronica Makowsky's comprehensive *Susan Glaspell's Century of American Women: A Critical Interpretation of
Her Work* (1993) and Linda Ben-Zvi's much-acclaimed *Susan Glaspell: Essays
on Her Theater and Fiction* (1995), an anthology informed by feminist
thoughts, the interest in Glaspell multiplied. Besides the hundreds of articles
that have appeared since then, Barbara Ozieblo published the first complete
biography of Glaspell, *Susan Glaspell: A Critical Biography* (2000), after the
pioneer biography Marcia Noe had published in 1983 under the title *Susan
Glaspell: Voice from the Heartland*. The coming out of yet another biography
in 2005, Linda Ben-Zvi's *Susan Glaspell: Her Life and Times*, proves that
scholars are eager to know more and more about this author. Lately, excellent
critical works have also come out; J. Ellen Gainor's *Susan Glaspell in Context:
American Theater, Culture and Politics, 1915–48* (2001) was the first work to
focus exclusively on the theater of Susan Glaspell, providing a brilliant and
quite exhaustive account of the conditions, ideologies, and critical reception
surrounding Glaspell's dramatic works. Needed as they were, soon other
anthologies appeared, notably, Martha C. Carpentier and Barbara Ozieblo's
Disclosing Intertextualities: The Stories, Plays, and Novels of Susan Glaspell
(2006), which indeed has opened up the scope of critical work to include
Glaspell's fiction.[2]

Equally important are Carpentier's *Susan Glaspell: New Directions in Critical Inquiry* (2006), an anthology that gathers brilliant essays on Glaspell's
theater and fiction, Kristina Hinz-Bode's *Susan Glaspell and the Anxiety of
Expression: Language and Isolation in the Plays* (2006), which focuses intensively
on Glaspell's use of language "both as theme and as a medium of artistic
expression" in her plays (2006b: 5), and Barbara Ozieblo and Jerry Dickey's
Susan Glaspell and Sophie Treadwell (2008), the first book to deal with
Glaspell's plays from a theatrical rather than literary perspective. Quite surely,
the recent publications of *Her America: "A Jury of Her Peers" and Other Stories
by Susan Glaspell* (2010), edited by Patricia L. Bryan and Martha C. Carpentier,
and *Susan Glaspell: The Complete Plays* (2010), edited by Linda Ben-Zvi and
J. Ellen Gainor, will bring about a third wave in Glaspell scholarship. The
recent productions of Glaspell's plays, such as *Inheritors* by the Metropolitan
Playhouse in 2005, *The Verge* by Performance Lab 115 at the experimental
Ontological-Hysteric Theater in 2009, and a collection of Glaspell's shorts,
Chains of Dew and *Alison's House*, at the Orange Tree Theatre in 2008 and
2009, prove that Susan Glaspell still has something to say to contemporary

spectators. I firmly believe Glaspell speaks to us in the 21st century with a renewed voice.

The aim of this book relates to the new wave in Glaspell criticism and treats one of the core elements of theater: space. The present study is the fruit of a long path, of profound ruminations on the careful configurations of the stage spaces Glaspell constructs in most of her plays. Interestingly, Glaspell once said about her drama, "There is no use repeating old forms. We are changing and we should reflect that change" (qtd. in Rohe 1921: 18). A woman seriously committed to her times, who proclaimed her interest "in all progressive movements, whether feminist, social or economic," and who took "very active part" through her writing (qtd. in Rohe 1921: 18), employed the stage space to mirror the changes she saw around her or the changes that she thought should be made.

Glaspell's innovative use of space cannot be separated from her own origins nor from the group she wrote most of her plays for: the Provincetown Players. Glaspell's provincial origins and her familiarity with the things of the earth affected her writings. But the modern outlook of the Greenwich Village bohemian also permeates her works. Both the ideological basis sustaining the Provincetown Players and its material boundaries marked Glaspell's plays. One of the main aims of the Provincetown Players was to create a true and *native* American drama. As Edna Kenton says, "We lamentably lacked a native drama—'native' meaning always that which is spontaneous, free, liberated and liberating, flowing through and from and again into the people and nation concerned" (1997: 18). This is how "the Provincetown aim was different; it was unique. To found a native stage for native playwrights" (1997: 27). The ideology behind the Provincetown Players defended the idea that American stages needed true and non-commercial drama, and that this drama had to be *native*, reflective of the American reality, and in continuous dialogue with its people.

As many scholars have argued, all the artistic forms that had exploded in Europe invaded the United States and influenced its little theater groups through different means. Some European artists and theater innovators traveled to the United States to lecture or to help to produce plays.[3] New York–based clubs, such as Heterodoxy, the A Club or the Liberal Club, also contributed enormously to the spread of new forms of art in the United States. Not only did these groups invite European lecturers, but they also became centers where new ideas were discussed.[4] Art exhibitions contributed to the spread of new artistic forms as well. Sam Hume's scenic design exhibitions, Alfred Stieglitz's avant-garde photography at his 291 Fifth Avenue, and the Group of Eight, which mounted the most important avant-garde art show prior to the Armory Show in 1908 at the Macbeth Gallery, provided new conceptions of art and also influenced the changes in the American stage spaces. The most significant art exhibition of the times was the Armory Show, which was organized by the Association of American Painters and Sculptors, and took place in New York City from February 15 to March 15, 1913, and later moved to Chicago and Boston.[5] The publicity aroused by the Armory Show was so great that salonist Mabel Dodge, closely connected to many of the Provincetown Players, wrote in a letter to Gertrude Stein that this exhibition "is the most important public event that has ever come off since the signing of the Declaration of Independence, and it is of the same nature.... There will be a riot and a revolution and things will never be quite the same afterwards" (qtd. in Watson 1991: 172). Most members of the Provincetown Players attended and admired the exhibition. Hutchins Hapgood, present at the foundation of the Provincetown Players, talked about it as he "would treat a great fire, an earthquake, or a political revolution; as a series of shattering events — shattering for the purpose of re-creation" (1939: 341).

The Irish Players had a very direct impact on the North American stage. The financial lawyer and art lover John Quinn, a big lender to the Armory Show, sponsored American tours of Irish lecturers and of Lady Gregory's Players in 1911–1912.[6] Susan Glaspell and George Cram Cook attended one of the Irish Players' performances in Chicago, an experience Glaspell recorded in *The Road to the Temple*:

> The Irish Players. Quite possibly there would have been no Provincetown Players had there not been Irish Players. What [Cook] saw done for Irish life he wanted for American life — no stage conventions in the way of projecting with humility true feeling.
>
> Pictures too — the new things. The shock of new forms, and hence awareness of form, the adventure of the great new chance for expressing what has not been formed [2005: 180].

Many American artists also traveled to Europe and came back home to share and practice what they had learned from European artists. For instance, among others, Hutchins Hapgood traveled around Europe, and so did Susan Glaspell. Two other theater practitioners who shared their knowledge of the modern European theater and exercised a great influence on the development of the modern American theater were George Pierce Baker and Robert Edmond Jones. Baker, a teacher at Harvard, Radcliffe and Yale, taught students who later became famous playwrights, such as Edward Sheldon and Eugene O'Neill.[7] Far from the escapist fashion of Broadway plays, one of the main pieces of advice Baker gave his students was: "Write what you know to be true about your characters, and write nothing that you do not know to be true," and "Get your material from what you see about" (qtd. in Gelb and Gelb 2000: 431). Certainly, this piece of advice became pivotal in the creation of native American drama, as seen in the goals stated by the Provincetown Players.

The development of the "New Stagecraft" in the United States is indebted to Robert Edmond Jones. Jones studied with Max Reinhard in Germany, and was a follower of Edward Gordon Craig, Adolphe Appia and Jacques Copeau. Indeed, his ideas about the creation of atmospheric stage spaces instead of realistic ones are quite similar to the ideas of the great European masters. Jones agrees with them that "when the curtain rises, it is the scenery that sets the key of the play. A stage setting is not a background; it is an environment. Players act in a setting, not against it" (1985: 23–24). Moreover, for him, "a setting is not just a beautiful thing, a collection of beautiful things. It is a presence, a mood, a warm wind fanning the drama to flame. It echoes, it enhances, it animates. It is an expectancy, a foreboding, a tension. It says nothing, but it gives everything" (1985: 26). As do Craig and Appia, Jones also gives lighting a leading role for the configuration of settings: "We use light as we use words, to elucidate ideas and emotions. Light becomes a tool, an instrument of expression" (1985:118–119).

Robert Edmond Jones was present at the very birth of the Provincetown Players. On the mythical summer night of 1915 when the Provincetown Players were born, Jones created the first scenery for Neith Boyce's *Constancy* and Susan Glaspell and George Cram Cook's *Suppressed Desires*. The theatrical event that night took place in the house of Neith Boyce and Hutchins Hapgood, "a rambling old house by the sea, with a great living room large enough to hold a few players and a fair audience" (Kenton 1997: 19). The very first productions of the Provincetown Players were already based on the factors which became the hallmarks of the group: simplicity, suggestive settings, and maximum exploitation of basic resources. Though the career of Jones developed mainly in big theaters, he would collaborate with the Provincetown Players. For instance, Jones worked with Cleon Throckmorton to design the settings of Eugene O'Neill's great success *The Hairy Ape* (1921), and he was O'Neill's main designer throughout his career.

Jones was also present at another key moment in the evolution of the stage space in the United States, a moment that also marked the Provincetown Players: the Paterson Strike Pageant, a great performance that took place in New York on June 7, 1913. The event showed the amazing possibilities that the North American stage had, in terms of what it could offer both thematically and formally. The main aims were to raise funds for the New Jersey strikers, and to bring the situation of the workers to the attention of New Yorkers. It constituted "a full integration of labor politics with bohemian theatrics" (Stansell 2000: 183). As Brenda Murphy puts it, "The aim [of the Paterson Strike Pageant] was the kind of authenticity, simplicity, and unity of effect that Gordon Craig and the practitioners of the New Stagecraft were calling for in Europe" (2005: 6). The pageant, as Watson points out, inspired Villagers to pursue their own theatrical vocation. He states that, for instance, George Cram Cook and Susan Glaspell "were so deeply moved by the event that they stayed up late into the night imagining what America's new theater could become" (1991: 149).

The Provincetown Players were born out of the members' conviction that the American stage had to be renewed, and in spite of their financial scarcity, the Provincetown Players endeavored to configure the stage spaces of their plays departing from the rules of Broadway and pure Realism. The varied formal interests of the members, which ranged from Symbolism, through Expressionism, to Realism, had their way on the Provincetown Players' stage. Naturalism can still be sensed in apparently deterministic sets, such as Rita Creighton Smith's *The Rescue* (1918) and Eugene O'Neill's *Bound East for Cardiff* (1916). But other sets, realistic at first sight, are indeed employed to subvert the drama of milieu, the determinism that race, gender, or social class enacted on physical places and the characters placed in them, as in the case of Glaspell's *Trifles*. The productions of the Provincetown Players also include the expressionist *The Emperor Jones*, by Eugene O'Neill, the symbolist *The Game* by Louise Bryant (1916), and the harlequinade *Aria da Capo* (1919) by Edna St. Vincent Millay.

While the first stage of the Provincetown Players was the Hapgoods' cottage in Provincetown, their second Provincetown stage revealed the importance the group granted to the physicality of the stage space and their aim to create native drama. Romantically, Edna Kenton recalls the Wharf Theatre in the following terms: "Old fish houses must have been constructed originally with some idea of a native theatre in mind — they are so native themselves to shore and sea" (1997: 20). Mary Heaton Vorse, the owner of the wharf, recalls this theater and its stage space: "A hundred feet long and fifty feet wide.[8] It had a dark, weathered look, and around the piles the waves always lapped except at extreme low tide. There was a huge door on rollers at the side and another at the end which made it possible to use the bay as a backdrop" (1991: 118). Costumes, props, lights and setting were borrowed from the players' houses. But as Edna Kenton points out, the "possibilities [of the Wharf Theatre] were never exhausted; it gave a variety of settings that was really remarkable for so small a stage" (1997: 21). Glaspell also says that the stage "was in four sections, so we could have different levels, could run it through the big sliding-door at the back, a variety of set surprising in quarters so small" (2005: 204). The fact that the Provincetown Players did not have many financial resources did not deter their aims, since all that mattered was that they did have a stage. As Cook summarized the Provincetown Players' enterprise: "Money cannot create a thing like this — it is born of the spirit" (qtd. in Glaspell 2005: 239).

Susan Glaspell's recollection of how she came to write *Trifles* denotes the importance that the stage space had for her. Protesting against her husband's announcement that she had a play for the next bill, when she had not any and she did not feel able to write a play on her own, George Cram Cook simply told her: "You've got a stage, haven't you?" (2005: 205). The story of the birth of *Trifles* deserves being quoted in full.

> So I went out on the wharf, sat alone on one of our wooden benches without a back, and looked a long time at the bare little stage. After a time the stage became a kitchen,—a kitchen there all by itself. I saw just where the stove was, the table, and the steps going upstairs. Then the doors at the back opened, and people all bundled up came in — two or three men, I wasn't sure which, but sure enough about the two women, who hung back, reluctant to enter the kitchen. When I was a newspaper reporter out in Iowa, I was sent down-state to do a murder trial, and I never forgot going into the kitchen of a woman locked up in town. I had meant to do it as a short story, but the stage took it for its own, so I hurried in from the wharf to write down what I had seen. Whenever I got stuck, I would run across the street to the old wharf, sit in the leaning little theater under which the sea sounded, until the play was ready to continue. Sometimes things written in my room would not form on the stage, and I must go home and cross them out. "What playwrights need is a stage," said Jig, "their own stage" [2005: 205–206].

Though it might be possible that Glaspell's memories of how she came to write *Trifles* were biased by the love she professed for her deceased husband, for indeed *The Road to the Temple* is a hagiography of George Cram Cook, Glaspell's explanation of her writing process does reveal the importance of the stage in her dramatic works. As seen above, the stage is such a powerful element that it "takes hold" of Susan Glaspell, and the idea she had kept for a short story becomes a play first. And then the bare stage space inspired her creation. Alone in the Wharf Theatre, the bare stage began to be imaginarily equipped with pieces of furniture, till finally characters appeared. Glaspell followed Cook's idea about the relationships between the stage and the kind of plays the Players produced: "The needs of our plays have suggested this new form of theatre; the new theatre will, in turn, suggest new forms of plays" (qtd. in Glaspell 2005: 240).

When the Provincetown Players moved to New York City in 1916, the place they rented at 139 MacDougal Street was not much better than the Wharf Theater. As Kenton claims, "Even the most modest of sets, the barest of stages, gave on our stage area of twelve feet by ten feet six inches, room for hardly more than a trio of players"[9] (1997: 51). Ben-Zvi comments, "By the standards of other acting spaces in New York, 139 was Spartan; in fact, it wasn't a theater at all but a series of three rooms, two parlors and a dining room" (2005: 180). As for the Players' final move to 133 MacDougal Street in

1918, Kenton emphasizes, "No, we had few resources, few actors, no money. All we had was a stage" (1997: 120). A former storehouse, the Players established their theater at a "a four-story dwelling of pre–Victorian days.... The ground floor became the stage and the auditorium. They cleaned it up, built a sloping floor, and installed benches, uncushioned, unnumbered and without backs" (Deutsch and Hanau 1972: 45). The new stage "measured 22' 10"— by — 22' deep" (Ben-Zvi 2005: 209). And more importantly,

> We installed house lights and finally succeeded in shading them; we installed a "dimmer" so that they could fade slowly out; we installed an extraordinarily large and dependable switchboard; we decided that we could not afford "rose lights." We had a curtain at last that worked smoothly and did not excite the audience to cheers by its eccentric hitchings along its rods [Kenton 1997: 86].

Little by little, the plays of the Provincetown Players counted on more sophisticated means for the places represented on the stage space. This of course depends enormously on finances, but it must be highlighted that, apart from the imagination of its playwrights, the Provincetown Players included artists from different realms ready to put their minds to work even with minimum resources. Besides Robert Edmond Jones and Cleon Throckmorton, many other artists, and most of them women who rarely appear in the stories about the Provincetown Players, also collaborated to shape superbly the stage space, as Cheryl Black details in *The Women of Provincetown* (2002). Famous painters who worked with the Provincetown Players included Brör Nordfelt, William Zorach and Wilbur Daniel Steele. And between 1916 and 1919 women who designed scenery for the Provincetown Players included Marguerite Zorach, Alice Hall, Margaret Swain, Edith Haynes Thompson, Louise Heelstrom, and Flossette Florence Heaton.

The Provincetown Players reached a climax as far as scenery is concerned with the construction of a dome. If up to 1920 the group had managed to explore the possibilities of the stage spaces they had, almost exclusively counting on their own inventiveness and the plastic qualities of the painters working with the group, George Cram Cook marked a turning point in the history of theater in the United States with his dome. After reading Eugene O'Neill's *The Emperor Jones*, Cook became obsessed with the idea that this play required a dome. Cook himself built the plaster cyclorama, which swallowed all the money the group then had. "Thanks only to him, *The Emperor Jones* had his dome, Gene had his dome, we had our dome, New York had its dome — the only one in all its packed Rialtos — and the rest is history" (Kenton 1997: 126). The success of *The Emperor Jones* owes a lot to the dome, and curiously, O'Neill's success marked the decline of the Provincetown Players. More and more often members of the group, and above all O'Neill, received proposals to have their plays produced in flashing Broadway. But the creation of the dome also meant new possibilities for later plays, since for instance it was used again in Glaspell's *The Verge*, whose expressionistic set design was also widely acclaimed.

Some scholars have suggested the importance that Glaspell gives to the places she recreates onstage in order to understand her characters or the main themes of some of her plays. J. Ellen Gainor has asserted, "One key achievement of [Glaspell's] drama is her ability to make the stage environment come alive as another player in performance" (2001: 7). Scholars' analyses of Glaspell's use of space have focused on specific plays. For instance, Marcia Noe has briefly analyzed Glaspell's use of region as a metaphor in *Trifles*, *Inheritors*, *The Outside* and *The Comic Artist*. Space has also been the focus of some articles by Karen Alkalay-Gut or John Kanthak, who claims that in *Trifles* the kitchen space sets the play in motion.[10] J. Ellen Gainor has observed a "thematic relation between setting and action, as, for example, the kitchen environment of *Trifles* and the almost anthropomorphized homes" of *Bernice* and *Alison's House* (2001: 75). Gainor has also pointed out that *The Verge* "makes use of the dramatic potential of her set" (1989: 82). And Klaus Schwank, among other scholars, has observed that in *The Outside* there is a strong symbolic relationship between the setting and the action of the play.[11]

Nevertheless, though space usually has a place in other scholars' works on Glaspell, this analysis has not been deep or comprehensive enough. The aim of this book is to show the titanic importance of Glaspell's settings. This book offers a deep analysis of Glaspell's onstage places and the relationships she establishes between these places, the dramatic development of her plays, and her usually pent-up characters. More concretely, given Glaspell's insistence on the relations between her characters and place, this book explores the dramatic concept of geopathology, a novel concept never applied to Glaspell's plays before and which Una Chaudhuri coined in 1995 to account for a common phenomenon in modern drama. In dramatic geopathology action relies heavily on the configuration of characters as victims of location and on their need to escape. The concept of geopathology is introduced and discussed in Chapter 1, together with the key terms and principles followed in this book. As my analyses develop, Chaudhuri's concept is systematized and enlarged, and given that most of Glaspell's protagonists are women, the discussion pays close attention to female characters.

This book is based on a semiotic system of analysis that enables an understanding of all the elements on stage as signs and thus determinants of the process of creation of dramatic geopathology. Careful attention is paid to a task not fully completed in previous works on Glaspell, and this is Glaspell's construction of settings through non-dynamic elements (doors, walls, windows, pieces of furniture and stage properties) as well as through the dynamic elements, such as characters and their configuration through costume, their kinesic relations to the place where they are, and to other characters. The methodology is mainly dramatic, instead of theatrical, and aims to argue how Susan Glaspell elevates setting to its rightful place, along with character and plot.

In detailed analyses which form the core of this book, the scope of study covers most of Glaspell's plays,[12] especially those set at home. Four plays will not occupy in an exhaustive way the corpus of my analysis: *The People* (1917), *Woman's Honor* (1918), *Tickless Time* (1918) and *Free Laughter* (1919). Although *The People* and *Woman's Honor* take place in closed spaces, they do not seem to offer many possibilities for the study of dramatic geopathology. *The People* is set in the office of a radical magazine and *Woman's Honor* in the house of the Sheriff. Though set in a house, *Tickless Time,* also written in collaboration with Cook, is constructed on the outside, the garden of an artist couple in Provincetown, and it does not seem to achieve the geopathic atmosphere of the other plays. *Free Laughter*, a lost one-act recovered in the latest edition of Glaspell's complete plays, illuminates Glaspell's political rhetoric, amply analyzed regarding *Inheritors.* The plays that are carefully scrutinized in this study are: *Suppressed Desires* (1915), written in collaboration with George Cram Cook, *Trifles* (1916), *The Outside* (1917), *Close the Book* (1917), *Bernice* (1919), *Chains of Dew* (1922), *Inheritors* (1921), *The Verge* (1921), *The Comic Artist* (1928), written in collaboration with Norman Matson, *Alison's House* (1930), and *Springs Eternal* (1943).[13] These plays share some spatial qualities that set in motion the mechanism of dramatic geopathology, namely, the close relationship between the fictional onstage place, the kind of characters Glaspell puts in these places and the dramatic development of these plays, as well as stunning spatial language. The plays of Glaspell show her struggle to find new theatrical forms and to give voice to the American woman whose anxieties were as valid in the America of the first decades of the 20th century as they are in the global world of today.

1

Towards Geopathology in Glaspell's Modern Drama

I can take any empty space and call it a bare space. A man walks across this empty space whilst somebody else is watching him, and this is all that is needed for an act of theatre to be engaged [Brook 1972: 11].

From the very birth of theater, space has always enjoyed a central role. As Peter Brook implies in the quotation above, space is a compulsory element in the theatrical event. Besides audience and actor, the theatrical experience is impossible unless there is a site. Borrowing Joanne Tompkins's words, while elements such as lights and props may be additional, theater "cannot exist without space: there must be a location, a venue of some sort in which theatre can occur or, rather, take 'place'" (2003: 537). But in spite of the centrality of the stage space for theater, it is surprising that it has not been until recently that theater theoreticians have begun to focus on the relevance of space in theater and drama studies. In the latest theater theories, a growing interest in developing the concept of "space" has arisen, and the works of philosophers such as G. W. F. Hegel, Karl Marx, Friedrich Nietzsche, Sigmund Freud, Jean-Paul Sartre, Michel Foucault or Henri Lefèbvre, to name just a few, have been discussed in relation to the implications of space and place in theater. However, one of the main problems when adopting this terminology comes from defining these very terms. These definitions are the starting point for this chapter.

Space and Place: Basic Definitions

Traditionally, definitions of space have developed according to two opposed conceptions of its nature. Newtonians have treated space as a real entity to be filled by atoms and planets. The view of Leibniz, however, was that space was an idea rather than a thing. Drawing on this opposition, two schools of thought have been identified: "spatial separatists" and "chorologists." The school of "spatial separatists" holds "that the spatial questions are about a separate subject matter — space; and that this subject matter required a separate kind of law or explanation — *spatial laws* and *explanations*" (Sack qtd. in Kirby 1982: 4, emphasis in original). Spatial separatists see space as a separate virtual abstraction. On the other hand, chorology, a counterpart of chronology, focuses on "the production of specific places, areas or regions, parallels the production of specific times such as era or epoch in history" (Sack qtd. in Kirby 1982: 4). While chorologists can draw upon any method or body of knowledge to assist in their study, the relativist view of space understands space as an object of study in its own right that requires the development of its own spatial laws.

The relativist view of space has lately been strongly attacked. Philosophers such as Edward Soja and Henri Lefèbvre reject the assumption that space can exist as an independent artifact. This rejection has paved the way for new theories. Whether taking space as a virtual abstraction, as Soja does, or as a reality, as it is Lefèbvre's standpoint, the common thread is that there is a strong relationship between space and social relations. Regarding spatial definitions, Dean Wilcox sets the differences between space and place: "Place is viewed as defined, specific, occupied, whereas space offers the potential for occupation, which endows it with the infinite quality of emptiness" (2003: 543). That is, space is a more abstract term, and place is the precise configuration of space at a particular time. The concept of space potentially offers the schema for social relations, while place provides the actual possibility to analyze such relations. For instance, cultural geographers see places as truthful and unavoidable traces of human evolution, or as Donald Meinig puts it, place is "a definite area, a fixed [and experiential] location" dependent upon "experience and purpose" (1979: 3). Similarly, Lefèbvre points out "*(social) space is a (social) product* [that] serves as a tool of thought and of action," and "it is also a means of control, and hence of domination, of power" (1991: 26, emphasis in original). Scholars such as Michael Keith, Steve Pile (1993) and Doreen Massey (1998) support Lefèbvre's standpoint about space as a social product or producer, but they prefer using the term "place" when referring to definite cases. These scholars agree with Michel Foucault that "Space was treated as the dead, the fixed, the undialectical, the immobile" (1988: 70). Contrary to the standpoint of cultural geographers such as Meinig, I side with this other idea that space/place cannot be construed as a fixed and unmovable terrain, as a mere reflection of human actions and thoughts. Space/place must be regarded as open and changing, provoking changes as well as reflecting them. Even if one takes place as a determinate configuration of space in time, and thus fixed, this is momentary. The configuration of such a place can be changed. And if one considers the identity of a place, this cannot be taken as fixed either, since, as Massey has affirmed, no place holds a coherent, seamless identity. Places do not mean the same for every one (1998: 151–155).

Foucault has suggested that the ideologies and strategies of space are so varied that they trigger a whole geopolitics made up of "tactics and strategies deployed through implantations, distributions, demarcations, control of territories and organisations of domains" (1988: 77), and whose analysis will help "to capture the process by which knowledge functions as a form of power and disseminates the effects of power" (1988: 69). That is, an analysis of space will disclose the ideology and form of power that exist in space. As Lefèbvre wonders, "What is an ideology without a space to which it refers, a space which it describes, whose vocabulary and links it makes use of, and whose code it embodies?" Ideology, therefore, is primarily shaped as a discourse upon social space, as a means of intervention (1991: 44). Consequently, space and place are both agent and product of social relations, as well as immediacy and mediation, where power and ideology are exercised.

Space and Place in Theater and Drama

In theater there is interplay between fictitious and real spaces and places that all together give birth to the third space of theater. But if univocal definitions of space and place have been difficult to reach in the general terms of philosophy, geography or politics, their definitions in terms of theater are not an easy matter, either. Indeed, the concept of space in theater is used in several domains; it can refer to "a play's setting, a theatre venue, scenography, [and] the socio-cultural milieu beyond a theatre building, which nevertheless intersects with theatrical action, and is an elemental aspect of theatre itself" (Tompkins 2003: 538). Anne Ubersfeld's writings (1977, 1981) constitute an excellent starting point for a study of the functions of space in theater and for initial clarifications of spatial terms in this field. Ubersfeld insists on the centrality of space in theatrical communication and she makes a preliminary distinction between theater space (*lieu théâtral*) and theatrical space (*espace théâtral*). Theatrical space is a general notion to refer to the whole complex function of space in the theater, an abstraction of theater space, which is the place of performance, the theater building. Ubersfeld's distinction between these two terms, with her emphasis on theater space as the starting ground for the meaning created onstage and perceived by the audience, has consequently been of great use in performance studies.

Beyond this first distinction between theater space and theatrical space, Ubersfeld also defines what she calls dramatic space. As Ubersfeld claims, "The task of the semiologist in the area of theatre is to find, within the text, the spatialized or spatializable elements that will provide a mediation between text and performance" (1989: 103). The fictional place created in the text gives way to a scenic place, and these two places together form the dramatic space, which, borrowing Gay McAuley's words, "is made up of both textual and performance signs; it is accessible to the reader of the playtext and, differently manifested, to the spectator experiencing the space as constructed by the given production" (2000: 19). I agree with McAuley when he says "Dramatic space is more than fictional space, even in the expanded sociological sense that [Ubersfeld] gives to the scenic place, for it involves the dramatic geography of the action as a whole and is indeed a means of conceptualizing the whole action or narrative content of the play" (2000: 19).

In *Reading Theatre*, Anne Ubersfeld argues that the dramatic text provides a spatial matrix, which is constituted by every linguistic spatial reference in the text. Ubersfeld proposes a method of textual analysis which not only includes all textual references to place and space, but also verbs of movement, adverbial phrases related to space and the occupation of space, all mentions of objects that could potentially be present onstage, and all prepositional phrases. Thus, there are two different but connected sets in Ubersfeld's semiotic method to analyze the underlying system of space in a play. On the one hand, by reading the text, one should be able to draw in their minds the exact configuration of the stage space as conceived by the author. Firstly, walls, floor, windows and doors must be taken into account. The material boundaries created through these basic elements are important for the dramatic development of the play, since windows and doors connect the onstage space with the offstage, and they can thus be used to link the localized onstage fictional place with the localized offstage place. Every piece of furniture and stage property must also be located. Chairs, tables, books, lamps, and ashtrays will help to further define the spatiality of the play, either by giving information about the milieu, about the character's identity, or by the uses that characters will make of them. The second set of elements to be taken into account for a proper semiotic analysis of spatiality relates to characters. From costume to hair color, the outward appearance of the character helps configure and gives information about the place where a character is. Equally important for a sound semiotic analysis of space is the way the character occupies the fictional place.

The nomenclature to deal with a character's occupation of space is complex and extensively detailed. Keir Elam defines kinesics as "the movement of the body" in the fictional dramatic place (2001: 69). Erika Fischer-Lichte divides kinesics into mimic, gestural and proxemic signs (1992: 30–62). Mimics details the movements characters make with their faces. Facial expressions, as well as looks, are important spatial acts. It is not only that as long as a character moves in a determinate place everything they do is spatial, but also that the author describes the character smiling or blinking *in* that fictional place and *related to* that very place. Elam has observed the deictic importance of a character's gestures, understood as the movements a character makes without changing their location; gesture "constitutes the essential mode of *ostending* body, stage and onstage action in (actual) space" (2001: 73, emphasis in original). Proxemics, the final integrating element in kinesics, describes the character's movements across space. As has been said, the meanings of this kind of movement vary enormously: "Movement may be meaningful in itself, or it may function rather to construct meaningful spatial groupings (either between performers or between performer and object or element of the set), and these, in turn, may convey ideas about character and fictional situation" (McAuley 2000: 105). That is, the very act of moving from one end of the stage to the other has a meaning in the dramatic development of the play, even more if this movement means appearing on or disappearing from the stage.

There is also a meaning in the whole range of possible proxemic relations that can be established between characters, characters and props or pieces of furniture, and characters and speech as well. As McAuley points out, a different position or movement may give the words uttered a different meaning (2000: 107). And besides material boundaries, stage properties, pieces of furniture, and characters as integrating elements within the configuration of the stage space, Erika Fischer-Lichte theorizes that the use of lighting and non-verbal acoustic signs (sound and music) must also be taken into account for an analysis of spatiality onstage (1992: 110–128). Sound and music as theater signs are not only used in their relation to characters and their activities, but they are also signs of the fictional place. For instance, if a character sings, the song is not only revealing about the character's attitude (happy, sad, moody, etc.), but that very song may also refer to space, to movement, to objects in the fictional place or to things that are happening onstage.

Despite the centrality of the stage space in the theatrical experience, scholars do not share a precise vocabulary to deal with it. To my knowledge, the taxonomy McAuley provides in *Space in Performance: Making Meaning in the Theatre* is the most comprehensive and useful to the moment. This taxonomy, which compounds theoretical frameworks and a method deriving from semiotics, phenomenology, sociology and ethnography, enables scholars to explore the multiple functions of this spatial reality in the construction and communication of theatrical meaning. This is McAuley's taxonomy of spatial functions in theater:

I. The Social Reality
    Theatre Space
        Audience Space
                                    Performance Space
            Practitioner Space
        Rehearsal Space
II. The Physical/Fictional Relationship
    Stage Space
    Presentational Space
    Fictional Place
III.   Location and Fiction
    Onstage Fictional Place
    Offstage Fictional Place
            Unlocalized in relation to Performance Space
            Localized in relation to Performance Space
                Contiguous/Remote Spectrum
                Audience Off
IV.   Textual Space
V. Thematic Space

[2000: 25]

Beginning with the fifth category, and though listed separately, thematic space brings together all the spatial signs and all the spatial functions from the other categories that will be explained next. As McAuley believes, "meaning merges only when all these functions are seen structurally as parts of a whole" (2000: 33). McAuley suggests that theater and performance spaces, two subcategories of the first category in his taxonomy, are preconditions to the theatrical experience, and that as such they will help to organize the stage space for a definite performance. That is to say, the exact configuration of the stage space that the audience will see is the complex product of the multiple interrelations between text, performance space, the actors' bodies and features of the rehearsal space. The second group includes the basic terms to analyze space in theater. These are: stage space, which is "the physical space of the stage"; presentational space, which is "the physical use made of this space in any given performance"; and fictional place, which "refers to the place or places presented, represented or evoked onstage and off" (2000: 29).

McAuley's third category, Location and Fiction, is so complex and fundamental for both theater and drama, and has evolved so much throughout the centuries, that McAuley grants it a whole category to account for all its subdivisions. The onstage fictional place is the recognizable place represented on the stage space. I agree on the importance that offstage fictional places deserve in the construction of theatrical meaning. What happens offstage is many times as important as or even more important for the theatrical experience than what happens before the eyes of spectators. Hence the necessity to include subcategories within the offstage fictional place. The localized off-stage fictional places are those places contiguous with those onstage, only separated by a door, a stairway or a window; and the unlocalized offstage fictional place is part of the geography of a play, but it is not physically present or contiguous offstage. A close analysis of these evoked places will reveal their iconic value and functionality regarding the onstage fictional place and the very dramatic development of the play. And McAuley's fourth category, the textual space, refers to the wealth of spatial references that the playtext itself contains, and which can be analyzed by the semiotic means discussed earlier.

Out of the different categories to be taken into account in a study of spatial functionality in theater, and depending on where research emphases are placed, Michael McKinnie has identified the three theatrical approaches that currently focus on geography in theater: one strand of thought, best exemplified by Una Chaudhuri's works, considers space and place as dramaturgical principles. Another strand, led by Richard Schechner, focuses on the phenomenological aspects of space. And the third strand of thought, illustrated by Marvin Carlson, decodes space from a semiotic optics to reveal how this space was part of the production and reception of a theater event.[1] The two latter approaches focus on the physical configuration of the space of the theater auditorium and the impact of such configuration on the relationship established between performers and audience. The very architectural and economical skeleton of the site of the performance, as well as the location of such a site, which connotes a determinate socio-economical and cultural status of the audience, are key factors for the perception and reception of a theatrical event. Theatrical approaches such as the ones proposed by Schechner and Carlson tend to focus deeper on the two first categories McAuley provides, i.e., Social Reality and the Physical/Fictional Relationship. This book, however, takes Chaudhuri's approach as its starting point. Chaudhuri considers space and place as themes and principles in dramatic narratives, mainly relying thus on McAuley's third category, Location and Fiction.

Dramatic Geopathology

Staging Place: The Geography of Modern Drama, first published in 1995, constitutes a very original approach to the conceptualization of space in theater studies. Chaudhuri reunites the meaning and role of place both in the social and theatrical experience. For her, as for many theater semioticians, space is not the mere background against which characters act, but indeed the essential element of every theatrical representation. For Chaudhuri, the dramatic structure is a reflection of the "mutually constructive relations between people and space," between "*where* one is and how one experiences that place" (2000: xii, emphasis in original). Consequently, the configuration of the stage space, the set, with all the elements which constitute it, is "as much a part of the contemporary theatre as such standard elements as character, plot, and dialogue" (Wilcox 2003: 542–543). I share Chaudhuri's premise that "objects that clutter the realist stage ... are, for want of a better word, *characters* in the play. Their significance is not confined to the short circuitry of symbolism; rather they exercise a direct, unmetaphorical power in the formulation of the dramatic action" (2000: 80, emphasis in original).

Una Chaudhuri's interest in the analysis of the theatrical representation of space in its relation to dramatic development leads her to coin a very interesting term first used in medical studies: *geopathology*. This term stands for the configuration of a stage space where place becomes a problem for characters. Two principles integrate the dramatic discourse of geopathology. The first one is *victimage of location*, a principle that describes place as the protagonists' fundamental problem. This spatial problem leads the characters to acknowledge their need for the second principle, which Chaudhuri calls *heroism of departure*. According to this principle, a character gains full independence and fulfills the creation of their own identity by disentangling themselves from the oppressive place they were fixed to.

After analyzing several modern American dramatic pieces, Chaudhuri concludes that home is "the core concept of traditional geopathology" (2000: 174). And at the same time, home is central to the traditional American realist drama. Brenda Murphy has analyzed in a brilliant way this kind of drama, and has asserted, "The writers of psychological plays sought a more indexical effect, using the setting to focus the audience's attention on specific qualities in the character" (1987: 151). Whether for comic or serious purposes, many of the Provincetown Players' early plays are located in interior settings that help us to understand the characters that inhabit these rooms. For instance, in *Contemporaries* (1915) Wilbur Daniel Steele puts his poor characters in a dark underground room in a congested quarter to make his social denunciation that the poor are in a kind of symbolic hell. In Pendleton King's *Cocaine* (1916–1917), the attic apartment where the drug addicts Joe and Nora live is as messy as their lives. Moreover, the fear of being evicted from this place triggers the tragic development of the play when they attempt suicide. And Rita Wellman's *Funiculi Funicula* (1917–1918) is set in a small Washington Square apartment, which is packed with books and modernist paintings and smells of tobacco, to represent the protagonists' bohemian lifestyle. Nevertheless, this use of the domestic setting to show a character's identity is only a minimal part of the function of this kind of setting in geopathic drama, where a character's identity is utterly affected by the set, and not solely the other way around. As Bert O. States says, "Rooms, like all [theater] images, must eventually justify their presence, they must inhabit the people who inhabit them" (1985: 46).

The figure of home is closely linked to American mythologies and gives way to an exceptional serious paradox. American materialism triggers an endless search to build a house one can call home, but then this house may evoke a deadly sense of fixity that can lead to pathology. "Progress, the idea of moving on — is an idea we are committed to as Americans. Yet we are also trying ever again to hold on, to sink roots, to build homes," says Pfefferkorn (1991: 120). As early as 1845, Margaret Fuller, who influenced enormously the feminist movement in the United States with her *Woman in the Nineteenth Century*, already emphasized the parallel importance of home and expansion. She says, "A house is no home unless it contain food and fire for the mind as well as for the body," and "human beings are not so constituted that they can live without expansion. If they do not get it one way, they must another, or perish" (1999: 15). In Fuller's discourse, the physical construction of a house only achieves the status of home once this house provides its inhabitants with both material and intellectual possibilities. To be a home, a house must not only provide physical security, but it should also assure that its dwellers can develop their inner selves. Fuller also points out humans' inherent necessity to expand, understood both in physical and intellectual terms. As in the case of a house, humans need to transcend, if not physically (moving out of the house), at least intellectually, and hence the importance of "food and fire for the mind." As this early feminist says, the accomplishment of this expansion is so vital that if it is not achieved, one perishes. In the dramatic discourse of geopathology, the action focuses on the moments previous to this fatal fate, on the moments when the house limits characters' expansion.

The vast majority of Susan Glaspell's plays are also set in houses that can rarely be called peaceful havens. While Robert K. Sarlós has pointed out that the realistic settings of the early plays of the Provincetown Players are determined by the group's financial shortcomings, and adds that these settings "did little to visually stimulate spectators" (1982: 162), I believe that Glaspell's preference for domestic interior settings is a deeply thought out decision she adhered to even when the Provincetown Players had more economic resources and more sophisticated theaters. Glaspell, indeed, elevates setting to its rightful place. As Barbara Ozieblo has affirmed, Glaspell's home sets "exemplify the various routes that modernism took in the theatre" (2006b: 7). Glaspell employed her home settings as stimulating starting points to make the audience think for themselves. As a follower of the new ideas of Craig and Appia, even though Glaspell's experimentation with light and music might be defined as uneven, she adheres to these practitioners' defense that evocation and symbolical representation were more stimulating than exact reproductions of reality.

The central role that home settings have in the development of Glaspell's plays responds to her own preoccupation with the idea of home in her life. In one unpublished fragment entitled "On Home," Glaspell writes, "Home — more than a house. Home of the spirit. Home is what we want to be. Where we feel at ease with ourselves. Home is faith — purpose. Many are homeless. Must get back home."[2] Here one can identify one of the dramatic principles behind the figure of home in drama: "the humanist yearning for a stable container for identity — a home for the self, a room of one's own" (Chaudhuri 2000: 59). Glaspell probably agreed with her friend Mary Heaton Vorse's idea of home:

> A woman may not be different to her house. It is part of her and serves her — or it is her enemy. Your house can destroy you; the very way the doors swing may kill your peace of mind. A house must give you the blessing of peace and privacy. Your room must be a sanctuary against the world. Many a woman has gone stale, has had her family turn upon her the faces of enemies, because her room gave her no defense against them [1991: 32].

As Ben-Zvi has acknowledged, "Susan also liked the idea of ordering and protecting her space. Even in a temporary home in Delphi, in the 1920s, she experienced 'that sense of a household which one keeps safe, that it may move on its destined way,' calling such a feeling 'more than other satisfactions'" (2005: 146). But interestingly, Glaspell's dramatic homes are not the protected and ordered places she dreamt of, but the physical media to show what Chaudhuri calls "the desire to deterritorialize the self" (2000: 59), the media to put onstage the tropes of belonging and exile, and the places where, as Heaton Vorse stated, family "turn[s] upon the faces of enemies."

Gender and Home

Contemporary feminist theories about home are also very useful for the analysis of the geography of Susan Glaspell's plays, given that most of her protagonists are female characters usually trapped in houses they cannot call homes, and characters who fight for a space of their own. As far as gender is concerned, Una Chaudhuri believes,

> Unlike gender, however, national and ethnic identities are often derived from or directed toward a *geography*; there is a *location* of identity based on race, nation, ethnicity, language — in short, all the elements that together or in part designate the notion of culture — that is often absent from the discourse of gender [2000: 3, emphasis in original].

Paradoxically, later Chaudhuri suggests the relationship between home, domesticity and women and its theatrical and dramatic relevance, though she never takes this point any further. At the same time that she acknowledges the work that feminist scholars carry out on the figure of home and gender politics, Chaudhuri highlights that modern humanism was inaugurated on the stage "by a decision not to remain in a home as artificial and stifling as a doll's house" (2000: 7). Indeed, the dramatic discourse of home shows that gender does have a geography, and that there is a location of gender identity. Henri Lefèbvre asserts that human beings know that they are active participants in space, and that their actions will give way to the whole net of social relations (1991: 294). As Andrew Kirby affirms, "In a very real sense, *where* you are dictates *what* you are" (1982: 72, emphasis in original). And more specifically, Judith Butler has claimed that gender is performative, "constructed by the reiteration of norms" (1993: 95). In *Gender Trouble*, Butler affirms that,

> gender is an identity tenuously constituted in time, instituted in an exterior space through a *stylised repetition of acts.* The effect of gender is produced though the stylisation of the body and, hence, must be understood as the mundane way in which bodily gestures, movements, and styles of various kinds constitute the illusion of an aiding gendered self [1999: 179, emphasis in original].

It is very interesting to notice that Butler includes the term "space" in her discourse on performativity. It is not only through the repetition of daily acts that gender is assumed, but also (and very importantly) that repetition of acts is always enacted in places, and places are also subdued to norms. Referring to the interplay between identity politics and location, Liz Bondi affirms succinctly, "'Who am I?' becomes 'Where am I?'" (1993: 98). Gender identity is instituted and constituted in space.

The emphasis that contemporary feminist geographers put on places and how these are gender-biased enhances this issue as a highly essential one for the study of dramatic geopathology. In *Perceiving Women* (1975), the Ardeners also agree that women have a different space, which they labeled "the wild zone." As Chávez-Candelaria explains, the Ardeners labeled women's separate space as a "zone" "to denote both its *physiology-derived* bounded space, as well as to capture the idea of the learned, *stereotype-derived* female space defined by the dominant structure" (1997: 249, emphasis in original). Chávez-Candelaria writes,

> The "wild zone" thesis thus identifies a fundamental paradox of female identity: on the one hand, a distinct female experiential, cultural space derived from an unrestricted ("wild") existence unmediated by inimical, imposed definitions of identity, and on the other the restricted women-space defined by and located within the englobing historical patriarchy without recognition of women's human potential or achievement [1997: 249].

Might thus the figure of home, the core of concept of geopathic drama, be considered a "wild zone"? McDowell and Sharp have stated that in the West the social construction of home has erected this figure "as a place of familial pleasures, a place of leisure and rest — for men a sylvan and tranquil respite from the rigours of the city or the workplace and for women a supposedly safe haven" (1997: 263). Nevertheless, for feminists scholars, "home may be as much a place of conflict (as well as of work) as of repose" (Massey 1998: 11), and this conflict may become greater once gender politics come into play. Soja and Hooper affirm that hegemonic power "actively *produces and reproduces difference* as a key strategy to create and maintain modes of social and spatial division that are advantageous to its continued empowerment," and that "otherness" is assigned by a means of social-spatial differentiations and divisions (1993: 184–185, emphasis in original).

Referring specifically to the geography of home, several scholars have discussed the uneven distribution of spaces and their gendered assumptions. Home has been constructed as woman's place, the source of stability, reliability and authenticity. "Home is where the heart is (if you happen to have the spatial mobility to have left) and where the woman (mother, lover-to-whom-you-will-one-day-return) is also" (Massey 1998: 180). And as D.A. Leslie says, "Feminine identity has tended to be more spatially confined than that of men. Whereas male subjectivity is defined in terms of control over space, female subjectivity becomes that which must be controlled by being bounded: the house itself may be seen as a system of control and surveillance" (1997: 304). In this manner, independent of whether women actually appropriate the house or not, that is, whether the house is woman's place or where woman is placed, the truth is that the figure of home consolidates female identity and can thus be read under the paradigm of the Ardeners' "wild zone" thesis. The figure of home identifies the spatial "paradox of female identity," since home simultaneously may restrict and confer her identity.

The link between home and the female has played a vital role in literature and literary theory. As Rosemary George states, "In literature and literary theory, until quite recently, most considerations of the home have occasioned examination of the status of women. The association of home and the female has served to present them as mutual handicaps, mutually disempowering" (1999: 19). This identification of women with home has led to a very important issue in the Western literary tradition: the differentiation between public and private spheres. Home, the private, woman's place, has thus appeared in literary pieces with very different goals.

On the one hand, in Virginia Woolf's "room of one's own" the private space appears as women's possibility to express their identities, and Woolf's influence upon women writers has a long history that includes Susan Glaspell.

On the other hand, the image of the room of one's own can also have a negative reading. Taking into account another of the most exploited feminist spatial metaphors, the attic, a room of one's own can also be negative when this is a room one has not created for herself and when she is forced to live there. The compulsory dwelling is inhabited by one of Woolf's fears: "I thought how unpleasant it is to be locked out; and I thought how it is worse perhaps to be locked in" (2000: 21).

After scrutinizing this crossroads between gender and home, Isabel Velázquez has called our attention to the possibility that although the house, the home, is a woman's place, its owner has usually been the man (1995: 124). Furthermore, the very architecture of the house is used to reflect power differences. Traditionally, rooms such as libraries, billiard rooms or studies were considered men's rooms, "less likely to be open to women than women's rooms to men," namely, drawing rooms and kitchens (Spain 1992: 112–114). At this point, it seems sensible to question the necessity of maintaining the traditional dichotomy between public and private spaces, a division into spheres respectively assigned to masculinity and femininity. Given that the private is controlled by the same social definitions working in the public arena (woman's roles, socializing practices, power relations, etc.), the long-held opposition between public and private spheres reveals itself as an artificial and deceiving trick.

This dichotomy is, borrowing Villegas-López and Domínguez-García's words, "inherently oppositional and hierarchical, and supports an ideology that is both patriarchal and capitalist at heart" (2004: 11–12). Sharing this point, I also consider dramatic homes as places of dramatic social interaction, where the same hegemonic power operates in the public and the private simultaneously. And as disclosed in the subsequent chapters of this book, hierarchization and gendered spatial assignments within houses are easily detectable in Susan Glaspell's drama through her preference for interior settings.

Geopathology, Realism and Feminism

Una Chaudhuri has accounted for the usefulness of the realistic interior setting for characterization and for setting the play in motion regarding dramatic geopathology. But before entering into Chaudhuri's catalogue of the dramatic elements that configure a geopathic setting, the convergence of the realistic domestic setting and geopathology must be further questioned. As is well-known, realistic settings were used to prove the environmental determinism that explained a character's psychological analysis. But the realistic theatricalization of the literalized home reveals "the crisis of its concept. One sign of the crisis is the violent ambiguity, in realism, of spatial signs" (Chaudhuri 2000: 8). As William Demastes has claimed, Realism has a "chameleon-like existence, changing colors at almost every turn and blending into a context appropriate to whatever needs a particular practitioner or critic deems appropriate for his or her goals" (1996: ix–x). Patricia Schroeder, nonetheless, provides a satisfactory definition of realistic theater:

> A realist play can thus be defined as one that reflects a specific social milieu in a particular era; that develops according to cause-and-effect sequences of actions; that ends with the resolution of some problem; that includes characters who react to the environment and action in complex and clearly motivated ways; and that attempts to convince the audience by all available theatrical means that the onstage action is, in fact, real (not fictitious) and occurring before them as they watch [1996: 17].

But as Chaudhuri affirms, in many plays which have been considered purely realistic, such as Ibsen's *A Doll's House*, spatial signs go beyond their literal deterministic meaning, coming closer to the modernist enhancement of space as a figure of its own, as happens with Nora's famous slamming of the door.

Similarly, most of Glaspell's dramatic works, except *The Verge* and *The Outside*, have usually been considered realistic. This long-held conviction has its origins in Gerhard Bach's early essay "Susan Glaspell: Provincetown Players," where he describes three phases of dramatic development in the Provincetown Players' existence: "the initial phase of social realism, leading to a phase of realism vs. symbolism (or the realistic prose play vs. the symbolistic verse play), leading again into the last phase of renewed social realism interspersed with experiments in expressionism" (1978: 36). Bach concludes that Glaspell's experimentation with dramatic form relied more heavily on ideology and characterization than on the dramatic structure itself. Nevertheless, as a few scholars have more recently argued, and as Hinz-Bode usefully summarizes, in her plays Glaspell acknowledged the wide range of artistic answers of her times:

> The realists' project of enacting stories of self-empowerment, the determinist stance of naturalism, the ecstatic insistence on a truth beyond surface reality that drives the works of German expressionism, the retreat into the individual consciousness evident in modernist aesthetics, the socialist and Marxist explanations of the world, and the intellectual and philosophical position that must fall silent in the atrocities of modern warfare and terror [2006c: 90].

One of Glaspell's dramatic hallmarks is, actually, the way she fuses the representational with the non-representational. This book, about Glaspell's use of space and its role in shaping her characters' identity, shows that

Glaspell's rooms are not merely representational and deterministic. On the contrary, her interior settings carry the more contemporary belief that identities are in a constant process of change, that they are "unfixed, contested and multiple" (Massey 1998: 5). The characters in Glaspell's dramatic works, as discussed in subsequent chapters, engage in a dialectical and proxemic dialogue with place, reworking, revising and altering the meaning and appearance of the fictional onstage places they inhabit.

Feminist dramatic theories are very useful in analyzing how Glaspell departs from Realism and her use of interior settings to explore dramatic geopathology. Given that Glaspell herself claimed that, as seen in the introduction, she was "interested in all progressive movements, whether feminist, social or economic" (qtd. in Rohe 1921: 18), a materialist feminist approach[3] seems the most appropriate perspective from which to explore the interplay between space and identity in her plays. It is extremely important to bear in mind the specific historical features surrounding Glaspell's life, her status as a bohemian white middle-class American woman, because her own context, brilliantly examined by J. Ellen Gainor in *Susan Glaspell in Context*, led Glaspell to write about specific kinds of women who belong to a particular class, race, and gender, and to write plays asking for a radical transformation of social and political structures. Edna Kenton, who joined the Provincetown Players in 1916, defined feminism as "a troop of departures from the established order of women's lives" (qtd. in Murphy 2005: 36), a definition Glaspell probably shared. The women of the Provincetown Players participated in the Feminist Alliance, a Greenwich Village organization that in 1914 declared that, "feminism is a movement, which demands the removal of all social, political, economic, and other discriminations which are based upon sex, and the award of all rights and duties in all fields on the basis of individual capacity alone" (qtd. in Murphy 2005: 37). Cheryl Black has explained how the women of the Provincetown Players, as active members of the feminist movement, used theater with this same goal.[4]

The materialist feminist perspective of this study is based upon my agreement with materialist feminist Michéle Barret, who says that "an analysis of gender ideology in which women are always innocent, always passive victims of patriarchal power, is patently not satisfactory" (1985: 81). Borrowing Jill Dolan's description of materialist feminism, I think that Glaspell makes us "look at women as a class oppressed by material conditions and social relations," and that she attempts "to denaturalize the dominant ideology that demands and maintains such oppressive social arrangements" (1988: 10–11), while never holding up the useless flag of women's assumed passiveness, innocence, and powerlessness.

The dramatic history of the compatibility of Realism and feminism is extensive. As many scholars have already pointed out, the debate on what makes a play feminist and on the appropriateness of using what is considered a "male form," that is, Realism, began around the 1930s. Critics such as Catherine Belsey, Sue-Ellen Case, who defines Realism as "the prisonhouse of art for women" (1988: 124), Jill Dolan, and Jeanine Forte, among many others, find the usage of this form intolerable from a feminist point of view.[5] They have argued that the classical conception of this form helps to maintain the fixity of the patriarchal world because this form tends to represent the reality and thus the power structure men usually hold in real life. For instance, Judith L. Stephens has claimed that Glaspell's adoption of standard dramatic conventions leads her to "reinforce the status quo" (1990: 285). According to Stephens, the fact that in *Trifles* the female characters are realistically placed inside the kitchen throughout the play makes the audience perceive that the kitchen is inevitably women's place. Nevertheless, this book discusses how in her plays Glaspell explores the feminist possibilities of Realism, subverting this form at the same time that she subverts the status quo.

Critics such as Elin Diamond, Judith Barlow, J. Ellen Gainor, and Patricia Schroeder have counter-argued the dismissal of Realism with feminist purposes.[6] The most simplistic defense of the use of Realism with feminist purposes, which is still totally logical, is that women playwrights may use this form to put onstage what must not be repeated in real life: "Depicting what is can help create what should be," says Schroeder (1989: 112). More interestingly, these critics also defend the use of Realism because "in realistic dramas, their realism adapted in sometimes subversive ways that merit detailed examination from a feminist standpoint" (Schroeder 1996: 8). Recently, feminist theater scholars have focused on feminist means of subversion of the theory of the "male gaze." The male gaze, a term made current in the 1980s by such feminist theorists as Laura Mulvey, Sue-Ellen Case, Teresa de Lauretis, and Jill Dolan, "describes as the controlling perspective of a theater performance that of the male spectator," usually white and middle-class, "who identifies with the male hero and sees women as passive beings created to support the male or as pretty toys 'dolled' up to heighten his viewing pleasure" (Burke 1996: 3). As many feminist critics believe, Realism is the best means of conforming to the desires of the male gaze, given that this form tends to represent the same subjugation and objectification of women in real life (Dolan 1988: 106). Glaspell, a Brechtian *avant la lettre*, makes use of a technique of estrangement later known as alienation-effect, whose aim, according to Brecht, consists of turning the object of attention "from something ordinary, familiar ... into something peculiar, striking and unexpected" (1997: 143), or as feminist critic Elin Diamond says, "to denaturalize and defamiliarize what ideology makes seem normal, acceptable, inescapable" (1988: 85). By analyzing Glaspell's plays, one discovers that the apparently realistic home settings she creates are used to denounce the problems triggered by women's entrapment in homes they do not want to be in, questioning their subjugation and objectification, and dismantling the male gaze.

The rooms Glaspell presents onstage do not respond to traditional mimesis but to feminist mimesis, as defined by Elin Diamond:

> A feminist mimesis, if there is such a thing, would take the relation to the real as productive, not referential, geared to change, not to reproducing the same. It would explore the tendency to tyrannical modeling (subjective/ideological projections masquerading as universal truths), even in its own operations. Finally, it would clarify the humanist sedi-mentation in the concept as a means of releasing the historical particularity and transgressive corporeality of the *mimos*, who, in mimesis, is always more and different than she seems [1997: xvi].

In her plays Glaspell takes the outside world not as an unmovable reference to copy, but as the ground for her feminist strategy. Glaspell's strategy is mimicry, "a representation of definition," "mimesis without a true referent — mimesis without truth" (Diamond 1989: 64). Though apparently her rooms stand for copies of real rooms from the outside world, inside these very rooms Glaspell keeps and shows how their spatial constituents, their walls, props, pieces of furniture, and even characters muffle the ideological apparatus of this outside (patriarchal) order. Most of the geopathic female characters in Glaspell's drama are the victims of gendered power relations that usually subdue women to men. And Glaspell uses the rooms they inhabit to display and reinforce these female characters' malady. Likewise, if an analysis of geopathology in Susan Glaspell's drama will uncover Glaspell's denouncing of power relations in the outside world, it is also in the rooms she puts onstage that the dramatic solution to geopathology will come, as the final chapter of this book discusses.

The Imagery of Dramatic Geopathology

Related to the home setting, Chaudhuri renders the images she considers pivotal in geopathology. As this scholar says, it is the very physicality of the rooms represented onstage that triggers the thematics of geopathology: "The structure of the room as a boundaried space, capable of keeping out as well as keeping in, allows it to function as a referent for such thematics as danger versus safety, infantile sexuality versus oedipal threat, political passivity versus active resistance" (2000: 93). In keeping with the American dichotomist yearning for a home but for movement at the same time, Chaudhuri claims that homes in modern drama are represented as either shelters or prisons, or both at the same time. As she says, "its status as both shelter and prison, security and as entrapment — is crucial to its dramatic meaning" (2000: 8).

In geopathic drama the belief that home is the place to anchor roots and to construct a fixed identity, and that home is the place that highlights the character's need for exile and exploration of new identities, coexist. Borrowing Massey's words, the home setting can be used in modern drama to reflect both "the comfort of Being" and "the project of Becoming" (1998: 117–124). Similarly, Chaudhuri explains how the experience afforded by geopathic drama "codes the world subjectively and binarily: here versus there, outside versus inside, belonging versus not belonging" (2000: 139). That is, the typical geopathic character wants to be there when they are here, outside when they are inside, and they want to belong when they do not, or vice versa. Closely linked to these images the dramatic representations of homecomings — usually failed — and dislocations appear. I agree with Chaudhuri's belief that the action of homecoming is used in modern drama "not to recuperate identity but rather to stage the difficulties, even impossibility, of such recuperation" (2000: 92). For instance, in Harold Pinter's *The Homecoming* (1965), Teddy comes back home only to face the shocking behavior of his family and to see how his wife abandons him to stay forever in the house as a powerful prostitute. With this play, Pinter reverses the traditional idea of homecoming, turning this figure into a device that reveals his geopathic representation of home.

The binary sets exposed above, as well as the figure of the failed homecoming, reveal another key issue in geopathic drama: the revision of the American Myth of Mobility, one of the main myths of American spatiality. A determinant milestone in the American Dream, and more specifically in the discourse of the Frontier Myth, the Myth of Mobility assured the infinite possibility to explore, to conquer, to progress. But as will be shown later, this foundational myth is used in geopathic drama to starkly confront the realistic closed home settings. Moreover, this figure is also questioned through the presence of immigration. Chaudhuri aptly argues that immigrant characters usually appear in geopathic drama to enlighten the binaries exposed before, since these characters do not belong to the place where they appear (2000: 174). Immigrant characters are left out; they are eternal others who wander endlessly while dreaming of their real place. As Rosemary George observes, "The subject status of the immigrant, especially that of the non-white immigrant to the west, forces another literary reinscription of the self and of home" (1999: 8).

Other key images and themes that can help to detect a geopathic home are generation confrontations, alcoholism, garbage, the destruction of nature, and the buried child. Given that home is usually equated with family, it seems sensible to think that in the geopathic home the concept of family could also be pathological. The most usual kind of confrontation is the generational problem: parents against children. When family is the source of confrontations, usually each generation supports a different and opposed point of view. In geopathic drama, this conflict is expressed in spatial terms. Family quarrels and fights take place within the walls of the house, and as the family members are forced to stay within these walls, a catch-22 situation is maintained. Plays such as Arthur Miller's *Death of a Salesman* (1948), Eugene O'Neill's *Long Day's Journey into Night* (1940), and Sam Shepard's *Buried Child* (1978) exemplify this common theme in American drama.

The pathological family is also commonly associated, according to Chaudhuri, with problems of alcoholism. O'Neill's *Long Day's Journey into Night* masterfully exemplifies both. Many times throughout the play Edmund and James drink heavily; firstly, to get away from the problems in the house, and secondly, they drink while they have arguments with the patriarchal figure. Similarly, the protagonists in Edward Albee's *Who's Afraid of Virginia Woolf* (1962) also drink to get away from the reality they cannot face: that their house, their family, is ruined, that the lie they had created to fulfill their sense of a family, their imaginary son, cannot not be sustained any longer. And the more they drink, the more they reveal the pathology of the place they inhabit. In extreme cases, alcoholism conjoins physical violence, and not just verbal violence. In *Buried Child*, the way the father is terrified as he has his head shaved again and again, causing him serious injuries, is a clear instance.

Significantly, alcohol addiction is the only factor Chaudhuri lists that Glaspell consciously avoids in her plays. A possible reason behind this is Jig Cook's heavy drinking. Glaspell's biographers Barbara Ozieblo and Linda Ben-Zvi tell of the many times that Glaspell had to mother her drunk husband, as she would later do with Norman Matson. Glaspell asserts in *The Road to the Temple*: "A woman who has never lived with a man who sometimes 'drinks to excess' has missed one of the satisfactions that is like a gift — taking care of the man she loves when he has this sweetness as a newborn soul" (2005: 252). Indeed, Glaspell saw drinking as a positive experience for the healthy growth of the Provincetown Players. Wine was never short at the meetings of the group, as it helped the group to "become one," and when they were running short of liquor, Cook would speed up: "'Give it all to me,' Jig would propose, 'and I guarantee to intoxicate all the rest of you.' He glowed at these parties" (Glaspell 2005: 212). As another of Glaspell's biographers has noted, "Susan was usually sympathetic to people who had problems with alcohol, perhaps because she herself did" (Noe 1983: 71). Nevertheless, though she enjoyed drinking and saw positive qualities in inebriation, Glaspell was aware of the fact that excessive consumption was not something to be proud of. One of Glaspell's greatest worries after publishing *The Road to the Temple* was that Cook's and her family might "make a fuss" over the excessive drinking she describes in her book (Glaspell qtd. in Ben-Zvi 2005: 315). Consequently, alcohol ingestion as a factor to detect a geopathic character is only suggested in one of her plays, *Alison's House*, where Eben shows his willingness to drink to forget his painful reality: that he cannot abandon his house and his wife to live the life he dreams of.

Images of garbage and the destruction of nature coincide with the depiction of place as a destructive force. When Chaudhuri points to images of garbage in geopathic drama, she refers in more general and symbolic terms to the idea that "America exemplifies a kind of prosperity whose history has already been written and whose residue is trash" (2000: 158). That is, if the land of opportunity has but garbage now, it can hardly offer nice places to inhabit. But reading images of trash in realistic settings, it could be said that this also symbolizes that the figure of home seen onstage can hardly be a healthy container of the self, given that disorder reigns all around and garbage stinks. In keeping with the relationship Chaudhuri establishes between the figure of America and trash, the figure of the destruction of nature answers to the dramatic representation of men's desire to control space, triggering the deadly image of a decaying world. Both figures appear metaphorically in Glaspell's plays.

The last figure Chaudhuri proposes to find a geopathic dramatic place is the image of the buried child, which Shepard epitomizes in his namesake play. The buried child is often used in modern American drama to point out the consequences of a place that triggers the death of the most fragile human beings. This image, which Chaudhuri defines as "privileged" and "obsessional," is deeply rooted in the modern American drama, and is employed to show the buried child's circumstance in terms of ill placement (2000: 18–19).

In the following chapters, Chaudhuri's semiotic approach to the analysis of dramatic geopathology is applied to Glaspell's plays. For this purpose, the images she proposes to configure a geopathic dramatic home are expanded and analyzed. Beginning with Glaspell's revision of some America geomyhtologies, the next chapters detail the way Glaspell constructs what can be called geodichotomies, that is, binary oppositions between home as shelter and prison, in and out, here and there, and belonging and not belonging. The generation conflict, the status of immigration, and the buried child will be examined throughout this book as well. And the final chapter discusses other feasible escapes from *victimage of location* beyond *heroism of departure*. In many cases Glaspell presents different means by which characters negotiate their identities with place, overcoming, quoting Chaudhuri, "the power of place," without being forced to abandon it.

2

American Geomythologies Revisited as Part of Dramatic Geopathology

Since its foundation the United States has relied on its geomythological configuration. America was seen by many as the Promised Land, the place where they could settle down, grow, and enjoy all the liberties the old Europe had denied them. The still valid, though much attacked, American Dream heavily relies on this idea that America is a country of opportunity, a place where chances to improve await across the road, a place of regeneration where everybody can move freely as golden opportunities of success wait around the corner. The present chapter on Susan Glaspell's revision of American geomythologies as part of dramatic geopathology focuses extensively on the American Myth of Mobility, treated simultaneously with other related American geomythologies, for their conjoined effect on contributing to the dramatic configuration of victimage of location.

One of the most obvious clues that leads one to start considering whether a character might be geopathic can be found in an analysis of that character's freedom or restriction regarding movement inside or outside places. As has been said, American literature has erected "the literary archetype of the American hero as a man in motion" (Chaudhuri 2000: 125). A look at Herman Melville's *Moby Dick* (1851) and Mark Twain's *The Adventures of Huckleberry Finn* (1885) suffice. Nonetheless, the American construction of travel as a powerful movement of adventure sometimes gets a negative transposition in its transfer to modern American drama. Plays such as Arthur Miller's *Death of a Salesman*, Sam Shepard's *Buried Child* and Tennessee Williams's *The Glass Menagerie* include a revision or critique of the American Myth of Mobility within the physical configuration of stage spaces which turn out as dramatically geopathic. Plays such as the ones mentioned are constructed upon "a painful sense of physical limitation" (Chaudhuri 2000: 126), and reveal the

31

impossibility of the American Myth of Mobility for the victims of place, those characters who are not entitled to pursue this myth inherent to the very land they inhabit.

In Glaspell's plays, the American Myth of Mobility appears as an appalling lie, especially for her female characters. As Doreen Massey claims, "The mobility of women does indeed seem to pose a threat to a settled patriarchal order" (1998: 11). Furthermore, an analysis of the Myth of Mobility promises to account for what has been called "Power geometry," a paradigm Massey explains as follows:

> For different social groups, and different individuals, are placed in very distinct ways in relation to these flows and interconnections. This point concerns not merely the issue of who moves and who doesn't, although that is an important element of it; it is also about the power in relation *to* the flows and the movement. Different social groups have distinct relationships to this anyway differentiated mobility: some people are more in charge of it than others, some initiate flows and movement, others don't; some are more on the receiving-end of it than others; some are effectively imprisoned by it [1998: 149, emphasis in original].

That is, an analysis of who moves and who does not, who initiates a flow and who does not, and who, as seen above, is imprisoned, will reveal that "mobility, and control over mobility, both reflects and reinforces power" (Massey 1998: 150). The beginnings of the Myth of Mobility, rooted in the American Frontier/Pioneer Myth, already implied women's abjection from this myth. This was a male adventure, and women, among other groups, "were left out of the initial dream" (Busby, Mogen and Bryan 1989: 6). This early American geomythology, the Frontier Myth, is thus charged by the power of gender politics. As Ben-Zvi states, "She is clearly *other*. If he is actor, she is passive recipient of his action; if he breaks new frontiers, she secures familiar ground; if he seeks adventure, she seeks security" (1989: 220, emphasis in original). Hence, reflecting on the implication of the Pioneer Myth seems pivotal in dramatic geopathology, since female characters, according to this myth, are mere unmovable accessories, secluded elements in a myth that, ironically, celebrates movement. One of the consequences of this myth in literary history, as Busby, Mogen and Bryan have noted, is that many women writers have used and inverted the same symbolic structures and images of the Frontier Myth with the aim to demonstrate women's exclusion from or even their fear regarding the frontier experience (1989: 6).

The Pioneer Myth always exerted a great influence on Susan Glaspell's works. Being herself the inheritor of a pioneer family, she admired her ancestors, and especially pioneer women. Talking about *Inheritors* in a 1921 interview, Glaspell acknowledges this influence: "My grandmother made the trip from Maine to Iowa in a prairie schooner. As a little girl she knew the Indians. With what regret I think that although I used to hang upon her words when she told of pioneer days and of pioneer upbuilding of a democracy I did not learn more from her" (qtd. in Rohe 1921: 18). The presence of pioneer women in Glaspell's plays constitutes her tribute to the stories she heard as a little girl, to those pieces of history she regrets not having paid closer attention to. Glaspell also had the influence of the stories about his ancestors that George Cram Cook used to tell, and which she collects in *The Road to the Temple*. Glaspell summarizes the pioneer experience in the following terms, where an especial emphasis on women's experience can already be perceived:

> Here is a queer thing: A man has a farm or an orchard or a mill in Massachusetts or New York. There is room enough for him where he is and he makes a comfortable living. But one day they get into a covered wagon, taking some of their things with them, but leaving most of them behind. The wife kisses her sisters goodbye. She puts the children in the wagon — the whip is cracked, and they start down the hill, away from the house where she came the day she was married — past the house where she played as a child and in which her mother died. For a while friends come to wave at them — but soon they do not know the people any more and after a while there are no people. They ride through wide lonely country on their way to country which has more days, weeks and months between it and the known world. They go to Indians, rattlesnakes, the back-breaking work of turning wilderness into productive land. They go to loneliness and the fears born in loneliness [2005: 33].

This excerpt deserves lengthy comment, since the source of the dramatic concept of geopathology appears here. In Glaspell's account, women's mobility within the American Dream is questioned regarding different aspects. Pioneer women are forced to leave the house they love, the place of their heritage, where their relatives still live, to settle down in a hostile and unknown environment, which is full of dangers. But far from submitting to a melodramatic view of women's role in the Pioneer Myth, where women appear as victims, Glaspell frequently takes the opportunity to praise the effort these women made in order to help tame the country, building and arranging their homes to fight victimage of location.

Pioneer women become leading characters in many of Glaspell's plays, such as *Trifles, Inheritors*, and *Close the Book*, as well as in some of her novels, such as *Brook Evans* (1928) and *Norma Ashe* (1942). In her amazing variation from the traditional version of the Pioneer Myth, Glaspell always emphasizes the importance that women had in settling frontiers, a task that was not carried out until the 1970s, when historical books about pioneer women started to be published.[1] In a 1896 article for *The Weekly Outlook*, Glaspell denounced the necessity of retelling the history from a feminist point of view: "despite the fact that histories have mostly been written by men, who slighted or ignored [women] altogether, [women] were well worthy a place in the foremost ranks of the world's patriots, philosophers and statesmen.... Truly we owe more to woman than we seem inclined to put in our school books" (qtd. in Ozieblo 2000: 21). Glaspell definitely assumed the role to (w)right the wrongs done to women in history books. With her emphasis on the pioneer female character, Glaspell asks to turn to the idealism and strength of these women from the past and to make use of these qualities in the present struggles for women's rights.

Glaspell's strongest example of pioneer woman is Grandmother Morton in *Inheritors*. *Inheritors* opens, symbolically, with Grandmother Morton sitting in her rocking chair. This character, who embodies the harshness and difficulties of the pioneer woman, is not the fearful, quiet and indoors pioneer woman that history books used to portray. She, like Mrs. Fejevary, deserves her place in the Pioneer Myth from which they have historically been removed. As a character, Grandmother Morton fights through her work and attitude the potential victimage of location the wilderness of the geographical site that the onstage fictional place, the American Midwest, poses. While at the beginning of the play she appears *"patching a boy's pants"* (181) and making cookies, actions that could make her fit into the traditional pioneer woman's pattern, in the words of Grandmother Morton, pioneer women worked as hard as men did, both inside and outside the farmhouse: "We worked. A country don't [*sic*] make itself. When the sun was up we were up, and when the sun went down we didn't" (183).

Grandmother Morton came to Iowa in 1820 in a wagon. She and her husband did not have a roof, a fire, a doctor, or shops. As J. Ellen Gainor suggests, Grandmother Morton is "a motif of female courage and strength" (2001: 118), and Glaspell emphasizes this strength as the other pioneer characters in this play acknowledge women's efforts. For instance, Felix Fejevary defines Grandmother Morton's strength as "a flame frailness can't put out. It's a great thing for us to have her,— this touch with life behind us" (186). Nevertheless, Glaspell highlights the usual rule that women had to travel accompanied by their husbands, erasing any hint of individuality for women within this myth. Grandmother Morton never went beyond the farm on her own, and she only got out of the walls of the farm to work with the animals or to help other farmers. This is also the case in *Close the Book*. Glaspell praises the effort of pioneer women as she describes Grandmother's journey with her husband from New York to Ohio, and this character's independence is hinted at as she travels alone from her present home in California to the Roots' house in the Midwest. But when Peyton raises the question whether Grandmother moved from New York to Ohio because she was having an illegitimate baby, he suggests that his grandmother's freedom of movement relates to her status as a fallen woman, a woman who has a baby outside of wedlock:

GRANDMOTHER: Am I to be told — at my age — that I gave birth to an illegitimate child?...

PEYTON: Well, it just came into my head that it was possible. You see, grandmother, your having moved — I do wish you could see that I meant nothing against your character. Absolutely the contrary. But you having *moved*—

GRANDMOTHER: My having moved where?

PEYTON: You having moved from New York State to Ohio at just that time —

GRANDMOTHER: I always did like to travel. Is that against a person's character? ... But I'd like to know right now what there is so immoral in moving from one state to another — even if you are going to have a baby? [43–44, emphasis in original].

When it turns out that Grandmother was indeed married before her journey to Ohio, and therefore her pregnancy respected the rules of decorum, Peyton produces *"A sigh of relief"* (44). Grandmother demonstrates that "a woman may move from one state to another without being dissolute" (44), suggesting then that in other cases it was "dissolute" women who were forced to move. This is what makes Peyton sigh with relief; his grandmother combined two things that seemed apparently incompatible to him: being a True Woman and traveling while pregnant. In terms of dramatic geopathology, in *Close the Book* and *Inheritors*, the pioneer female characters' problem with place may originate in their disentitlement to move freely, as the American Myth of Mobility promised. They must always travel accompanied by their husbands if they want to be considered proper women.

It is in *Trifles* where Glaspell most poignantly deconstructs the Myth of Mobility within the Pioneer Myth. In this short one-act play, Glaspell makes even more explicit than in the above plays that mobility is a gendered mythology. While in *Inheritors* Glaspell celebrates the effort made by pioneer women, in *Trifles* the most negative side of this effort comes to the fore as it materializes in spatial confinement. Mrs. Hale and Mrs. Peters are trapped in the Wrights' kitchen, symbolizing pioneer women's entrapment at their farms. Glaspell symbolizes Minnie Wright's confinement to the kitchen in her rocking chair. As Daphne Spain has warned, even chairs are subdued to gender hierarchies in the geography of home. Armchairs and easy chairs were usually linked to men, while smaller chairs and rocking chairs usually belonged to women.[2] Spain's point about the relationship between hierarchy and chairs is relevant to a semiotic analysis of dramatic geopathology, since the chairs that appear onstage, their typology and the possibility of an analysis of what characters use what chairs, can be revealing about gender politics. In *Trifles*, the rocking chair is Minnie's. Firstly, it must be noted that the typical conception of the rocking chair on the outside porch vanishes here; the rocking chair is inside the farmhouse. The rocking chair is thus not the comfortable piece of furniture to enjoy looking at the landscape. Instead, it appears as a deceitful device to reproduce movement while being spatially trapped. When describing how he found out that John Wright was dead, and how Mrs. Wright had told him so, Mr. Hale says:

> HALE: and there in that rocker — [*Pointing to it.*] sat Mrs. Wright. [*They all look at the rocker.*]
> COUNTY ATTORNEY: What — was she doing?
> HALE: She was rockin' back and forth. She had her apron in her hand and was kind of— pleating it.
> COUNTY ATTORNEY: And how did she — look?
> HALE: Well, she looked queer [27].

Minnie's movement back and forth in her rocking chair represents her impossibility to move beyond. She, like the protagonist of Samuel Beckett's *Rockaby* (1980), is trapped in space, and simply awaiting death. A bit later, Minnie does swap chairs and sits in a small chair in the corner. As Minnie realizes that she will be sent to prison, that any possibility that the Myth of Movement could open up for her has vanished, she chooses a quieter chair, "*a small chair in the corner*" (27) that does not reproduce any kind of movement. Glaspell enhances the symbolism of the rocking chair when Mrs. Hale is about to sit down in it and then steps back. In her proxemic relation to the rocking chair Mrs. Hale avoids Minnie's entrapment. Although Mrs. Hale can be considered another prisoner in the kitchen, at least she escapes from the symbolic prison this rocking chair stands for.

In stark contrast to Minnie's rocking chair and the women's fixity inside the kitchen, the male characters move all around the farm, going upstairs and to the barn, symbolizing their mobility outside, too. But while the kitchen appears as the place women cannot leave, this place is also invaded by the male characters. Mrs. Hale sees in the way the male characters move around the kitchen a shameful invasion of Minnie's space. When the County Attorney complains about the dirty towels, Mrs. Hale answers back: "Those towels get dirty awful quick. Men's hands aren't always as clean as they might be" (28). Moreover, there is also the possibility that Frank, the Sheriff's assistant, who had been sent to the farm early that morning in order to make a fire, could have stained the towel after using the stove. Mrs. Hale observes: "Duty's all right, but I guess that deputy sheriff that came out to make the fire might have got a little of this on. [*Gives the roller towel a pull*]" (29). According to Mrs. Hale, the male characters invade and spoil the work done in the kitchen. This is why she arranges the pans under the sink, which the County Attorney "*had shoved out of place*" (29). Thus, it is not only that the female characters in this play are not entitled to participate in the American Myth of Mobility, but they also have to stand invasions in their very places, what can be said to enhance their victimage of location.

But unlike Mrs. Hale and Mrs. Peters, who at least can go to church and join the quilting bee, Minnie Wright could not even attend either of these events. This is the reason why Minnie's quilt is one of the main symbols of the play, a symbol closely related to the Myth of Mobility, and which can be regarded as one of the clues to Minnie's victimage of location. As Karen Stein points out, "In the quilt patterns and the names for them ... women told the stories of their lives" (1987: 255). Significantly, Minnie's pattern is a log cabin:

> The log cabin pattern is constructed of repetitions of a basic block, which is built up of narrow overlapping strips of fabric, all emanating from a central square. That square, traditionally done in red cloth, came to represent the hearth fire within the cabin, with the strips surrounding it becoming the "logs" of which the cabin was built.... [T]he log cabin quilt came to symbolize both the hardships and the heroisms of pioneer life [Hedges 1995: 64].

In Glaspell's dramatic strategy, Minnie's quilt is meaningfully erratic, half is "nice and even," but then "it looks as if she didn't know what she was about" (30). Mrs. Peters and Mrs. Hale read these erratic stitches as Minnie's rebellion against the lie of the Pioneer Myth, symbolized in the log cabin, since in her contribution to the Pioneer Myth her hardship goes unnoticed and her heroism is silenced. Furthermore, the log cabin quilt pattern is a geometrical construction that represents the geographical enclosure that Minnie suffered. Minnie's inability to move out of the farm is symbolized in the perfectly closed square lines of the quilt. Thus, Minnie's destruction of the quilt pattern could be interpreted as her yearning to escape from the enclosing form of the farm and her need to move beyond its walls. As many scholars have extensively analyzed, it is precisely Minnie's erratic stitches that make Mrs. Hale and Mrs. Peters come to think that Minnie's life was really miserable.[3] This moment of recognition triggers a sudden change in the passive behavior of the other two women in the play, prompting them to delete the incriminatory evidence they find.

Given that in *Trifles* quilting is also used to signify the common threads in pioneer women's lives, since all pioneer women found quilting absolutely necessary as "a uniquely American solution to the dilemma of keeping warm in an economy of scarcity before the introduction of central heating" (Stein 1987: 254), Mrs. Peters easily puts herself in Minnie's place and states that "I don't know as she was so nervous. I sometimes sew awful queer when I'm just tired" (31). The meaning of this affirmation is twofold. On the one hand, it points out the vast amount of work these women had to complete in very hard living conditions. On the other hand, this "tired" can be read in a more metaphorical dimension as being tired of something or even someone, being tired of such an entrapment within her roles, the kitchen, and the farmhouse, and even being tired of her husband. The myth of the log cabin and all it stands for, that is, the American Dream, the cornucopia, the idea of going from rags to riches, and also the idea of mobility represents a big lie to Minnie and to the other women in the play.

From Mrs. Hale and Mrs. Peters's perspective, Mrs. Wright was so overcome by this lie that this could be the reason why she had not sewn delicately or why she had spoiled this log cabin pattern. How can a red block stand for the hearth fire when she does not even have a working stove? How can she endure her life when all the hardships of her work exceed her expectations? And, finally, how can she be proud of being a pioneer woman when there is nobody to celebrate her effort? Moreover, the fact that the men in the play laugh at Mrs. Hale and Mrs. Peters's debate on whether Minnie was going to quilt or to knot her patchwork demonstrates that the men do not celebrate their women's effort, which is embodied in the quilt. So in *Trifles*, Glaspell uses the Pioneer Myth and the relative Myth of Mobility to dramatically develop her female characters' victimage of location: firstly, as Glaspell does in *Close the Book* and *Inheritors*, to highlight the place that women should have in the Pioneer Myth; and secondly, to point out the problem some pioneer women had with place when they were not allowed to move freely and instead they were kept trapped inside their farmhouses.

Glaspell insists on questioning the Myth of Mobility for women other than pioneers. Dotty, in *Chains of Dew*, is only allowed to go to certain places, such as the Tuesday Club. In contrast, her husband, Seymore, regularly travels to New York, as Craig does to New York and Europe in *Bernice*, while his wife always stays at home. Craig's and Seymore's trips are justified on the basis of their literary careers, as was the fashion among many bohemians; they traveled to gather with other artists to find inspiration for their writings, and on many occasions these male characters traveled to meet their lovers. Craig's and Seymore's trips are seen as the moments of relief from their ordinary "trapping" homes. But the matter of their wives' need to move outside the house is completely ignored, as well as their need for intellectual development. Dotty is eventually allowed to go to New York too, but she can only do it as long as her husband goes with her and as long as she behaves as a proper woman, that is, as the ideal wife Seymore wants:

> DOTTY: When you go to New York, I want to go too. That is, sometimes....
> SEYMORE: Well, of course Dotty shall go to New York, if Dotty Dimple wants to go to New York. But not on wild goose chases, where she has to be rescued, shooing off friends who have meant much to me [178].

Seymore accepts taking Dotty with him "sometimes," as long as she goes as Dotty Dimple. The pet name implies that Dotty is allowed to come if she behaves as Seymore wants her to: as a submissive wife that will keep apart from the new ideas his friends could exert on her. In like manner, in *Alison's House*, Alison only left home once and she did it with her father. She went to Harvard, where she met her lover (349). After this trip Alison stayed at the Stanhope homestead her whole life. In Dotty's case, as well as in Alison's, it is quite clear that freedom of movement is a highly gendered issue, and that those female characters who care about being labeled other than proper women, take extreme care to travel only accompanied by a patriarchal figure.

It is sensible to consider that the Myth of Mobility should have opened up for women after the appearance of the New Woman, and even more after the peak moment of 1920, when women won the vote in the United States. But an analysis of this issue in Glaspell's plays reveals that she felt dubious about its consistency. In *The Verge*, Elizabeth seems a New Woman character, but as soon as she announces that she has been to Europe on a school trip, our belief in her as a free character dissolves. It is not only that Elizabeth has traveled with her older teacher, Miss Lane, that is, under surveillance, but since she summarizes her trip as "awfully amusing," unable to explain what she liked about Europe, her words suggest that her trip is just what "all the girls" do (244), not a self-motivated trip, to learn, to see the world, or simply for the fun of traveling. Moreover, when Elizabeth comes to visit her mother, she again travels accompanied by an older character, her aunt Adelaide. Considering Jhansi a New Woman in *Close the Book* is also revealing about her commitment to defend her freedom of movement. Whereas throughout the play she insists on taking the "open road," it is suspicious that her boyfriend, Peyton, convinces her easily to give up her wish. Though this will be analyzed in the final chapter of this book, it is interesting to say at this point that Jhansi abandons her ideals for the comfort that staying in the wealthy Root house provides.

Dramatic geopathology in conjunction with revisions of the Myth of Mobility also appear in the case of characters who do move freely. Indeed, in several of her plays Glaspell puts onstage female characters who enjoy the Myth of Movement without restraint, but their movements have sound dramatic implications, fostering as well the development of victimage of location. Mrs. Patrick in *The Outside* could be regarded as a woman entitled to move. Importantly, Mrs. Patrick has no husband, which makes her freer. But as Mrs. Patrick discusses with Allie Mayo why she came from New York to the derelict old life-saving station in Provincetown, Mrs. Patrick reveals that her change of location was not a self-motivated movement: "I didn't *go* to the Outside.

I was left there. I'm only — trying to get along" (64, emphasis in original). After being abandoned by her husband, Mrs. Patrick had no place to go, and the most derelict place she could find was the Outside. Moreover, when she came to buy the old life-saving station, she let people believe that Mr. Patrick had died. Mrs. Patrick's concealment of the truth suggests that at that time traveling alone was acceptable in the case of widows, but not so much in the case of abandoned women. Even so, the way in which Mrs. Patrick is treated by Provincetowners also implies that seeing a woman traveling alone is unnatural. As McBride claims, "Although Mr. and Mrs. Patrick were initially welcomed as transitional members of the community, as summer folks with money, when Mrs. Patrick showed up later alone and wanted to set up housekeeping, the local people were more resistant to and curious about her presence as an unattached woman" (2006: 167). Thus, Mrs. Patrick could travel to Provincetown when she did so with her husband, but now that she is alone her movements are regarded with suspicion. It is as if, as an alleged widow, she should have stayed imprisoned at home, and maybe in mourning.

Although Glaspell portrays more intensely cases where women have movement restrictions, some of her male characters experience this restriction too. In Glaspell's very first play, the idea that male characters can also be negatively affected by the politics of location arises. Steve in *Suppressed Desires* is a geopathic character to some extent. He is almost forced to leave the place he lives in and that he loves because his wife, who wants to occupy his place, has turned his workplace into a battlefield. It might be the case that Glaspell's commitment to the feminist cause had broadened by this time to take into account how some of the moral issues tying women to place also tie men, or maybe it was Cook who wanted to reflect men as victims of locations. According to Hinz-Bode, many of Glaspell's male characters "share her female protagonists' sense of imprisonment and express a similar urge to rebel against the existing social order" (2006a: 202). This is clearly the case of *Alison's House*. It seems plausible that Stanhope rejects so utterly Elsa's departure from the family estate because she did what he wanted to do but could not. As revealed towards the end of the play, in the past Stanhope had renounced his elopement with his real love, Ann's mother. He felt obliged to stay because he was the head of the family, a role he despises: "Sometimes I wish there weren't any family" (316). Likewise, his son Eben sometimes wants to "run away from all this" (322), from a wife he does not love and from the tedious and respectful life he leads:

> EBEN: Sometimes I feel I want something else.
> STANHOPE: What?
> EBEN: I don't know.
> STANHOPE: And what about your family?

EBEN: Oh that's why I'm going.
STANHOPE: You are not going!
EBEN: Probably not.
STANHOPE: Going where?
EBEN: I don't know. Somewhere — where things are different.
STANHOPE: Things are not different anywhere [330].

This quotation discloses a lie implied in the Myth of Mobility, which is that, in this play, no character, male or female, can move freely when family and tradition interfere. Though these issues will be analyzed in depth later on, at this point it is interesting to highlight how these male characters are also forced to stay within the walls of the house that suffocates them. Both Stanhope and Eben are victims of spatial determinism because of their obligations, their social, moral, and family duties. Both had to follow the family business and became lawyers. And Ted, Stanhope's youngest son, though he would rather enter into the rubber wheel business, is also obliged to study law and enter the family office. Glaspell visualizes in spatial terms the impossibility of these characters moving out of the house by placing them all in the library, since "there's no other room to go to. They're all torn up" (318). The impossibility to move out physically is, however, just a part of the relations between the Myth of Mobility and dramatic geopathology. Many are the consequences of movement, and actually, the trope of invasion constitutes a cornerstone of ill-placement in Glaspell's plays.

The Trope of Invasion in Dramatic Geopathology

Displacement is one of the most interesting aspects that can be found in Glaspell's plays regarding the relationship between dramatic geopathology and female characters who move without restraint. For the present analysis, displacement is understood as Keith and Pile define it, as a status where these characters are "out of place" (1993: 225). Before entering into the analysis of the role of displaced female characters in dramatic victimage of location, it is interesting to consider briefly the kind of woman these female characters stand for. Una Chaudhuri has pointed out that in pre–Ibsenesque drama there was a certain type of female character that was allowed to move. This character was the Fallen Woman, or the woman with a past (2000: 61). Female characters who deviated from their traditional roles, above all in sexual terms (such as prostitutes or unfaithful women), moved without any trouble, mainly because these women, considered social outcasts, had no place in society. Interestingly, in *A Doll's House* Ibsen reworks this kind of character to present the downfall of a female character. Significantly, Nora's fault is not sexual misbehavior; her

Scene from *Chains of Dew*, Act I. Ruth Everett as Nora Powers and Charles Daish as Leon Whittaker. Orange Tree Theatre production, 2008. Director: Kate Saxon. Photograph © Robert Day.

shameful past deals with her deviation from gender roles and social rules: she dared to tackle finances, an enterprise her husband should have been left alone to solve.

Glaspell portrays the experience of displacement through modern women, that is, through women that under patriarchal lights could be seen as "fallen" because of their deviation from traditional gender roles. In her treatment of displaced female characters, Glaspell reveals two phenomena regarding the politics of location. On the one hand, the use of displacement to define a character evinces that character's own geopathology. That is, if a character is "out of place," it is quite easy to conclude that this character might have a problem with place. On the other hand, sometimes Glaspell employs the displacement of a character precisely to bring a sense of displacement to the places that character goes to, that is, to places that belong to other characters who probably will be affected, maybe even reaching geopathology, by that sense of "placelessness" someone brought.

Rosemary George has observed that in contemporary literature the idea of home is usually reworked through homeless, displaced, characters. According to George, "The sentiment accompanying the absence of home — homesickness — can cut in two ways: it could be a yearning for the authentic home (situated in the past or in the future) or it could be the recognition of the inauthenticity or the created aura of all homes" (1999: 175). Glaspell offers a third way to confront homesickness. In her plays, displaced characters, dispossessed of a place of their own, endeavor to destroy other characters' homes by invading and showing disgust at their houses. Nora in *Chains of Dew* and Nina and Luella in *The Comic Artist* are female characters that have an active role within the Myth of Mobility, but who suffer from a sense of displacement that makes one regard them as invaders, losing the positive essence of this myth.

In the fist act of *Chains of Dew*, it seems that Nora has a place of her own, her office. The birth control posters, the excess family exhibit, the lots of books, the working-table, the telephone and the mimeograph help to configure this place as Nora's, since they represent Nora's strong belief in and commitment to birth control. But the early appearance of the male characters, who are totally entitled to move, dispossesses Nora of the control over her place. Even in her office, she is told to shut up. Leon says, "Nora, will you let conversation be possible?" (136), and "No use trying to interview a man with Nora around" (140). Leon behaves as if this were *his* office. After complaining about Nora's disruptions, he opens the door at the side and invites O'Brien to come in for the interview (140). Furthermore, while throughout this act we see Nora working with her mimeograph, listening to its sound, feeding it, taking and examining papers, and answering the phone, her work is mocked in her very place. Seymore and Leon laugh at Nora when she gets enthusiastic about the phone call telling that Mrs. Arnold will donate a thousand dollars for birth control (141–142). Nora's place is invaded by the male characters in the same way that Nora will invade Seymore's place in the following acts.

It is at this point that one wonders whether Nora is the sympathetic character most critics agree on. For instance, Barbara Ozieblo defines Nora as "the courageous realist with a will to transform society" (2006b: 17), and Kristina Hinz-Bode believes that Nora "is presented as a likeable and energetic woman who meets her fellow human beings in an open, straightforward way" (2006b: 141). While I agree with some of these descriptions, such as Nora's courage and energy, some doubts arise regarding her likeability and sympathy. Glaspell herself was rather ambivalent regarding some New Women. Caroline Fletcher has pointed out that Glaspell did not completely agree with the radical women of Heterodoxy, evidenced by her irregular attendance at the Saturday luncheons of the club, and her commitment to the club, which was not as unreserved as other members.'[4] Though a New Woman herself in looks and ideas — Glaspell was the first woman to have her hair bobbed in Provincetown [5] —the fact that as a young, and yet anonymous girl in Davenport, her middle-class background prevented her from joining other women's clubs, could have made her suspicious of the reasons behind some women's clubs. Taking this background into account, I find it possible that Glaspell displays an ambivalent position towards Nora, wavering between sympathy and suspicion, being aware of the good Nora could bring to Bluff City, but also avoiding an straightforward definition of Nora's motives and means.

On the one hand, Nora's decision to go to Bluff City is based upon her commitment to birth control and the need to spread the movement to the Midwest. On the other hand, there is another reason that makes Nora go to Bluff City, a reason that hardly makes her appear as a nice character. She hopes to ruin Seymore's home life so that he goes to live permanently to New York, where they have a relationship. Thus, Nora can be regarded as a negative invader since a point in her agenda is to break up Seymore's home, a home where his wife and his mother also live. As Nora says referring to Bluff City inhabitants, "[*With fervor.*] I will disturb ten thousand toads," and "I will forget birth control!" (143). If as she says, she will forget birth control, then it becomes clearer that she has primarily come for Seymore.

When Nora arrives in Bluff City, she begins invading Seymore's house little by little, and her appearance is her first strategy. Glaspell employs Nora's bobbed hair as a marker of the New Woman, the one involved in politics and women's rights. Her hair is a representation of her own identity and matches the office of the Birth Control League. Glaspell describes Nora as follows; she "*has short hair. This does not mean she's eccentric — it is not that kind of short hair. It curls and is young and vital and charming short hair. NORA also is young and vital and charming — devotion to a cause really doesn't hurt her looks in the least*" (127). Glaspell enhances the contrast between this New Woman and the Midwestern house she is ready to alter through Nora's look, and especially, her hair, which is a shock to Midwesterners. When she appears in Bluff City, Mrs. MacIntyre, Edith and Dotty "*look at her hair, which snuggles up round the face in just the slant SEYMORE gave the doll*" (152).

Nora's body language is also part of her invasion. A proxemic analysis of the way Nora arrives at the Standishes' and how she moves in this place reveals her out-of-placedness. Firstly, Nora comes to Bluff City even though she has not been invited. The first time Seymore sees her here, he cannot but utter in astonishment, "*Nora! You here?*" (155, emphasis in original). As soon as she is in the room she articulates her wish to rule over this space, to change its configuration: "Here is a table all prepared for me. [*Going to the bridge table.*] But not in the presence of mine enemy, I hope. [*Taking some circulars from her bag*]" (154). After this verbal statement of invasion, Nora physically invades the room. Throughout Act II, scene 1, Nora displays her birth control circulars. The quiet and traditional library of the Standishes becomes little by little a portion of bohemian New York in Act II, scene 2, until it is turned into the headquarters of the birth control league. For this purpose, Nora's posters, the large family exhibit and literature on birth control are taken out of the packing box throughout the scene. The excess family exhibit is put on a corner of Seymore's desk, as he helplessly witnesses how the "room where we see people — the people who come to see us" (156) is being transformed in front of his eyes. That the room is altogether changed is also evident in the Maid's hesitation about whether it is appropriate to bring visitors into the room. She asks whether she is to bring O'Brien and Leon "in — here?" (161), and whether she is to "bring Mrs MacIntyre in *here*?" (162, emphasis in original).

That the appearance of the library resembles more closely New York than the Midwest is also clear when O'Brien remarks, "But even dolls have bobbed hair out here.... I didn't know the West was like *this*" (162, emphasis in original). By Act III, Nora's New York has totally invaded the room. The birth control pictures on the wall say so. Mrs. MacIntyre, a very conservative female character, notices that Nora is breaking down the Standishes' shelter, so she says to Nora: "Have you no idea of the sanctity of the home?" to which Nora answers, "Don't let me detain you. If you are going out" (154). It is not only that Nora has occupied space as she has pleased, but she also feels entitled to rudely invite people to leave the house she has invaded.

It is interesting to note that, out of the three dwellers of the house, Nora's invasion only troubles Seymore. While he admits "I do not understand this invasion" (158), Dotty and Mother feel very happy about Nora's intrusion. Glaspell shows physically that these two characters were tired of being trapped in Midwestern structures and that they welcome the liberation that Nora brings from New York in the way they eagerly help to display the family exhibit and the posters. Through Nora's displacement and her invasion of Seymore's house, Dotty reacts and acknowledges her own need of a place of her own, a place where she can work for birth control. And it is from this standpoint that Nora can be regarded as a positive invader.

In other plays, Glaspell exploits costumes and particular looks to suggest problems with place regarding displaced characters, invader characters, and those characters who find their places occupied. In *The Comic Artist*, Luella and Nina are visually configured as invaders through their costumes. Luella is described as "*a slight, chic woman*" (270). And the stage directions say, "*Luella occupies herself with her vanity case, fixes her curly, bobbed hair under her hat. In the clearer light LUELLA looks her age. She is dressed too youthfully*" (271). She has dyed hair (273), and later is "*inappropriately dressed in silk; very high heels*" (297). Her daughter, Nina, who is announced onstage by the car horn, a symbol of her modernity and mobility, "*is so beautiful that all look at her for a moment—she pleased, seeming a little shy*" (278). But she is not shy at all. She is a kind of Helen of Troy whose beauty will confront two brothers,

Stephen and Karl. "[M]en would destroy themselves for beauty such as hers," says Stephen (277), an ominous remark that foreshadows the metaphorical destruction that Eleanor and Stephen's home will undergo subsequent to Nina's arrival, as well as Karl's death. In sharp contrast, Eleanor, Stephen's dutiful wife, is wearing comfortable costume, "*what apparently were the things nearest at hand when she started out— a man's blue coat over her sweater, a man's grey cap*" (270). Luella's and Nina's astounding costumes of silk and fur coats, respectively, begin to make Eleanor feel attacked in her own house.

Eleanor is more bluntly attacked in the way her space is despised. While she endeavors to arrange the room, removing her baby's clothes, lighting the fire and the lamp, Luella examines the room "*with unfriendly curiosity*" and with "*A half articulated expression of disdain*" (270), and she does not even sit when Eleanor invites her to do it. Nina's first remark about the house is as unpleasant as her mother's: "And this is your house — the house we've heard so much about. [*A glance around, uncertain what to say*]" (278). And when she finds out what to say about the house, she refers to it as "Way out here?" (279). Nina overtly admits she has come to invade Eleanor's house. After an argument about Nina's intrusion into their lives, Stephen and Eleanor tenderly become reconciled. However, Nina interrupts abruptly this intimate moment: "Was I — [*Seeing the intimacy of the moment and more angry, but trying to control it.*] Oh — pardon me. I am intruding. Was I wrong in thinking I was posing for you?" (304). Nina acknowledges she is "intruding," and hypocritically apologizes, only to bring back the issue about which Eleanor was so angry, that Nina was posing for Stephen, symbolically occupying Eleanor's place. Nina not only exerts her mobility by occupying a place that does not belong to her, but she wants to go further and invade Eleanor's personal space, her position as Stephen's wife.

Considering the reasons why Luella and Nina mistreat Eleanor, Nina and Luella's problem is not simply that they feel superior to Eleanor, but that they are displaced characters also beyond Eleanor's house. They do not have a place they can call home, and thus they defend themselves by attacking the one who is trying to maintain hers. Nina and Luella come from big cities; Luella from the Latin Quarter in Paris, and Nina from New York, places where they have a great social life but no real friends, and less a place called home. Luella is the first one to acknowledge that she has no place: "There never seems any place for me" (302), and she has no place to go. She would love to go to New York to live with her daughter. But Nina despises her mother for having abandoned her in Paris. Nina has been raised on displacement, so she has no place she can call home either. She chooses, thus, to invade Eleanor's shelter. This is totally obvious in the scene when Nina wants to take Eleanor's place as Stephen's model. On purpose, Nina takes the chair where Eleanor had sat to pose for Stephen, and *"moves the jug ELEANOR left on floor beside the chair"* (289). Symbolically, Nina moves the jug out of its place as she is also trying to move Eleanor out of hers. But Nina's eagerness to put Eleanor out of her way does not end there. She leads Stephen to contribute to Eleanor's displacement. Suggestively posing for him, Stephen then *"Examin[es] the picture of ELEANOR again — impersonally. Takes it off easel, sets it on floor, against the wall, face inward"* (49). Eleanor's picture is located facing the wall, and its place on the easel is replaced by the white canvas that will rank Nina above Eleanor in a metaphorical way.

In *The Comic Artist*, Glaspell and Matson provide their displaced characters with an extremely important feature that helps to understand geopathology, and this is their fear of solitude. For these characters not only lack a place of their own, but they also have problems keeping acquaintances. Because people are usually linked to places, and friendships are created in locations, it is highly difficult for these displaced characters to maintain their friendships. Nina and Luella clearly share this fear of solitude. The dramatic devices Glaspell and Matson employ are diverse. Games, which appear very consistently in Glaspell's dramaturgy, are the first of these. Luella is always forced to play cards alone (297), and although she asks the others to join her for a bridge game, she never succeeds (284, 307). Moreover, Luella is left alone in the house, something she cannot stand: "Why do you always leave me behind? I'm afraid in there alone.... Oh, do come in the house. It's gloomy out here" (297). Nina cannot be left alone either. When Stephen leaves her all by herself in the barn, she later complains, "Leaving me out there posing in an empty barn" (304). This solitude is symbolic of how she usually finds herself. As Eleanor believes, "I'm afraid you would often find yourself posing in an empty barn" (305).

A very interesting case to analyze in terms of regarding Glaspell's revision of the Myth of Mobility in conjunction with the dramatic strategy of invasion is Henrietta in *Suppressed Desires*. As Gainor has observed, "Much of the literary criticism of Cook and Glaspell's farce has been lightly dismissive, based on a view of the play as amusing but not aesthetically substantive" (2001: 21). Unlike other critics who have seen this play as a mere spoof on psychoanalysis, Gainor has demonstrated the importance of this play read in its context, revealing Cook and Glaspell's portrait of "the tension between the lingering Victorian values of monogamous marriage and the merging bohemian code of free love" (2001: 20).

But what no critic to my knowledge has ever pointed out is that a subtle topic Glaspell and Cook deal with in this play is the dramatic representation of struggles for space, a pivotal issue in the relations between self and space. Henrietta is not the dutiful traditional wife, but a modern New York woman interested in the new kinds of ideas treated at the Liberal Club, where she is an active member. Her husband, Steve, apparently respects his wife's bohemianism. Although it has been said that both Henrietta and Steve are "freethinkers," the typical bohemian couple (Eisenhauer 2006: 122), I do not think that Steve is such a freethinker. Indeed, very early in the play Henrietta tells her husband, "You're all inhibited. You're no longer open to new ideas" (13). Even if Henrietta is *too* bohemian, the fact that she reproaches her husband means that Steve's commitment to radical streams is not as satisfactory to Henrietta as it was before. At most, Steve tolerates his wife's bohemianism, but only up to the point when this begins troubling his own life and his own space.

Glaspell and Cook introduced a variation in the onstage place of the living room that could have supported Steve's bohemianism. In an earlier version of the play,[6] there was a divan with a leopard's skin on the stage, a clear symbol of the couple's equal embrace of modernity, because of the fabric, and even of psychoanalysis, given that this is a divan. Moreover, as it is Henrietta who writes on psychoanalysis, this divan could be a representation of her right to be in this living room. However, by having removed the divan from subsequent versions of *Suppressed Desires*, the issues of Steve's commitment to his wife's ideals, as well as the ownership of the living room, complicate the play.

The play opens in the living room of Henrietta and Steve's studio apartment. The order of territoriality is evident in a clear dividing line that can be drawn between the zone of Steve's work table, at the rear, and the breakfast table, at the front. This breakfast table works as a metonymical extension of the kitchen that will help to place the female characters in this play. At the beginning, Henrietta and Mabel only move around this table and to the kitchen. In a spatially dialogical way, in this first scene Steve only moves around his work table, representative of his concern for his profession. The table sports his architecture tools: his drawings, blue prints, dividing compasses, square, ruler, etc. And a close survey of the way the characters relate to space suggests that the whole living room is Steve's place. Firstly, Steve shows a kind of affective relationship with the room. When he wonders about quitting the apartment, following Dr. Russell's recommendation to leave Henrietta, he says that he will miss the view (19), an affective relationship with this place that Henrietta never displays. Moreover, when Mabel realizes that their conversation on psychoanalysis disturbs Steve, she claims, "Don't you think it would be a good thing, Henrietta, if we went somewhere else?" (17). Likewise, this is a place Henrietta lets Mabel stay in only when Steve is not there, again certifying that this place is Steve's: "Well, if he's gone, you might as well stay here" (18). Interestingly, Henrietta has her own room, which implies that there are different locations for different owners in this apartment.

Scene from *Suppressed Desires*. Ruth Everett as Henrietta Brewster and Pia de Keyser as Mabel. Orange Tree Theatre production, 2008. Director: Phoebe Barran. Photograph © Robert Day.

The living room is Steve's, and Henrietta has a room of her own that she does not use to write her paper.

Steve's work table becomes a symbol of the struggle for space in the play. Contrary to Steve's desire to possess the table, this table is not absolutely his own. As the play opens, the table is already occupied by some material which is not his. On one end of the table there are Steve's assets, as described before, but the other end is loaded with Henrietta's "*serious-looking books and austere scientific periodicals*" (13). Henrietta's endeavor to occupy Steve's working table is more evident in scene 2. As the curtain rises Henrietta "*is at the psychoanalytical end of Steve's work-table, surrounded by open books and periodicals, writing*" her paper for the Liberal Club (18). The relation established between these characters and the stage properties in this place shows their subtle struggle for the room. Importantly, Henrietta is not attempting to occupy Steve's place for the sake of invasion. Her primary purpose, writing her paper, is as serious as Steve's work; with this occupation Henrietta suggests that what she does must be considered as important as her husband's job. I believe that through Henrietta, Cook and Glaspell argue how even a woman conscious of her right to the Myth of Movement, and who, as a New Woman, can move freely out, still has the need to move to places that do not belong to her, maybe a dramatic representation of the New Woman's anxiety to prove that she can occupy a man's place. As such, this little invasion visualizes Henrietta's demand that the extant power geometry be reworked.

Thus, in *Suppressed Desires* Glaspell and Cook employ the trope of invasion to show that women are also entitled to the Myth of Mobility, but that the cost of this mobility might be marital trouble. But unlike the cases of Nina and Luella in *The Comic Artist*, the manner in which invasion is carried out in *Suppressed Desires* makes one wonder about the female character's need for invasion. To overcome her victimage of location, Henrietta has to occupy another place, even if the casualty of this occupation is her husband's own geopathology. Given that this play is a comedy, Henrietta does not have to pay a high price for her adventure; many other characters who dared to fight for their right to move to escape their victimage of location are punished in Glaspell's dramaturgy.

Casualties of the Myth of Mobility

There are a few instances in which Glaspell shows onstage female characters making good use of the American Myth of Mobility. However, it is difficult, not to say hardly possible, to find an example where a female character makes good use of the possibilities the Myth of Mobility provides without receiving some kind of punishment. Margaret in *Bernice* is a New Woman who freely enjoys the Myth of Mobility, and she usually travels alone, as is the case when she comes to the Nortons' house as the play opens. Though Margaret is a likable character, Laura's attack shows the difficulties to be faced by modern women who want to move freely: "You who have not cared what people thought of you — who have not had the sense of fitness — the taste — to hold the place you were born to" (102). Likewise, in *Alison's House*, Elsa has also exercised her right to move, but only to find herself dislocated and alienated when she comes back to her old house. Her story is a failed homecoming. When she first appears, she needs to ask:

> ELSA: Father, may I — come in? [*One hand, palm up. Goes out towards him, timidly, but eloquent.*]
> LOUISE: Certainly, you may not — not while [*But is afraid to go on, STANHOPE is staring so strangely at his daughter.*]
> ELSA: Perhaps I shouldn't have come ... I thought — perhaps it's too much to ask — but hoped you would let me stay here. Just tonight ... [*Advancing a little to her father*] [322].

Elsa's homecoming reveals her personal displacement. She had moved out of the family estate with her married lover, and when she comes back she is ostracized. She fails when she tries to approach her father physically. And Elsa fails again when she seeks reconciliation with her aunt Agatha, the one who never forgave that "Elsa went away" (323). When "*Elsa brings a footstool*" for Agatha, she disregards it (339), proxemically enacting her rejection. As seen in the cases of Margaret and Elsa, Glaspell shows that there is a price female characters have to pay for making use of their right to move, for stepping out of the places they have been given in society, for attempting to leave behind their victimage of location. These female characters turn into victims of location, by being, to greater or lesser degrees, verbally or physically punished in places they thought they would be re-accepted after their departure.

If one kind of character is clearly punished in Glaspell's dramaturgy, this is the ethnically "Other." In the same way that Glaspell revisits the Myth of Mobility concerning female characters who move, in one of her plays she touches the theme of racially marked immigration. Indeed, one of the main topics in *Inheritors* is the lie of the Myth of Mobility for immigrants, a theme that serves Glaspell to revise the conceptualization of America as an open and tolerant place. Actually, Glaspell employs immigrant characters in her plays to demonstrate the high price of the American myths of spatiality, for the price is, borrowing Chaudhuri's words, "a crushing, numbing homogeneity," "the weak spot in the omnipotent figure of America" that "fails to conceal its antipathy to the very projects — of individualism and self-determination" that apparently it supports (2000: 204). Significantly, in *Inheritors*, place is not only a problem for unwanted immigrants, but also for the female protagonist who cannot bear to see how her place rejects the immigrants it welcomed so heartedly before, and who cannot stand that the American geomythologies have been subverted in order to reject the different and the individual in favor of a homogeneous community.

With the purpose of showing that in contemporary America immigrants have a problem with place, Glaspell opens *Inheritors* at a more idyllic time, at least as far as immigration is concerned. The play opens in 1879, forty-one years before subsequent acts. Glaspell employs this dramatic structure as a device to explore the different responses of her characters to similar problems and concerns, and more concretely, to show that place constitutes a problem in the present while it did not to the same extent in the past. In the first act, Glaspell puts onstage pioneer characters from diverse backgrounds in order to show that it was the peaceful coexistence and collaboration among immigrants and settlers that enabled the colonization of America. In Glaspell's version of the Melting Pot, the Mortons, white Anglo-Saxons, "laid this country at [the Hungarian Fejevary]'s feet — as if that was what this country was for" (210). They fought together in the American Civil War, and they worked together for "the dreams of a million years" (193), to make their country a better place. Their descendants also mixed; Ira Morton married Madeline Fejevary. But Glaspell's version of the Melting Pot does not respond to the traditional assimilation of every culture into the WASP archetype. Glaspell does not make immigrants renounce their values to emulate the Mortons, but each group offers what good they have, in this case, the Fejevarys their culture, and the Mortons their soil and ideals.

The idyllic community created by these characters responds to some extent to what Bachelard has identified as *topophilia* in the literary tradition, to the images of "felicitous space" (1994: xxxv) which are opposite to the images that nurture dramatic geopathology.[7] The fictional place in the first act of *Inheritors* can be considered a felicitous place because, in spite of the difficult moments the pioneer characters experience, the act ends as they dream of a better future, and this future materializes in space through the construction of Morton College. Silas's land conjoins Fejevary's knowledge to create a place that is meant to signify the cultivation of the landscape. The manifesto of Silas Morton and Felix Fejevary's college reads:

> Born of the fight for freedom and the aspiration to richer living, we believe that Morton College — rising as from the soil itself — may strengthen all those here and everywhere who fight for the life there is in freedom, and may, to the measure it can, loosen for America the beauty that breathes from knowledge [205].

That is, Morton College is envisioned as a microcosm of what these pioneers want America to be: the land where everybody is welcome, and where further mixtures of immigrants and Americans go on making this country better and better. As a place of renewal where the mistakes made in the old Europe could be avoided, the possibility of victimage of location could be at least diminished in America.

Interestingly, Glaspell reworks at this point a crucial geomythology in American history: the spatial metaphor of the City upon the Hill. As Barbara Ozieblo has pointed out, Morton College is a new "City upon the Hill" (1990: 69). In *Inheritors*, the hill is relevant both in terms of space and as far as the plot is concerned. Dramatically the hill is important since it will give a place for the following acts to happen, once the college has been built there, and as far as what this hill and this college should mean for the community. Glaspell suggests this dramatic importance through her characters' kinesic language. In the opening act the hill cannot be seen from the front, but many stage directions describe how characters are continuously positioning themselves in front of the window or at the door so that they can contemplate the hill. Its relevance is confirmed in the following acts, when characters call attention to the privileged position of Morton College, looking down on the growing town: "This is a great site for a college. You can see it from the whole country around" (198).

It seems obvious that Glaspell uses as a basis the image John Winthrop created in 1630 referring to the Pilgrim Fathers. In "A Model of Christian Charity" (1838), Winthrop declares enthusiastically: "For wee must Consider that we shall be as a City upon a hill. The eies of all people are upon us" (1989: 41). Morton College is located on a hill so that everybody can see it from the fields:

> SILAS: A college should be on a hill. They can see it then from far around. See it as they go out to the barn in the morning, see it when they're shutting up at night. 'T will make a difference, even to them that never go [189].

Morton College is a new version of the City upon the Hill because, in Silas's respect, the hill is not a model, the place to look at, but "a hill of vision," where "visions of a better world [shall come]" (190). Glaspell gives another turn of the screw to the trope of "the City upon the hill" and the "hill of vision" when it is due to the physical location and status of Morton college that Madeline will rebel against the community. It is when Madeline is up in the library of Morton College that she looks through the window and sees the abuses committed against the immigrant students. Madeline is forced to have the "vision" of what her place is, and she will react accordingly.

Silas's dream of the felicitous place is shattered, as in the following acts Morton College is a problematic location for the immigrant characters. Up on the hill, there are violent confrontations between Morton College students, aided by police forces, and Hindu students, which result in the Hindu students being injured and sent to prison, where they are given a taste of federal prisons before being deported. Linda Ben-Zvi has identified that "The model for the aliens in the play, who are being threatened with arrest and deportation, came from the numerous trials of Hindus, which were widely reported at the time" (2006: 289). In post–World War I America, political fundamentalism, whose leading mark is the artificial promotion of a sense of oneness, especially closes up the Melting Pot to any racially-marked individual. Mary Heaton Vorse recalls, "Intolerance, hatred of foreigners, fear and prosecution of Negroes, spread like poison through the country" (1991: 159). In *Inheritors*, Aunt Isabel says, "These are days when we have to stand close together — all of us who are the same kind of people must stand together because the thing that makes us the same kind of people is threatened" (218). The Hindu boys will never be considered integrated parts of the community, since "This college is for Americans. I'm not going to have foreign revolutionists come here," as Felix Fejevary states (207). But as this character also acknowledges regarding Bakhshish, one of these students, "It is not what he did. It's what he is."

Bakhshish and the other Hindu characters "are the wrong kind of strangers" (211). That is, it is not that they were giving out leaflets on the right of India to be free from the British rule, but that they are racially-marked outsiders. The Hindu students break the illusion of homogeneity that helps racist characters be comfortable with the place they inhabit and enjoy their sense of topophilia.

According to Beverly Smith, in *Inheritors* Glaspell predisposes "audience members to tolerate marginalization and see [foreign-born individuals] in society's midst as 'other'" (2003: 137). In Smith's discussion, the Hindu characters are marginalized because they do not appear onstage, and neither does their culture, so they are never seen onstage forming part of an American group. Smith has also highlighted that one of the main modes of marginalization appears when "even those qualities appropriated by the mainstream can be interpreted negatively when exhibited by foreign-born characters" (2003: 133). In *Inheritors*, Glaspell makes the Hindu students appropriate the words of an American icon, Abraham Lincoln, causing the immediate rage of some of the American-born characters. A reason the Hindu students use to state their right to express their discontent with the situation in India and with the isolationist policy of the United States is backed up by Abraham Lincoln's "First Inaugural Address to the Congress" (March 4, 1861). In this speech, Lincoln justified a revolution when "by the mere force of numbers, a majority should deprive a minority of any clearly written constitutional right" (1989: 219). Tellingly enough, the Hindu students have also quoted Lincoln's famous line: "Whenever they shall grow weary of the existing government, they can exercise their constitutional right of amending it, ... or their *revolutionary* right to dismember or overthrow it" (198, emphasis in original). Horace, Fejevary the Second, and Senator Lewis believe that the Hindu students do not hold the right to quote Lincoln because "he was speaking in another age," "Terms change their significance from generation to generation," and "The fact that they are quoting it shows it's being misapplied" (198). But these arguments do not show that the American-born characters appropriate Lincoln's words better. Horace Fejevary really embodies the inferiority of some American-born characters regarding the appropriation of what they consider purely American. He says, "But gee — Lincoln oughta been more careful what he said. Ignorant people don't know how to take such things" (199), revealing his own ignorance and stupidity. No matter how well-educated these immigrants are, these modern Americans, regardless of their own origins, see them merely as "foreign elements" threatening the safety of their country. Thus, far from fostering ethnic marginalization, Glaspell reworks the American geomythology that this country welcomes everybody. The racially marked others do not even appear onstage as a symbolic representation of their common erasure from the American map. Borrowing Gainor's words, Glaspell literalizes marginalization by having the Hindu characters never appear onstage, "Nevertheless, she forces us to recognize the figures society has ostracized by making them integral, if invisible, to the action" (2001: 127).

As regards the topic of immigrants and the community, it is interesting to consider George Revill's discourse on the role of the community in establishing and fixing identity between people and places. According to this scholar, the concept of community is strongly linked to place, and the identity of a community only survives if identified with an area. This identification allows the community to define ownership of that area and to defend it against those seen as "invaders" (1993: 120). This is nowhere more evident than in the way "the one-hundred-per-cent" American characters in *Inheritors* see the land as theirs. "People are a bit absurd out of their own places. We need to be held in our relationships — against our background — or we are — I don't know — grotesque," says Aunt Isabel (219). Given that characters such as Horace, Fejevary the Second, or Aunt Isabel cannot identify themselves with the racially-marked Hindu characters, these must also be expelled from their place so that their community identity remains undamaged. In the same way that these Hindu characters do not belong to this place, Glaspell also introduces verbally other immigrants who do not belong to it either. The following dialogue is revealing about this point:

> HORACE: I'll show those dirty dagoes where they get off!...
> FEJEVARY: Are you talking about the Hindus?
> HORACE: Yes, the dirty dagoes.
> FEJEVARY: Hindus aren't dagoes you know, Horace.
> HORACE: Well, what's the difference? This foreign element gets my goat.
> SENATOR: My boy, you talk like an American [197].

Horace cannot tell the difference between dagoes and Hindus. For Horace, as for Senator Lewis, Spanish, Portuguese, Italian and Hindu people are defined merely in terms of how different they are from Anglo-Saxon Americans; they are just the disturbing elements attempting to demolish the "felicitous place" America is.

In the way Glaspell depicts America in *Inheritors*, it is America itself which opened its territories to these immigrants, only to marginalize them once inside. Glaspell puts her finger on the spot, and deconstructs an important American geomythology as she makes the only character who truly defends foreign-born characters, Madeline, claim, "They're people from the other side of the world who came here believing in us, drawn from the far side of world by things we say about ourselves. Well, I'm going to pretend — just for fun — that the things we say about ourselves are true" (212). Glaspell criticizes how unfair it is to advertise America as the land of opportunity where everybody has a place to simply reject newcomers once they are there.

Even ethnic American-born characters are attacked in this play. Ira Morton will never forgive the fact that his wife died when assisting a neighbor, to whom he scornfully refers as "that immigrant woman": Ira's wife "choked to death in that Swede's house. They lived" (223). For this motive, Ira Morton hates the natural fact that his corn flies to the Johnsons, "them Swedes" (225), representative of their symbolic union, and he cannot stand the idea that his daughter, Madeline, befriends Emil Johnson.

Going deeper into the interplay between revisions of the Myth of Mobility and racially marked characters in Glaspell's theater, the cases of African Americans and Native Americans must be considered. The physical absence of these characters from the stage, as in the case of the Hindu students in *Inheritors*, symbolizes their ostracism and, at the same time, suggests that, in spite of what other "genuine" American characters can think, say, or feel, non–Anglo Saxon Americans are indeed rightful inhabitants of America. Though African Americans do not usually appear in Glaspell's writings,[8] in *Inheritors* they appear symbolically in two ways. Firstly, the portrait of Abraham Lincoln hanging on the wall of the Morton farm echoes the Civil War fought, among other political and economic reasons, for the right of African Americans to have a rightful place in American society. Secondly, Glaspell shows that even if some Americans reject the idea of African Americans being part of the country, they are. When in Act II jingoistic Horace Fejevary is in the library dancing with Doris and Fussie, they practice some new jazz steps. Jazz music, a craze at that time, is of African American origin.

From the basic standpoint of who was here first, Native Americans should be considered one hundred percent Americans. They are not immigrants, but in Glaspell's *Inheritors* they suffer the same kind of marginalization as the Hindu characters. Displaced from their land and confined to secluded areas, Native Americans become the victims of the white colonizer's Myth of Mobility. All the details of the absent Native American characters Glaspell provides are based upon historical data, showing a level of accuracy that cannot but explain that the author aimed to praise these people that once helped colonizers to survive, at the same time that she condemns what was done to them afterwards. The Native Americans of *Inheritors*, the Sacs, actually occupied the part in the Mississippi Valley the play is located in, an area Glaspell knew well. Furthermore, Glaspell's depiction of the Sacs and their Chief Black Hawk seems to be influenced by George Cram Cook. There is a clear similarity between the portrait of Native Americans in *Inheritors*, and their portrait in Cook's accounts quoted in Glaspell's *The Road to the Temple*, as well as in his play *The Spring* (1921).[9] *Inheritors* is set in what was the territory of the Sacs:

> GRANDMOTHER: This very land — land you want to buy — was the land they
> loved — Blackhawk and his Indians. They came here for their games. This was

where their fathers — as they called 'em — were buried. I've seen my husband
and Blackhawk climb that hill together. [*A backward point right.*] He used to
love that hill — Blackhawk [182].

But after the Black Hawk War (1832), Native Americans were paid "not a
fancy price" (182) for this land. And as Glaspell echoes in the play, Native
Americans were also mistreated when they were put on reservations or exhibited in Wild West Shows. This was the case of Black Hawk, who in real life,
as well as in Glaspell's play, was exploited in a show. Black Hawk was taken
to Washington, Philadelphia, and New York. He did move, but not in the
free manner white colonizers would; Black Hawk was forced to move, only
to have his heart broken, as Grandmother Morton laments (182).

The main excuse to justify why Native Americans were excluded from
the Myth of Mobility relies on their conceptualization as "tragic figures whose
inability to adapt ... necessitated their removal" (Moy 1995: 192). This alleged
inability to adapt was further enlarged by the way Native Americans were
portrayed in literature, so that the American geomythology could justify the
erasure of Native Americans from their territories. Given that what Glaspell
questions is the necessity of their removal, and thus, the concept of American
geomythology as has been historically transmitted, she avoids any traditional
binary description of Native Americans in terms of either evilness or nobleness.
Indeed, I believe that the disappearance of Native Americans from the landscape is the only obstacle for the pioneer characters' absolute *topophilia* in the
first act. Glaspell's pioneer characters emphasize that nobleness is the main
feature of the Sacs, and not their evilness.

Chief Black Hawk is referred to as "Noble. Noble like the forests" (188).
Moreover, this nobleness becomes overt in Glaspell's reference to the American
celebration of Thanksgiving. "The way they wiped us out was to bring fish
and corn. We'd starved to death that first winter hadn't been for the Indians"
(182), states Grandmother Morton. But the Sacs are also presented as violent
men. Their violence, however, has been learnt from the white man. Confrontations with the Sacs began "after other white folks had roiled them up —
white folks that didn't know how to treat 'em" (182), recalls Grandmother
Morton. And Silas says, "I can't forget the Indians. We killed their joy before
we killed them. We made them less" (193). Furthermore, Glaspell suggests
Native Americans' superiority through Silas's belief that "'Twould 'a done
something for us to have *been* Indians a little more" (187, emphasis in original).
In Glaspell's depiction of the encounter between pioneers and Native Americans, there was space for everybody. But in exchange for their good intentions,
Native Americans were expelled from their own territories, put on reservations
and ignored in the community. And this is why Glaspell makes Silas Morton
feel ashamed of owning a piece of land that belonged to Black Hawk. Silas

reconciles with the Sacs in spatial terms: "That's what the hill is for! [*Pointing*.] Don't you see it? ... Plant a college, so's after we are gone that college says for us, says in people learning has made more: 'This is why we took this land'" (189). But as pointed out earlier, the absence of Native American characters in subsequent acts shows that Silas's dream has vanished. In the present time, Silas's place goes on being purely for whites, while Native Americans, as with other racially-marked characters, are displaced.

This chapter closes with a brief analysis of *Free Laughter*, an allegorical parody of the Red Scare, and a blunt attack on the suppression of free speech and the jingoistic spirit of the so called one hundred percent Americans. In *Free Laughter*, as in *Inheritors*, Glaspell denounces the attempt to erase all those who are not one hundred percent Americans and dissenters alike from the United States. In the same way that *Inheritors* starts symbolically with the celebrations of the July 4 holiday, *Free Laughter* opens with the preparations for the thirdtennial celebrations of the Wildflower, a parody of the Mayflower. The Trend of the Times, sitting on a throne, passes a law forbidding laughter, a comic revision of the suppression of free speech that *Inheritors* also criticizes. In contrast to the Wildflower, the Garbage Fleet is ready to deport those who dissent from the norm. The two ships frame the great American paradox. While the Wildflower was full of dreams and possibilities — it headed to "the land where men could think" — the Garbage Fleet ironically takes "men because they thought" (122). With just a short time separating both plays, several lines from *Free Laughter* echo in the later *Inheritors*. A girl character called the Spirit of Laughter, who is about to be deported and resembles Madeline in *Inheritors* quite closely, claims, "I can be silent/ And yet be heard" (120), a similar remark to that of Madeline about being in prison freer than outside, since in prison she will go on defending her right to speak freely. Another character, the Native-born, is also locked up: "Locked men have sometimes been more free than Man has ever been" (123). As Madeline, the Native-born prefers to celebrate the 300th anniversary of the Wildflower in prison, where the love of liberty dwells in his heart, rather than somewhere else. A character called the Foreign-born denounces, as Madeline does, that immigrants came to the United States because this was supposed to be a free country: "I heard you laughed more here" (181). But as seen in *Inheritors*, the Others do not fit within the homogenizing American map, and thus, one hundred percent Americans required their departure. Having discussed how Glaspell's revision of American geomytholgies are fine indicators of many of her characters' victimage of location, the following chapter focuses on the relationship between the geopathic character that cannot move out and dichotomist conceptions of dramatic spaces: isolation vs. communality; the configuration of home as either prison or shelter; and inside vs. outside.

3

Geodichotomies in the Configuration of Dramatic Geopathology

Home is a place to escape to and a place to escape from [George 1999: 9].

The configuration of place as a problem relies heavily on subjective and binary geographical dichotomies such as here vs. there, inside vs. outside, and enclosure vs. boundlessness. Before going deeper into the analysis of dramatic geodichotomies in Susan Glaspell's dramatic homes, it seems appropriate to analyze in the first place the very geography of the sets Glaspell presents onstage. Glaspell's favorite setting, which is typically a geographically isolated one, implies a first geodichotomy; the dramatic representation of isolation vs. community. This geographical isolation has a pivotal role in understanding the following geographical dichotomies that appear in Glaspell's plays: the configuration of home as either prison or shelter, and the character's urge to be inside or outside these locations, hallmark geodichotomies in the configuration of place as a problem in modern drama.

Geographical Isolation in the Face of the Community

In Chaudhuri's paradigm to detect dramatic geopathology there is no mention of the significance of physical isolation, which is actually a determining factor. One of the problems a character may have with the place they dwell in is precisely the feeling of isolation. This isolation is part of a long-held dichotomy, that between individualism and communality. Indeed, this geodichotomy is at the core of American Transcendentalism, a tradition that heavily influenced the writings of Susan Glaspell. For Transcendentalism places the individual first, but always trying to come to terms with the community. In her book *Susan Glaspell and the Anxiety of Expression*, Kristina Hinz-Bode focuses on the dichotomy individuality vs. communality regarding language and communication: "In many of her plays her protagonists are presented as individuals whose well-being is threatened as they struggle to both free themselves of and at the same time define themselves within a web of communicational contacts which create the notions of self and other in a constant reciprocal process" (2006b: 31). Regarding this relationship among character, identity, and community, Marcia Noe has included location in the matrix that Glaspell employs to present her characters. Noe's preliminary observation that Glaspell employs isolated regions to show "the effect of isolation upon the human spirit" (1981: 79) is the starting point for the construction of problematic places in Glaspell's plays. Beyond what Noe calls Glaspell's "regional drama" (*Trifles, Inheritors, The Outside,* and *The Comic Artist*), geographical isolation appears in some other plays with similar purposes.

The impact of isolation for the construction of geopathic homes and characters is already evident in Glaspell's *Trifles*. In her analysis of the setting of Susan Glaspell's *A Jury of Her Peers,* the short story version of *Trifles,* Elaine Hedges concludes that the story "refers to the prairie and plains country that stretches across Iowa into Nebraska — a country of open, level or rolling land, and few trees" (1995: 52).Within this isolated region, the very location of the Wrights' farm is even more isolated given that "it is down in a hollow and you don't see the road. I dunno what it is, but it's a lonesome place and always was" (31), as Mrs. Hale describes it. Susan Koprince highlights the dichotomy existing between the isolation of the farm and community as she says, "the desolate farmhouse in *Trifles* becomes symbolic of the protagonist's repression and alienation" (2006: 68), that is, Minnie's exclusion from the community is heavily given by the spatial isolation of the place she inhabits. Indeed, in an undated typewritten draft of *Trifles*,[1] Glaspell had made this point clearer by making Mr. Hale say, "She was always nice when anybody came in — poor thing, she used to seem grateful"(3), verbally enhancing Minnie's isolation as Mr. Hale recalls how grateful Minnie looked when someone dropped by.

Glaspell also makes use of this landscape of isolation in other plays set in the Midwest. *Inheritors* opens in *"the Mortons' farmhouse in the Middle West— on the rolling prairie just back from the Mississippi"* (181). The windows open *"looking out on a generous land"* (181). Grandmother Morton describes how "houses are sparse" (183) and how they were alone in the area but for the Owens, "ten miles down the river" (182). It must be noted, however, that although in the first act Glaspell recreates in spatial terms a feeling of isolation similar to that perceived in *Trifles,* in *Inheritors* this feeling is less acute, probably because what Glaspell intended in this play was to celebrate pioneer life and to use to some extent the values of that time as a model to follow. The subsequent acts, taking place forty-one years later, still show the Mortons' farm as an isolated place, alien to the industrialization of the area. Morton College, "up on the hill" in the middle of cornfields, marks a symbolic relationship between its physical isolation and the isolationist policy characters such as Senator Lewis and Horace Fejevary defend. And the Stanhopes' house of *Alison's House* is also apart from town. The stage direction describes it as follows, "*There is a river village near-by, and the small city where the other Stanhopes now live is about ten miles up the river*" (312). Nature further isolates the place. The river and the vast vegetation around the house help to suffocate it and keep it apart from civilization, also marking a spatial hindrance to human communality with those outside the estate.

Significantly, Glaspell's plays set in New England also share this device of isolated location. The plays set on Cape Cod represent lonely places. The old life-saving station of *The Outside* is "a buried house, you might say, off here on the outside shore — way across the sand from man or beast" (61). Precisely, Mrs. Patrick and Allie chose this isolated place to live in, since this isolation guaranteed the abjection from the community, symbolized in the town of Provincetown, that they long for. Similarly, in *The Comic Artist* several characters acknowledge the isolated location of Eleanor and Stephen's house. Luella considers the house as a "no place": "the road seemed to go to no place at all" (270), and "[*She says in comment on the lonely house...*] My God!" (271). Moreover, Luella and Nina refer several times to the location of the house as "Way out here," as seen in the previous chapter. Karl also emphasizes the isolation of this place when he admits, "This is the kind of place I'd like. It would be lonely for Nina, though. [*Cheerfully*.] In New York I'll think of you having this good light and space, and this heavenly quiet" (288). Interestingly, in Karl's words place in itself is not the only source for victimage of location. The isolating conditions of Eleanor and Stephen's house would not be a problem for Karl; on the contrary, he would enjoy its quietness. For his wife Nina, however, this place would be a problem. In like manner, Stephen, who seemed to be pleased with his house at the beginning of the play, also sees its isolating condition. He says to his wife, "We've been here in isolation too long" (302). Probably, the fact that Eleanor and Stephen had lived in isolation for a long time predisposes the tragic confrontation that takes place when the community, embodied in Luella and Nina, arrives at this place, turning it upside down.

The house setting in *Bernice* is also apart from civilization. It is located in an unnamed New England town, two hours from Boston. It is "in the country" (94), and up on a hill, determining factors for isolation. As Laura points out, "It's a pity you couldn't get a doctor. That's the worst part of living way up here by one's self" (100). As the Stanhopes' place in *Alison's House*, the house in *Bernice* is also surrounded by nature, making it more inaccessible to humans. Bernice's house is amidst woods. As regards Bernice's home, Jackie Czerepinski has asserted, "The home is isolated, difficult to get to but well worth the trip, just as Bernice was 'off by herself'—beyond the understanding of most" (1995: 147). Certainly, the isolation of the house is Bernice's metaphorical representation. Nonetheless, Czerepinski's appreciation that the house "is well worth the trip" cannot be left uncontested. One of the most interesting points in the study of geopathology in this play precisely focuses on the matter of isolation. Though it has been pointed out that Bernice lived "content in her isolation" (Hinz-Bode 2006b: 113), this cannot be taken for granted, since it is more probable that Bernice, indeed, did not live content in isolation. Bernice's father at one point thinks about his daughter's detachment: "I think it wasn't that she—wanted it that way" (112), and her maid suggests that Bernice's alleged happiness was fake: "If all those years ... there was something she hid, and if she seemed to feel—what she didn't feel. She did it well, didn't she?" (110). The two characters who lived with Bernice have serious doubts about her happiness in isolation.

In dramatic geopathology hard climatic conditions add to isolated fictional places to multiply the feeling of isolation. On the whole, Glaspell shows a predilection for autumn and winter scenes. *Inheritors* (Acts II and III) and *Bernice* take place in October and *Alison's House* in December. Since Mrs. Patrick is wearing a coat and a scarf (62), *The Outside* also takes place in a cold season. And so does *The Comic Artist*, taking into account the outside "September hills" (272), the characters' costume, the mist and the wind. It is not a matter of coincidence that Glaspell's plays where the tone is more dramatic, and geopathology more easily detectable, show harder climatic conditions, mainly *Trifles* and *The Verge*. *Trifles* begins with the men rushing towards the stove and rubbing their hands because of the intense coldness. Indeed, "it dropped to zero last night" (26). This low temperature is also indicative of the isolation and scarce social life of characters inhabiting this place; coldness is a hindrance to social life. In *The Verge* Glaspell does not describe the geographical location of the house as an isolated one straightforwardly. Because of what the characters say, we know that the house is somewhere in New England. The isolating atmosphere is provided by the snow piling up against the lower greenhouse and the "stormy wind" (230). Maybe the greenhouse is not so difficult to arrive at, as Dr. Emmons, Adelaide and Elizabeth do reach the house, but the snow and wind create an impression that this place is difficult to reach.

Glaspell's dramatic use of geographical isolation does not directly lead to geopathology. Geographical isolation is employed to dramatize the confrontation between the isolated individual and the community. As Kristina Hinz-Bode claims, this dichotomy is one Glaspell employs frequently as one of life's essentials: communality is both "a prison for the individual" and "a chance to change life for better" (2006b: 229). Next I discuss whether the geopathology attributed to the characters placed in isolation comes from their need to defend their isolation and escape from communality; or, on the contrary, from their urge to embrace the community, thus ending their isolation. The key geodichotomy is, therefore, the representation of home as prison or shelter.

Dramatic Representations of Home as Prison and Shelter

The dramatic representations of home as either prison or shelter respond to the different ways characters understand the figure of home. This geodichotomy comprises a paradox inherent to American culture: the need to have a shelter that provides security for identity, and the need to move beyond the house. Dichotomist representations of home are closely related to other issues seen earlier, especially to Glaspell's revision of the different aspects of the American Myth of Mobility. For if a geopathic character cannot move freely, surely their geopathology will increase if the place they are in resembles a prison. And vice versa, if a character constructs a shelter in their house, in dramatic geopathology this same character may have to cope with the threat that invaders pose, struggling against those characters that, exerting their right to the Myth of Mobility, want to occupy their place.

A very consistent device to suggest a prison-like dimension is to relate the onstage to unlocalized offstage fictional prisons. In some of Glaspell's plays, absent characters are imprisoned paralleling the actual prison that the place seen onstage represents metaphorically. *Trifles* has been amply discussed in this respect. Minnie Wright is in an offstage prison, but as Mrs. Hale and Mrs. Peters interpret her farm, this is a prison too. A stage property, Minnie's apron, is a pivotal element that draws the connection between both prisons: "She said she wanted an apron. Funny thing to want, for there isn't much to get you dirty in jail, goodness knows. But I suppose just to make her feel more natural" (29). As Elaine Hedges has said, the fact that Minnie asks for her apron means that with her apron she will feel in prison as at home (1995: 65). As Mrs. Hale and Mrs. Peters agree that the apron will make Minnie feel "more natural," more at home in the sheriff's house, they come to understand that Minnie's kitchen was her prison. And since they are in the kitchen all the time, one cannot but wonder if they consider their kitchens their prisons too. Hedges has seen Minnie's kitchen as "the limited and limiting space of her female sphere" (1995: 54). This kitchen not only represents Minnie's "limited and limiting" space, but also the space of most pioneer women, since all shared the same chores and obligations on the farm, and most of these obligations were geographically located inside the kitchen. Reconsidering that the male characters move freely inside the farmhouse, while the women remain all the time in the kitchen, this stage space makes itself evident as a prison for Mrs. Hale and Mrs. Peters. Closed doors and windows reinforce the configuration of this place as a prison.

Glaspell employs a similar technique in *Inheritors*. Here Glaspell also draws the connection between an unlocalized offstage prison and the prison that home becomes for Madeline. The offstage prison in *Inheritors* is not portrayed as a fair institution where offenders are punished and rehabilitated if possible. On the contrary, the prison Glaspell evokes in *Inheritors* appears as a place of torture and injustice, which, on the whole, does not follow the principles of the democracy the United States claims to defend, as Professor Holden says: "A society which permits things to go on which I can prove go on in our federal prisons had better stop and take a fresh look at itself" (207). Glaspell leads us to imagine the conditions of an American prison at the time. In the same way that there is a spatial connection between the offstage prison and the kitchen in *Trifles* through a prop, in *Inheritors* Glaspell utilizes another stage prop for similar purposes: the letter Fred Jordan sends to Madeline from jail, in which he tells her about the configuration of his cell:

> MADELINE: He got this letter out to me — written on this scrap of paper. They don't give him paper. [*Peering.*] Written so fine I can hardly read it. He's in what they call "the hole," father — a punishment cell. [*With difficulty reading it.*] It's two and a half feet at one end, three feet at the other, and six feet long. He'd been there ten days when he wrote this. He gets two slices of bread a day; he gets water; that's all he gets [214].

Glaspell might have been influenced by a real letter J. H. Collins, a conscientious objector, sent from jail to *The Masses*[2] in 1917. Writing from Hordcott Camp, Wilton and Schubury, Collins's letter reads,

> I do not expect I shall be able to write again for some time, because when we are under sentence, we are not allowed to have letters unless they are censored. We are not allowed to read, or to write to friends or to have visitors except when serving time, and we have only half rations. I can assure you that the life of a conscientious objector is almost unbearable [1917: 30].

Collins's words seem to reverberate in what Madeline says after reading Fred Jordan's letter from prison. Jordan's account parallels Collins's "unbearable" life under sentence, with limited paper, censored reading, and scarce food.[3]

At the same time that the offstage prison helps suggest that the onstage places, the Morton farm and Morton College, are geopathic, Glaspell is here displaying a brave political commitment to denounce the problem of place in American prisons, not only because of the bad state and inhuman conditions of these buildings, but also because of the reasons why people were incarcerated at that time. Fred Jordan's and the Hindu students' incarcerations in *Inheritors* respond to America's problem with place. Hindu students are in jail because of American xenophobia and isolationist policy after World War I, revealing that in America there is no place for everybody. And Jordan is imprisoned under the Espionage Act and the Sedition Act, passed by Congress in 1917 and 1918, respectively, which "forbade any expression of contempt for the government, Constitution, flag, or military uniform" (Wainscott 1997: 12). Glaspell shows that America, as anywhere else, is a place where governmental rules, either good or bad, have to be respected. Imprisonment awaits dissenters. In *Inheritors*, one of the problems Madeline and Fred have with place is that they cannot speak freely where they are. Fred was thought to be an anarchist and imprisoned for defining himself as a conscientious objector. And when Madeline denounces the unfairness of the Hindu students' imprisonment, she is warned, "Do you know that in America today there are women in our prisons for saying no more than you've said here to me!" (213). Actually, besides her final movement towards prison at the end of the play, Madeline is sent to prison twice for defending the Hindu students.

But prisons are not only physical presences in Glaspell's plays, and the metaphorical representation of home as prison is part of a long tradition to which Glaspell is a heiress. Gilbert and Gubar in *The Madwoman in the Attic* acknowledge the core role of "images of enclosure" in women's literary tradition (1979: xi). Glaspell adheres to this tradition, for in many of her plays she turns home into metaphors of entrapment which make home look more like a prison than a safe haven. To present home as a prison Glaspell employs different devices: through what the audience can see onstage, through the relationship between characters and place, and through what characters say about these places. As shown earlier, Madeline in *Inheritors* is affected by Fred's physical imprisonment. Glaspell underlines the symbolic connection between this offstage prison and the farm by making Madeline construct a metaphorical prison onstage in front of the audience's eyes. The most powerful moment in this play happens when Madeline takes a piece of chalk and reproduces Fred's cell:

> *On the floor she marks off FRED JORDAN's cell. Slowly, at the end left unchalked, as for a door, she goes in. Her hand goes up, as against a wall; looks at the other hand, sees it is out too far, brings it in, giving herself the width of the cell. Walks its length, halts, looks up.... In the moment she stands there, she is in that cell; she is all the people who are in those cells* [215].

As Christine Dymkowski has observed, "because the focus is on Madeline's attempt to experience Fred's confinement, the audience's mental and emotional engagement is greater than it would have been if he were actually shown on stage in his cell" (1988: 99–100). I share Dymkowski's belief in the emotional impact on the audience, but the image gets greater transcendence as Madeline's imagination and concern go further than his friend's cell. The cell is not merely Fred's, but the cell of "all the people." As Madeline experiences all those prisoners' confinement, she does not feel entitled to look out through the window. Reflecting upon this political issue made personal, the reasons why Madeline cannot look through the window seem at least twofold. On the one hand, as these prisoners do not have a window to look through, she wants to identify with them and thus she denies herself this privilege. "I used to tramp with Fred Jordan. This is where he is now. [*Stepping inside the cell.*] He doesn't even see out," says Madeline (220). On the other hand, it might be possible that Madeline feels so ashamed of the extreme isolationist and nationalistic policy of some Americans that she cannot look on the American land with the same eyes she did before. She cannot enjoy her country as she did before, not after realizing what is happening to other people who dissent against the government and who do not enjoy the freedom she has.

Visually, the image of the prison goes beyond the cell drawn on the floor and metaphorically occupies the whole farm in the following scene:

> MADELINE: Detachment. [*Pause.*] This is one thing they do at that place. [*She moves to the open door.*] Chain them up to the bars — just like this. [*In the doorway where her two grandfathers once pledged faith with the dreams of a million years, she raises clasped hands as high as they will go.*] Eight hours a day — day after day. Just hold your arms up like this one hour then sit down and think about — [*As if tortured by all those who have been so tortured, her body begins to give with sobs, arms drop, the last word is a sob.*] detachment [223].

As Madeline has come to understand that her problem with place in America is that it is an ideological prison, the representation of what happens inside cells is not limited to the chalk cell. Madeline becomes here the Every (wo)man of expressionistic theater. Her *Schrei*, however, is silenced and killed by a sob because she is exhausted from repeating the tortures Every (wo)man experiences. The power of place seems to defeat her.

Other plays where Glaspell builds prison-like homes, such as *Chains of Dew*, *Alison's House*, and *Trifles* are not as political as *Inheritors*, or *Free Laughter*, in terms of Glaspell's criticism of America, its immigration policy, its jingoism, and its xenophobia, but they focus more explicitly on the idea of home as a metaphorical prison for some of the dwellers. The imprisoned characters of these plays are ill-affected by the power of an enclosing location that does not allow their identity to change or even show. Very early in *Chains of Dew*,

Seymore opens up the topic of his home as a prison, as he makes the general comment that when "You're *in* a certain place. Holding it down — and up. Too many things fall if you let go" (137, emphasis in original). In Seymore's discourse, home looks like a prison because this is a place that keeps one tied to it because of its many family obligations. Glaspell underlines Seymore's feeling of geopathology by making him a free character when he is in New York, free of the chains that keep him tied to his home. There he is a man let out of prison, released from "bondage" (134). But as the play develops, the audience becomes more and more aware of how fake Seymore's bondage is, as fake as his geopathology. In this regard, the title of the play is worth analyzing. Seymore's *chains*, the metaphor of his social and family obligations, which deter him from living the free and satisfying life he would like to lead as a full-time poet, "are as ephemeral as dew" (Gainor 2001: 185). Playing with the phonetic similarity between "dew" and "due," Glaspell's title already makes us question whether Seymore's chains to his family, which Leon nicely labels "chains of affection" (172), are actual obligations or just weak ties Seymore has invented to continue being the martyr of the family. I agree with Kristina Hinz-Bode's statement that Seymore "is a conceited prig who casts his family and social circles in the role of 'burden' so that he can sustain the theme of 'longing for freedom' which is the essence of his poetry" (2006a: 213). Thus, what Glaspell merges here is the dichotomy between the representation of home as prison or shelter. As it becomes evident that Seymore's home is not his prison, one cannot but assert that this is, actually and contrary to what he actually says, his shelter. As he says that it is his prison-house that prevents him from being a good and free poet, his house is his shelter to justify that he is not the great poet he claims he could be.

Agatha in *Alison's House* is another character that has configured her home as a prison. Indeed, she has named herself the guardian of this prison-house, as she repeatedly implies with her words: "I won't have people looking through Alison's room. I've guarded it for eighteen years" (317); "Me leave this house — while it is still this house? I shall be the last to step from the door" (318). Agatha's obsession with being the guardian of the house, and of Alison's secret poems, makes her a geopathic character. The rest of the family, although unaware of the existence of these poems, realizes Agatha's problem with the house, and this is the reason why they are moving: "Agatha cannot be left here. Her heart's feeble, and her mind — not what it was. If the place remained, she'd come back here" (330), says Stanhope. Here Glaspell shows again that the geodichotomy of home as prison and home as shelter can blend. Agatha's eagerness to protect the house, to keep its status of shelter, has turned into the source of her pathology: the house has become a prison too. For as she has played the role of Alison's guard during and after Alison's life, Agatha has also developed a role of prisoner herself. At one point Agatha wonders, "I'm no *prisoner*, am I? Why should I stay up in my room if I don't want to?" (339, emphasis added). Glaspell complicates this issue of the status of the house as prison and shelter, and plainly presents Agatha as a geopathic character, in the solution Agatha finds to remain Alison's eternal keeper: burning the house down. When the fire is announced, Agatha re-enters the stage and is described as a pathological character. She is "*white, rigid,*" entering the room "*in a curious, fixed state*" (323). She confidently states her wish to see the house burnt down, "Burning. All burning. All at once" (323). Regardless of the damages she might cause to herself or her family, Agatha needs to demolish the whole house in order to destroy Alison's secret poems.

In as much as Agatha is the guardian of Alison's poems, the imprisoned poems are a posthumous extension of the seclusion Alison endured all her life. I agree with Karen H. Gardiner's idea that Alison "was walled in by the conventionality of her family during her life. After her death, her poetry was also walled in, hidden away in a closet, still carefully guarded by sister Agatha" (2006: 196). Even before the content of the poems is revealed, when the other characters learn what they had only intuited before — that Alison felt as a prisoner in the house — Alison arises as a geopathic character through her association with what can be considered a commonplace geopathic location in women's literature: the closet, the symbolic location where Agatha starts the fire. Before seeing this closet in Act III, Glaspell has made several references throughout the play to the fact that Alison's room has a closet, which implies that the physicality of this closet does not answer to a mere functional or realistic dimension. Glaspell erects the closet within the room in Alison's house as a prison, within the prison of the room, within the prison of the house.

Alison's poems are never read aloud in the play, but Glaspell dramatically suggests the imprisonment this character experienced through other means that add to the symbolic closet. Glaspell recreates Alison's entrapment within her room through the stories and memories that the Stanhopes recall. At no point in the play do they tell of any memory of Alison that took place outside her room. In the following scene Stanhope, Eben, and Elsa are in Alison's room, and Eben recalls a time when he told Alison of Jimmy Miles, who had knocked over Eben's mud house. Alison comforted her nephew by saying: "You can build a fort, and put him in it. She tells me the story of the bumble bee that got drunk on larkspur and set out to see how drunk you could get in heaven" (344–345). Elsa has her story, too. She remembers when she pounded "with fists" to enter Alison's room to tell her that "Aunt Agatha won't give me a cookie, because I pulled the cat's tail." As Elsa recalls, Alison "stands at the door so that Aunt Agatha can't get in, but God, she says, could come down the chimney" (345). In the little stories Alison told her niece and nephew to console them, two images underline her feeling of entrapment. Firstly, the "sand fort" in which Alison suggests Jimmy be put reveals how her mind would work on prison images, possibly influenced by her own imprisonment. Furthermore, right after telling about the fort, Alison went on to tell a story about a "bumble bee." In the poet's mind, and in stark contrast to her entrapment in the room, this insect that can fly free and reach heaven is a metaphor for freedom. Secondly, when Elsa recalls how she sought refuge from Agatha in Alison's room, this room erects itself as a fort, a shelter. Nevertheless, Elsa remembers that Alison used the door to block Agatha's entry, and that her aunt was aware that God "could come down the chimney." For the geopathic Alison, no room is a shelter. It is also significant that Elsa and Eben remember all these seclusion stories and references just as they are about to discover Alison's poems. By following the rules of respectability, Alison accepted imprisonment within the house. Years later, when her nephew asserts, "We can't keep Alison in a prison," her sister Agatha is prompt to reply, "Who kept Alison in a prison? What do you mean — a prison? She was where she wanted to be, wasn't she?" (318). But Alison was not where she wanted to be, and the years she spent separated from her lover, confined to the house, constituted a chain of painful days she hid from her family. It is only when Stanhope, Eben, and Elsa read the secret poems that they realize all the pain Alison went through when she stayed at home instead of eloping with her lover; her writing is the proof of her painful experience of the inside: "[*slowly, as if trying to realize it.*] And all of that — went on in this room," says Eben; and Stanhope adds, "If I had known it was as much as this — I would not have asked her to stay" (349).

The metaphorical usage of images of seclusion for dramatic geopathology is perhaps nowhere more obvious than in the symbolic allusions to cages in Glaspell's plays. For instance, in *Close the Book* Glaspell employs this image to verbalize Jhansi's feeling of entrapment within the Roots' library, her geopathology. "[W]alls stifle me. You come of people who have been walled all their lives. It doesn't *cage* you. But me — I am a gypsy!" says Jhansi (37, emphasis added). The cage enters straightforwardly in opposition to Jhansi's alleged ancestors: "right behind me — all those wanderers, people who were never caught; feel them behind me pushing me away from all this!" (37). The walls, elsewhere used as "metaphors of social oppression in general" and of "conventionality" (Gardiner 2006: 185, 196), have a physical dimension not to be forgotten. Walls, besides being metaphors of social control, physically prevent the free exit of geopathic characters who cannot move out. Though it is true that Jhansi's geopathology, as in the case of Seymore in *Chains of Dew*, seems fake, for other characters, such as Alison in *Alison's House*, the physicality of the walls is a boundary as uncrossable as their metaphorical allusion to social norms.

In *Trifles*, the birdcage is more than an illusion that helps Mrs. Hale and Mrs. Peters see Minnie as a prisoner at the farm. Here the birdcage is a real stage property with a physical presence onstage, as well as the dead canary that the other female characters come to see as a metaphor of Minnie. Both the cage and the canary have been extensively analyzed as symbols of imprisonment.[4] In the same way that in *Alison's House* Glaspell organizes images of imprisonment as a set of Russian nesting dolls (the closet inside the room inside the house), in *Trifles* Glaspell places the cage within the kitchen, within the farmhouse. All three are prisons in themselves, and when all three are seen together they contribute to a greater sense of entrapment.

Glaspell gives the cage a central role as she makes Mrs. Peters and Mrs. Hale touch and talk about it, turning this stage prop into one of the main devices in the play to understand its dramatic geopathology. As they examine the cage closely, Mrs. Peters notes, "Why, look at this door. It's broke. One hinge is pulled apart," and Mrs. Hale adds, "Looks as if someone must have been rough with it" (31). Most scholars believe that both women see in this broken cage the clear evidence of John Wright's roughness. This is, at least, the way Mrs. Peters and Mrs. Hale see it.[5] However, since both Minnie and John are absent characters, it is impossible to ascertain if John was a battering husband, and neither can we assert that John broke the cage. It is Mrs. Hale and Mrs. Peters who lead the audience to think that these are the cases. Mrs. Hale makes the explicit connection between a singing bird, the one that supposedly inhabited the cage, and which has not been found yet, and the choir girl Minnie was. Reconsidering the point that Minnie might be a geopathic character trapped in the cage/at the farm, there seems to be a parallelism between wanting to escape from the farm and murdering her husband, and between feeling trapped within the farmhouse and breaking the cage. Both the murder and the breaking of the cage are violent acts. In this manner, another possibility opens up: what if Minnie broke the birdcage hoping somebody could see it as evidence of her own entrapment and longing for freedom? In the same way that Mrs. Hale and Mrs. Peters see Minnie's wrong quilt stitches or the messy kitchen as indicative of her pitiful life, the broken cage might be a sign Minnie leaves in her kitchen on purpose.

Metaphors of entrapment are consistent in Glaspell's dramatic homes. Might this mean that no home is a shelter in Glaspell's plays? Indeed, few are the characters in Glaspell's dramaturgy who see their homes as their shelters. In general terms, those characters who endeavor to keep their long-held family identity, embodied in the house where they live, do find a shelter in their house, such as the Roots in *Close the Book*. Characters such as the pioneers

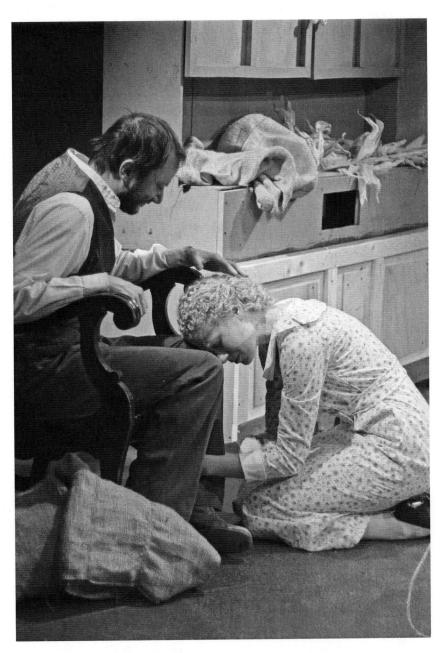

Scene from *Inheritors*, Act III. David G. Fraioli as Ira Morton and Margaret L. Robinson as Madeline Morton Fejevary. Metropolitan Playhouse production, 2005. Director: Yvonne Opffer Conybeare. Lighting design: Alexander Senchak. Set design: Ryan Scott. Photograph © Michelle DeBlasi.

in *Inheritors*, who had fought with all their strength against nature and the Native Americans to tame the land they inhabit, also find a shelter in their house. But there is a feeling that, above all, and with a few exceptions, characters that construct shelters in their houses are not very sympathetic ones. And in some other cases, those characters who construct a shelter to come to terms with place do so only to see their places invaded by other characters or to see how these places eventually become their own prisons.

Ira in *Inheritors* is the main instance of the kind of character whose geopathology comes from considering the onstage place his fort. He finds that staying at home is the safest means of keeping alive, since those who left the house died. Having witnessed the deaths of many relatives, Ira has come to equate going outside the farm with death. His wife, Madeline, died when she went to help the Johnsons: "*Out of this house* she ran.... She stumbled in the rough field — fell to her knees. That was the last I saw of her" (223, emphasis added). And Ira's son, Fred, also found death outside the farm. Ira says, "Gone —[*Snaps his fingers.*] like that. I told him not to go to war. He didn't have to.... But no, — he must — make the world safe for democracy! Well, you see how safe he made it, don't you? Now I'm alone on the farm and he — buried on some Frenchman's farm" (224). Ira is a victim of place, as he wrongly believes that the farm will protect him from life's unfortunate facts. He blames the deaths of his wife and son on the outside, on their departure from the house. This explains why he does not want Madeline to go out. "Don't you leave me — all alone in this house" (224), Ira tells his daughter. All his sufferings come from his inability to comprehend that "Nothing stays at home" (224), that going out, as Madeline is about to do, is something necessary for her to fulfill her own identity and leave her geopathology behind.

Eleanor in *The Comic Artist* is one of Glaspell's characters who struggles the most to keep her house as her shelter. She chose the house herself and decorated it, shaping it according to her identity and as a tribute to her past. Eleanor's victimage of location precisely originates in her engagement in the defense of her place. Interestingly, early in the play she has had a premonition that her house was being invaded: "Oh, what has come into our house!" "Will it ever be gone?" (292). Eleanor notices that Nina and Luella are going to destroy her home, but her love for Stephen and her brother-in-law, Karl, deters her from expelling them: "It keeps me from saying to her — I want you to leave my house!" (304). She asks her husband to do the manly thing, to protect their home and expel invaders. I partially agree with Ozieblo's remark that *The Comic Artist* lacks the hallmark of Glaspell's plays, "the determined woman who consciously molds her own life" (2000: 234). Eleanor succeeds in modeling her life as she models the house, making her house mirror the identity she wants to have, but at this point she is not the typical female protagonist; she is not strong enough to defend her place without the aid of a man. In a very symbolic scene, Eleanor asks Stephen to protect her as a man should protect his wife, affirming that her security, her happiness, and her freedom come from this protection. The scene ends as Eleanor offers Stephen a goblet, explicitly underlining Eleanor's worship and materializing their union and reconciliation.

Nonetheless, it is interesting to note that seeing that her husband will not help her to recover her house, Eleanor admits, "I asked Stephen to do something for me. It was cowardly. I must do it myself" (305). For a brief moment, Eleanor equals other female protagonists in Glaspell's dramaturgy and tries to take command of her own life. Eleanor unsuccessfully attempts to convince Nina to love Karl and forget Stephen. But as suggested in Eleanor's earlier wondering, whether after the invasion the house will be their house again, that is, whether it can be again the safe shelter Eleanor had created, is not clear. Through the invasion performed by the displaced characters, Glaspell and Matson make us re-consider the possibility of the home-shelter. In *The Comic Artist*, the point seems to be that, even after intruders have been expelled, no house can be a shelter against painful and reviving memories of the past. Eleanor has learned that Stephen had an affair with Nina, when she was just seventeen years old, and that he let his brother Karl marry her although he knew the kind of selfish woman she was. Moreover, these women have made Stephen think that the shelter his wife had constructed, and which he had cherished for so long, is but a source of solitude, a deadly enemy of the artist he is.

Mrs. Patrick in *The Outside* resembles other Glaspell characters in her effort to create a shelter. But unlike Ira in *Inheritors* or Seymore in *Chains of Dew*, who create their shelters to protect themselves from the outside, or Eleanor in *The Comic Artist*, who had created a shelter to live, Mrs. Patrick wants a shelter to let herself die. Mrs. Patrick has chosen an abandoned place to equal the feeling of abandonment she experiences, and she has not made any change to turn this place into what could be called a home, giving no hint that this can be a shelter in the traditional sense. Bradford tells the other male characters that he once heard the Patricks comment, "They was goin' to put in a fire-place and they was goin' to paint it bright colors, and have parties over here — summer folk notions" (61). That is, when the Patricks were together and planned to take over this place, they wanted to turn the old life-saving station into a joyful and homely site. When Mrs. Patrick finds herself alone, she decides to take this place, but she keeps it as far as possible from the image she had constructed with her husband. Indeed, according to the stage directions, there is no piece of furniture, but a bench in a corner. The almost derelict state of Mrs. Patrick's home is her suitable shelter, metaphorical of the fact that she wants to let herself die, since she cannot find any joy in life after being abandoned by her husband.

Regardless of the kind of metaphorical shelter Glaspell constructs in this fictional onstage place, the important issue regarding dramatic geopathology is that Mrs. Patrick's shelter is invaded. The male characters intrude into Mrs. Patrick's place without any restraint. Bradford tells how he had entered the old life-saving station to try to resuscitate the drowned sailor he had found: "So I kicked this door open with my foot [*Jerking his hand toward the room where the CAPTAIN is seen bending over the man.*] and got him *away*" (60, emphasis in original). So it is not only that the men had invaded the old life-saving station by entering it, but Bradford also makes explicit his use of violence to move deeper into Mrs. Patrick's space. The old life-saving station has become a battlefield, and Mrs. Patrick has to defend the place she rightfully owns:

> MRS PATRICK: You have no right here. This isn't the life-saving station any more. Just because it used to be — I don't see why you should think — This is my house! And — I want my house to myself! [60].
> CAPTAIN: You'll get your house to yourself when I've made up my mind there's no more life in this man. ...[A]nd if there's any chance of bringing one more back from the dead, the fact that you own the house ain't going to make a damn bit difference to me! [61].

The way the men rule over Mrs. Patrick's space is also evidenced by the fact that the Captain, at his will, opens and closes the sliding door that joins the main room, where the action takes place, with the adjoining room where the men are working over the sailor's corpse. He behaves as if he were in the life-saving station, not in Mrs. Patrick's house.

Kristina Hinz-Bode asserts that all three men "are drawn as decidedly sympathetic figures in their struggle for life, in their interactions amongst themselves, and even in their attitude towards the women" (2006b: 92). While I agree that Glaspell grants the men in this play a very positive role — to resuscitate the sailor, which indeed will serve as a metaphor for the symbolic resuscitation of Mrs. Patrick at the end of the play — the men's attitude towards the women cannot be considered sympathetic. Both Mrs. Patrick and Allie feel attacked by the male characters' violent presence in the house. Bradford describes how when he came to the house, Allie "backs off and stands lookin' at [them]" (60). Glaspell suggests Allie's fear through movement and body language, by making this woman step back in space and through her paralyzed body; she can only stand there, just looking at the invaders. Glaspell makes this case more obvious when, close to the end of the play, the male characters re-enter the stage, and Allie "*shrinks into her corner*" (64), making a shelter out of this corner.

In his interesting analysis of the poetics of corners, Gaston Bachelard claims, "The corner is a haven that ensures us one of the things we prize most highly — immobility. It is the sure place, the place next to my immobility. The corner is a sort of half-box, part walls, part door" (1994: 137). The corner, for Bachelard, is a shelter, "a symbol of solitude for the imagination" and "a negation of the Universe" (1994: 136). The use Glaspell makes of the physical corner of the stage space to place Allie reveals all these complexities. Allie's retreat to the corner when the men appear stands for her negation of the male universe she resists joining. It is the symbolic and theatrical representation of Allie's search of a shelter in the very place where she lives. In this manner, I believe that in *The Outside*, Glaspell states a clear case of gender politics of location, about how men do not usually respect women's places. Would the Captain behave in the same rude and despotic manner if there were a Mr. Patrick onstage? Probably, if Mr. Patrick were onstage, there would have been neither kicks on doors nor rude words, and the old life-saving station would not have been invaded.

In *The Verge*, Glaspell explores most radically the interplay in the configuration of the stage space as prison and shelter. Indeed, when referring to the fictional places Glaspell presents in this play, critics divide into those who believe that these sets constitute an "emblem of the socially restricted and shielded" spaces which trap the protagonist (Ozieblo 2000: 185–186), those who see these sets as "'womb-like' sanctums" (Papke 1993: 60) and "creative vaginal spaces" (Carpentier 2006a: 43), those who regard the sets as "physical projections of Claire's mental state" (Gainor 2001: 154), and those who claim that the sets stand for "alienating environments" (Ben-Zvi 2006: 292). And all of these versions are valid, since they all reflect on different aspects of the stage space configuration in *The Verge*, and all together contribute to Claire's problem with place.

In Claire Archer, Glaspell creates a female character that is exceptionally and fully conscious of the need to have a home that is a stable container of the self. As has been claimed, "*The Verge* takes place in Claire's territories, her greenhouse and her tower" (Galbus 2000: 86). To create Claire's territories, Glaspell constructs onstage places that expressionistically represent Claire's main feature: her rejection of traditional forms. Bringing together Claire's rejection of conventions and her will to escape from the prison a domestic setting represents for her, *The Verge* "occupies the outer perimeters of the domestic space. Both the greenhouse and the tower are sites separated from the main house" (Stufft 2006: 89). Claire has constructed several rooms of her own, apparently several shelters, by dividing the space where she wants to be and where she allows the other characters to stay. The very first division can be found in the separation between the proper house, which never appears on stage, and the greenhouse. The latter is Claire's work place, her place of creation. A glass partition separates the area within the greenhouse, where the other characters can stay, from the inner room, where she and her employee, Anthony, work on the flower "Breath of Life." Furthermore, Claire also has a room downstairs accessible from a trap door in the floor, and whose importance is highlighted when the play opens and a ray of light comes from this low room. As metaphors of her efforts to control the power geometry of her places, Claire keeps the key to this room and the greenhouse door. While the configuration of the greenhouse enables Claire to have her shelter, as Glaspell does with other home-shelters, there is a constant threat of invasion on the part of the other characters. Despite her control over keys, Claire sees her spaces invaded at different points throughout the play. Early in Act I, and against Claire's specific statement "I'll not have you in my place" (232), Harry and Dick gather in the greenhouse to have breakfast. As the play opens the greenhouse is a laboratory, but little by little stage props begin changing the identity Claire has provided to her place. An electric toaster, eggs, and pepper shakers displace Claire's plants. All of these stage props, related to the cult of domesticity Claire so utterly hates, and which are so out of place in this greenhouse, are placed on Claire's table in a symbolic invasion of her place.

After seeing her greenhouse invaded for a second time, when Dick also enters, Claire starts showing her wish to control her places more seriously, being in command of doors and keys. Once Dick is inside, "*She shuts the door and leans against it*" (232). In the third attempt of invasion, when Tom tries to enter, even knocking on the door with the revolver and firing it (237), Harry says,

> HARRY: Why — it's Tom! What the —? [*Going to the door.*] He's locked out. And Claire's got the key. [*Goes to the inner door, tries it.*] And she's locked in! [*Trying to see her in there.*] Claire! Claire! [*Returning to the outer door.*] Claire's got the key — and I can't get to Claire. [*Makes a futile attempt at getting the door open without the key, goes back to inner door — peers, pounds.*] Claire! Are you there? Didn't you hear the revolver? Has she gone down cellar? [*Tries the trap-door.*] Bolted! Well, I love the way she keeps people locked out!
> DICK: And in [237–238].

As Dick remarks, it is not only that Claire has locked Tom out and herself in, but she has also left Dick and Harry locked in. Here there is an expansion of the dramatic possibilities of geopathic representations of home as shelter or prison as these merge in a pathological way. In *The Verge*, the female protagonist's need to have her shelter leads her to turn her house into a prison.

While it could be pointed out that Claire's pathology is similar to Agatha's in *Alison's House*— both turn their houses into prisons — it must be noted that Glaspell made Agatha unaware of her problem with place. But Claire is very conscious of the dangers of being locked in. It is in her endeavor to protect her space that she has to trap the other characters as well as herself. This explains why Claire wants to keep Tom locked out, even freezing under the snow:

> HARRY: Claire, have you no ideas of hospitality? Let him in!
> CLAIRE: In? Perhaps that isn't hospitality.
> HARRY: Well, whatever hospitality is, what is out there is snow — the wind — and our guest — who was asked to come here for his breakfast. To think a man has to *say* such things.
> CLAIRE: I'm going to let him in. Though I like his looks out there. [*She takes the key from her pocket*] [238, emphasis in original].

Comic as it may seem, letting Tom outside the greenhouse is Claire's act of love for Tom. She likes his looks outside because he is free outside the walls of the house. Claire's idea of hospitality is to let people be free and outside.

As her refuge within the house, Claire's "thwarted tower" is the place which most clearly represents Claire's self and her rejection of traditional forms. The tower is described as "*a tower which is thought to be round but does not complete the circle. The back is curved, then jagged lines break from that, and the front is a queer bulging window — in a curve that leans. The whole structure is as if given a twist by some terrific force — like something wrung*" (247). For the traditional Adelaide, the tower "lacks form" (258), since "a round tower should go on being round" (248). But precisely what Claire likes about the tower is that it represents the deviation from old forms she tries to find both for her plants and for her own life. The tower is a "free" building, free from the prison of traditional forms. Indeed, "she bought the house because" of the thwarted tower (248).

Glaspell also articulates Claire's problem with enclosing and traditional forms through Claire's metaphorical language. In the following scene Claire tries to explain to Adelaide her vision of the world:

> CLAIRE: Here is the circle we are in. [*Describes a big circle.*] Being gay. It shoots little darts through the circle, and a minute later — gayety all gone, and you looking through that little hole gayety left.... [*Moved, but eyes shining with a queer bright loneliness.*] But never one of you — once — looked with me through the little pricks the gayety made — never one of you — once, looked with me at the queer light that came in through the pricks....
> ADELAIDE: You must see yourself that you haven't the poise of people who are held — well, within the circle, if you choose to put it that way [250–251].

Making use of the circle as a metaphor of entrapment, Claire explains how she feels trapped in this perfect and enclosing form. Only little darts, moments of vision beyond her prison, can give Claire some relief. But Claire is afraid and lonely looking through the hole. And she will go on being so, since her sister cannot understand Claire's metaphor, and instead urges her to stay calmly "within the circle," that is, within the gates of society. Unable to make Adelaide understand her point, Claire cannot but confront her and, making use of her body language, she destroys the imaginary circle: "*CLAIRE, after looking intently at ADELAIDE, slowly, smiling a little, describes a circle. With deftly used hands makes a quick, vicious break in the circle which is there in the air*" (251). It is not coincidence then that the thwarted tower Claire loves so much shares with this circle image the little pricks in the wall that let the light come in. The tower is "*lighted by an old-fashioned watchman's lantern hanging from the ceiling, the innumerable pricks and slits in the metal throw a marvelous pattern on the curved wall, like some masonry that hasn't been*" (248). The pricks and slits in the metal lantern project these patterns on the whole wall, becoming the holes though which Claire dreams of looking beyond. And at the same time the patterns formed on the wall constitute the deviation from form Claire longs for. The shape is "*like some masonry that hasn't been.*" That is, it is a form that is not conventional.

Turning to Claire's tower as a spatial representation of her need to transcend traditional geographical places, and to reflect upon her places and her own subjectivity, David Sievers, in his psychoanalytical study of *The Verge*, describes this strange tower as "a room shaped in curves with a bulging window like a womb. This apparently marks the first expressionistic distortion of scenery in our theater for a subjective effect — that of unconscious 'regression to the womb'" (1955: 71). Several feminist scholars have followed Sievers's point, seeing the tower as a womb, the self-chosen reclusive place where Claire feels safe. This tower also holds a certain resemblance to the medieval and romantic quiet places where artists retreated to think and write, a place separated from the world but with a window allowing dwellers to look out. A distorted rail of a spiral staircase leads to this place. In purely physical terms, this spiral case is meant to be an obstacle to intruders, since for instance Adelaide has some difficulties climbing them, and it is also symbolic of the difficulties most characters have to understand Claire's inner self.

For the close reader and for the attentive member of the audience, however, Glaspell leaves a physical clue which reveals that Claire's tower will never be an example of *topophilia*, of a felicitous shelter, but rather a transparent prison. It is noteworthy that "*the huge ominous window*" in the tower separates the stage space from the audience, a glass partition materializing the theatrical fourth wall.[6] Glaspell literally encloses Claire within the walls of the stage space "with an actual physical barrier rather than a merely imagined fourth wall" (Dymkowsky 1988: 101). That is, from the point of view of the audience's experience, and regarding its relevance for dramatic geopathology, the tower is, from the very beginning, a prison for Claire. And given that the tower is only accessible through a trap door on the floor, Claire's possibilities of escaping in the case of invasion diminish.

As happened in the greenhouse, the tower clearly ceases to be a shelter when it is invaded. Adelaide is the first to intrude, and to this first invasion of her tower, Claire answers in a mocking way. She approaches the window, the threshold to the outside. As if she were a medieval maid shut in a tower, Claire opens the window and calls Tom to save her: "Tom! *Tom!* Quick! Up here! I'm in trouble!" (252, emphasis in original). Likewise, when they leave, Claire asks Tom, "Will you stay with me a while? I want to purify the tower" (253). Her place has not been respected and she feels it requires purification. But the purification does not last long. A bit later Dick, Harry, Adelaide, and Dr. Emmons are all in the tower, and, even though she had invited "Everybody — up here!" (257), Claire feels her place has been invaded. This is shown proximemically as Claire backs "*against the curved wall, as far as possible from them*" (258), as Allie does in *The Outside*. Claire's collapse in the face of this invasion is so great that after getting out of the tower, she runs to lock herself in her room. Analyzing Claire's movements in these fictional places, it is observed that Claire tries to have her shelters protected, but these are invaded or turned into prisons in crescendo.

There is, however, only one place that is preserved intact throughout the play. Claire's downstairs room, the one accessible through the trapdoor in the greenhouse, is never invaded. Significantly, this room resembles the location of Hell in medieval morality plays, which is also accessible through a trapdoor in the floor. This is a place where Claire can be herself, where she can work without being disturbed. Glaspell locates Claire twice on the threshold between this downstairs room and the greenhouse, and the analysis of these scenes is very interesting because they reveal Claire's resistance to join her family, representative of the society she rejects, and those who try to make a proper woman out of her; that is, Claire's resistance to be imprisoned in "forms molded for us." The threshold between these two rooms, the one downstairs and the greenhouse, functions as a kind of protective space where Claire aims to avoid imprisonment. The first time Claire locates herself here occurs when Harry thinks Tom is going to shoot himself if he is not allowed to get into the greenhouse. Answering to Harry's desperate calls, "*the trap-door lifts, and CLAIRE comes half-way up*" (238). She stays a while in this position, enjoying the power she thinks she has over her space as she watches Harry's futile attempts to communicate with Tom through mimics. The next time the trap-door is used as threshold in *The Verge* visualizes Claire's rejection to be imprisoned in her maternal role. Her daughter Elizabeth has just arrived:

[*The trap door begins to move. CLAIRE's head appears.*]
 ELIZABETH: Mother! It's been so long — [*She tries to overcome the difficulties and embrace her mother.*]
 CLAIRE: [*Protecting a box she has.*] Careful, Elizabeth. We mustn't upset the lice.... [*Calling.*] Anthony! [*He comes.*] The lice. [*He takes them from her.*]
 [*CLAIRE, who has not fully ascended, looks at ELIZABETH, hesitates, then suddenly starts back down the stairs.*]
 HARRY: [*Outraged.*] Claire! [*Slowly she re-ascends — sits on the top step. After a long pause in which he has waited for CLAIRE to open a conversation with her daughter.*] Well, and what have you been doing at school all this time?
 ELIZABETH: Oh — studying.
 CLAIRE: Studying what?
 ELIZABETH: Why — the things one studies, mother.
 CLAIRE: Oh! The things one studies. [*Looks down cellar again*] [243–244].

Unnaturally for a mother who sees her daughter after a long time, Claire only shows her head. She is not interested enough in her daughter or in respecting conventions about how a mother should greet her daughter. Therefore, she does not come up completely from the downstairs room. As Elizabeth tries to embrace Claire, a difficult task given that Claire has not ascended, the rejection becomes more evident, and even more so when she prefers the well-being of "the lice" rather than greeting Elizabeth. Glaspell makes Claire retreat even a bit lower, sitting on the last step. The geography of this last step represents that Claire does not want to fully enter the social space her greenhouse has turned into. While sitting there and talking to her daughter, Claire looks down several times. A few sentences serve Claire to realize that Elizabeth is just a common social being who studies "the things one studies" and who does "the things one does." Her own daughter is imprisoned in form. Claire would rather be downstairs, in her domain where she experiments with life, with the lice that will turn her plants into new forms, than in the deadly domain with her daughter and other social beings. Significantly, on the occasion when Claire finally goes up, she will try to hit her daughter, a climax for the geopathic character who cannot stand being imprisoned in given roles. It seems that no shelter can protect Claire. For the geopathic character, there is no place to hide eternally from family, as Claire eventually comes up to the greenhouse and meets her relatives.

 It is interesting to see that in *The Verge* Glaspell reworks some conventional metaphors of shelter. While shells and caves are usually metaphors of protection, Claire expresses her fear of imprisonment by using these images as trapping spaces. Claire states that she is in "a cave," which has sometimes opened allowing her to see "immensity" (255), a metaphor that mirrors the image of the circle and the darts that allowed her to see beyond the boundaries of home and the family. For what Claire struggles to achieve during the play is to escape from the cave itself, the places she created as shelters, but which have become prisons. Her conception of place was new, and shelter-assuring; buildings which do not look like any building seen before, places that reflect their owner's creativity and self. But once she has set the pattern, the form is not new any more, and besides, her shelters are invaded again and again. The metaphor of the shell is what eventually leads Claire to kill Tom at the end of *The Verge*. Tom proposes: "As there you made a shell for life within, make yourself a life in which to live. It must be so" (264). Tom commits a fatal mistake; he offers Claire protection and the promise of being kept. As he uses the image of the shell, Tom is offering Claire what Gaston Bachelard has called "day-dreams of refuge" (1994: 107): "You will stay with me!" "I can keep you. I will keep you — safe" (265), says Tom. Turning to spatial metaphors, the confused Claire at first sees Tom as a gate in positive terms: "*You fill the place — should be a gate.* [*In agony.*] Oh, that it is *you* — fill the place — should be a gate! My darling! That it should be you who — " (265, emphasis in original). As Tom offers her the shell, a shelter, Claire responds with a spatial metaphor too: Tom should be a gate, a metaphor of liberation. Thus, Tom's shell is not a shelter, but a prison for Claire. Bachelard has also argued that "there is a sign of violence in all these figures in which an over-excited creature emerges from a lifeless shell" (1994: 111). In a later chapter I shall have the opportunity to show that Claire eventually realizes Tom is not an open gate, but a closing one, and so she will become violent and kill Tom. For Claire, to be safe and protected is just a prison in disguise.

A key spatial aspect Glaspell exploits is the changing geodichotomy of representations of home as shelter or prison. Glaspell deconstructs the fictional places of her plays to show that no home is a shelter, since the utopian home-shelter is under question constantly. Glaspell presents dramatically many reasons why none of her characters should consider their homes unassailable shelters, and "stable containers of their selves," but the main one is that, basically, every home is a prison in itself. Indeed, most of the characters that endeavor to see their homes as a shelter end up mad, dead, or disheartened by the fact that their places are turned into battlefields where invaders attempt to hold strong. After reaching the conclusion that in geopathic drama, home as shelter is but a dream and that one of the main features of geopathic characters is their entrapment, next I will focus on another geodichotomy, that between inside and outside.

Dramatic Geodichotomy between Inside and Outside

This third geodichotomy, inside vs. outside, forms part of the subjective coding of the world and must be understood both in physical and symbolic terms. That is, inside/outside, on the one hand, refers to the physical theatrical reality of being onstage or offstage. On the other hand, inside/outside also refers, in linguistic terms, to those metaphors characters employ to refer either to abstract offstage places (the idea of "the outside," devoid of an identifiable referential location) or to abstract ideas, such as being free or alien to society. Linda Ben-Zvi has identified Glaspell's emphatic usage of the words "out" and "outside," a metaphor she continually "uses in her writing to signify both alienation from society and freedom from the restrictions it imposes" (2006: 280). Thus, "in" and "inside" are usually metaphors of community adherence and the subjection to the rules it inflicts.

Close the Book is constructed upon the geodichotomy inside/outside as a metaphor of belonging or not belonging to this idea of society. Indeed, it is the characters' opposing views about this geodichotomy which shape the plot of the play. Ben-Zvi has summarized the theme of *Close the Book* as "the fear of the outsider" (2006: 285). But this play is also about the outsider's fear of the inside. Glaspell physically places Jhansi, the "outsider," inside the walls of the onstage location representing the Roots' library, in constant opposition to her verbal references to the outside. Jhansi's very first words in this play set the geodichotomy inside/outside: "[*Springing up.*] It's absurd that I should be *here*!" (37, emphasis added). Jhansi does not want to be "here," inside the library, and with her body makes her first attempt to go "out there." In opposition to the "here" she despises, the Root home, the family and the university as a fixed institution, she says to Peyton, "I should take you by the hand and you and I should walk together down the open road" (38). This open road symbolizes for her the freedom she wants and the link to what she thinks is her heritage: the gypsies. She would love to take the open road and live in a covered wagon, a metaphor of Jhansi's wish to be free, as "a wanderer," and "an outlaw" (43). Jhansi, who describes herself with "I am not a part of your society," but "an outsider" (41), has formed her identity as a gypsy. This identity is what gives her pride, and hence her apparent rejection of everything conventional, and of society, and her need to be outside this house.

But with *Close the Book*, Glaspell reworks the idea that the dichotomy inside/outside is unmovable, for in this play borders are movable and outsiders can be brought in very easily. In contrast to Jhansi's need to be outside, her fiancé's family endeavors to bring her inside, to metaphorically integrate her inside society. Bessie's efforts to find out Jhansi's real origins reveal the Roots' necessity of ensuring that the new member is an insider. When Bessie tells Jhansi that she is the daughter of a respectable Baptist family, she says "Welcome Within!" "You must not stand outside society! You belong *within* the gates," "You are one of us!" and "as respectable as we are" (42, emphasis in original). It is interesting to note that Glaspell capitalizes "Within" to symbolize the respectful status that belonging to society represents, in contrast to the "outside society" status Jhansi had before.

In Glaspell's spatial metaphors in *Close the Book*, society has gates, and these have been opened for Jhansi to come back to where she belonged by birth. Clara and Grandmother had talked earlier about Jhansi's foster parents, who were also Anglo-Saxon and respected members of the community, and their attempt to bring her "within":

> GRANDMOTHER: How did this gypsy get here?
> MRS ROOT: She was brought up by a family named Mason. But it seems she was a gypsy child, who got lost or something, and those Masons took her *in*. I'm sure it was very good of them, and it's too bad they weren't able to make her more Christian. She is coming to have a following in the university! There are people who seem to think because you're *outside* society you have some superior information about it [39, emphasis added].

This is a short and sharp dialogue regarding the politics of location. Grandmother's question, referring to Jhansi as "this gypsy," already locates the girl as an outsider, who got "here." Thus, Glaspell employs Jhansi's ethnic difference, as in the case of the Hindu students or the Native American absent characters in *Inheritors*, to present victimage of location, in the sense that ethnically different characters are primarily considered outsiders. Moreover, Glaspell uses the uncertainty of Jhansi's spatial origins to further locate her outside. She was "lost" somewhere, and the Masons "took her in." Jhansi, nevertheless, was not brought in enough, according to Mrs. Root. That is, she has not been assimilated into the community. Before discovering that Jhansi is indeed Anglo-Saxon, a legitimate member of the inside, Peyton's family had been considering bringing her metaphorically within the community: "She won't be a gypsy after she's Peyton's wife. She'll be a married woman" (40), says Mrs. Root. That is, by means of her marriage to an Anglo-Saxon man, Jhansi had to be part of the inside, like it or not, and forget her gypsy outsider identity in favor of that of the married-to-an-Anglo-Saxon insider. As in others of Glaspell's plays, gender plays a great role in the politics of location. Marriage, understood at this time as the woman's adherence to the man's place, could destroy the dichotomy inside/outside easily.

Glaspell reworks the dialectics between inside and outside as metaphors of belonging to society or being alienated from a political point of view in *Inheritors*. As in *Close the Book*, Glaspell metamorphosizes society into a room with gates:

> HOLDEN: I hate to see you, so young, close a door on so much of life. I'm being just as honest with you as I know how. I myself am making compromises to stay within. I don't like it, but there are — reasons for doing it. I can't see you leave that main body without telling you all it is you are leaving. It's

not a clean-cut case — the side of the world or the side of the angels. I hate to
see you lose the — fullness of life.... I think there is danger to you in — so
young, becoming alien to society....
     MADELINE: As great as the danger of staying within — and becoming like
the thing I'm within? [222].

Professor Holden warns Madeline about the dangers of being outside society
when he says, "It's not a clean-cut case." Glaspell complicates here the geodichotomy inside outside; this is not a simple, binary fight against "the side
of the world," the mundane inside, against "the side of the angels," the outside,
or a fight of evil vs. good. While Kristina Hinz-Bode claims that "it seems
that the experience of life as lived in a web of social relations is understood
as a purely negative phenomenon in this play" (2006b: 239), I believe that
the point Glaspell expresses through Holden is that there must be something
good inside, as well as some evil outside. Glaspell creates in Holden a character
that suffers from the same geopathology as Madeline does, a need to be outside
society, but who unlike Madeline chooses the inside. Glaspell justifies Holden's
decision to stay inside society for his love for his wife. "If you sell your soul"
to stay inside, says Holden, "it's to love you sell it" (223).

     Besides this verbal discourse for the "outside," Glaspell also makes Made-
line physically state her case for being outside. In the climax of Act III, Madeline has to fight to reach the outside, the offstage campus. In this scene, her
uncle Felix Fejevary is trying to convince Madeline to be a respectable girl,
to stay inside society, and consequently, to stop her demonstrations for the
Hindu students. Then, Glaspell makes the outside reach the inside as some
offstage noise interrupts the onstage dialogue. Madeline listens to the offstage
confrontations between the Hindu students and the police, and she rushes to
open the window. The act of opening the window breaks the barrier between
inside and outside, the frontier between conforming to the rules and breaking
them. Leaning her body through this window, Madeline shouts:

> You're not what this place is for! [*Her uncle comes up behind, right, and tries to
> close the window — she holds it out.*] My grandfather gave this hill to Morton
> College — a place where anybody — from any land — can come and say what he
> believes to be true!... Oh, let me *down* there! [*Springs down, would go off right,
> her uncle spreads out his arms to block the passage. She turns to go the other way*]
> [214, emphasis in original].

Despite Felix Fejevary's efforts to keep Madeline physically inside the library,
a metaphorical extension of her uncle's wish to keep her inside society and
under control, "in here," the female protagonist struggles to go "out there"
and fight for what she thinks is right, for the freedom the Hindu students
must have to state their beliefs in the free country the United States is supposed
to be. The patriarchal forces, incarnated in Fejevary and Holden, try to stop

the emerging strong female character. With the superior strength of their male bodies, Fejevary and Holden block Madeline's rush to the outside. Holden eventually steps aside for Madeline to pass. In this proxemic discourse, Holden accepts Madeline's idea that it is better to be alienated and outside a society that rejects those who do not conform to homogeneity, either racial or ideological. Madeline's slam at the end of this scene is a straightforward reference to Ibsen's Nora. At this very moment, Madeline emerges as a New Woman. Her fight for defending outsiders has become her only principle, a principle that has placed her outside the gates of society.

The Verge is very special regarding Glaspell's revision of the geodichotomy inside/outside. In this play the boundaries between inside and outside and what they might represent completely blur, contributing to the complexity and greatness of this play. Some scholars have focused on some of the binaries appearing in this play, and have affirmed that Glaspell creates binaries that Claire needs to destroy in order to be the free individual she struggles to be throughout the play.[7] Indeed, Claire's effort to destroy the opposition between inside and outside is based on her rejection of what the inside represents: order, society, and family ties. However, what cannot be denied is that Claire only attempts to break the barrier between inside and outside, but never succeeds, and that her attacks on the inside are basically verbal. Claire's position on the outside is not physical, as we have seen in the previous section; she is on the inside, the greenhouse and the tower, unable to escape from these places and the community/family that wants her inside. Thus, the geodichotomy between inside and outside is much a rhetorical device in Claire's hands.

The very set confounds the inside and the outside, so that one could wonder if there is a real inside and a real outside one can escape from or to, the existence of a promised land where one can be free. Regarding physical boundaries, Henri Lefèbvre claims, "Visible boundaries, such as walls or enclosures in general, give rise for their part to an appearance of separation between spaces where in fact what exists is an ambiguous continuity" (1991: 87). This is exactly what Glaspell constructs in *The Verge*. The setting of the play is already constructed on a geodichotomy that blurs. Klaus Schwank has pointed out that in *The Verge* there is a clear boundary between the inside, the greenhouse, and the outside (1989: 419). Nevertheless, glass makes this boundary fragile, not only because of the symbolic connotation of having an easily breakable material separating both zones — Claire actually breaks the glass partition when she is strangling Tom — but also because glass allows the conception of this space in a continuum, as Lefèbvre affirms. And the boundary between inside and outside in the tower is also fragile. As seen, at one point Claire opens the window, physically breaking the barrier between inside and outside. Nevertheless, this act is insignificant regarding "outness," since even though Claire's body is partly out, she is still trapped in the tower, "the inside." The most important issue is that Claire still needs the concept of the inside so that she can maintain her identity as an outsider trapped on the inside. As Kristina Hinz-Bode believes, Claire "essentially depends on the very concept of the detested 'inside' as it enables her to position herself on the 'outside,' and to give this space significance in the first place" (2006b: 174). I agree with Hinz-Bode, as I think that in *The Verge* Glaspell shows that geodichotomies are needed to shape her characters' identities, and that they cannot be destroyed, but only attacked. Claire's failed attempts to reach outside, physically and metaphorically, prove this.

Together with Claire's entrapment in the onstage place that the audience witnesses, verbal references to the outside contribute to our perception of Claire's victimage of location. In order to express her need to be outside, that is, outside society and traditional roles and places, Claire employs some images that appear as synecdoche extensions of the outside. In sharp contrast to the closed doors and trapping spaces that characterize the setting of *The Verge*, Claire wants to "feel the limitless — out there — a sea just over the hill" (247). It is interesting to note that Gaston Bachelard has identified hill and sea images with the representation of immensity, and that according to this philosopher, "immensity is the movement of the motionless man" (1994: 184). Thus, Claire's insistence upon the hill and the sea further manifest her urge to reach outside, to move out of the house and what being inside/outside represents. Glaspell, nevertheless, makes Claire destroy the possibility of achieving freedom through the images of the hill and the sea. Claire dreams of going to these offstage places with Tom:

> CLAIRE: [*Raising her head, called by promised gladness.*] We'll run around together. [*Lovingly he nods.*] Up hills. All night on hills.
> TOM: [*Tenderly.*] All night on hills.
> CLAIRE: We'll go on the sea in a little boat.
> TOM: On the sea in a little boat.
> CLAIRE: But — there are other boats on other seas. [*Drawing back from him, troubled.*] There are other boats on other seas [264].

For a moment Claire rejoices in the idea of living outside, up on hills and on the sea. However, her joy vanishes when she realizes that "there are other boats on other seas." These boats on other seas represent society. That is, Claire will never be out in the sense of being different that she longs for so eagerly. There will always be other people around her, people who will make being on the sea or up on hills something conventional, turning these places into traditional ones, too.

Claire's utter dream for the outside is represented in the gutter. Claire's statement, "All I ask is to die in the gutter with everyone spitting on me" (259), epitomizes her geopathology. Mary Papke sees the importance of this moment in the play: "Claire asks only 'to die in the gutter with everyone spitting' on her so that she might at least feel something" (2006: 32). Given Claire's complete rejection of society, interpreting this spitting as her need to feel would make her part of society. I think, however, that what Claire expresses through this spitting is precisely total alienation, the acknowledgement that society ("everyone") feels disgust at her. Moreover, the gutter as location is a very interesting site; the gutter is the most marginal place of the outside. It is on the edge, the verge, of the main road. If, in *Close the Book*, Jhansi verbalizes her need to be outside through the open road, in *The Verge*, for Claire, who suffers the victimage of location more painfully than the gypsy-turned-into-Anglo-Saxon character, the open road is not open enough. Glaspell makes Claire word her yearning for the outside by placing herself in this marginal space where all the dirt of the open road collects, that is, where the most alienated people can meet. In fact, Claire employs the gutter as a placement of renewal: "From the gutter I rise again, refreshed" (261). As if she were a phoenix, the gutter contains the ashes from where Claire raises again after her collapse in Act II.

Glaspell also exploits the geodichotomy between inside and outside in *The Verge* through Claire's insistence upon being in the air to verbalize her need to be outside. Her very name includes the noun "air," as if to express Claire's inherent need to be on the outside. Claire says, "To fly. To be free in the air. To look from above on the world of all my days. Be where man has never been!" (239). Claire proposes to escape her victimage of location through flying, leaving the earth. Henry F. May has highlighted the symbolic power the airplane had for the moderns. As he says, "A fragile thing of wire and canvas, looping the loop at county fairs, it was to some of the younger generation a *symbol of magical hopes*. To some conservatives, man in flight was a disturbing sight: *if he could do this, what natural law could he not break*? (1960: 335, emphasis added). As a member of this younger generation, Claire perceives the magical power of the airplane, and she uses it to express her desire to break other "natural laws," the laws that society has created about propriety and fixity, also mirrored on Claire's plants.

Perhaps the most evident symbol of the struggle between the inside and the outside in *The Verge* is Claire's experiments with plants. As Claire finds it impossible to leave the inside by actually leaving the place she lives in, or by flying—her aviator-husband stopped flying—she tries to reach the outside through her plants, with which she aims to demonstrate that "there is outness—and otherness" (235). These plants, in Claire's words, have "broken from the forms in which they found themselves. They are alien. Outside.

That's it, outside, if you — know what I mean.... Out there — [*Giving it with her hands.*] lies all that's not been touched — lies life that waits. Back here — the old pattern, done again, again and again" (246). This summarizes the significance of the geodichotomy between inside and outside for Claire. The inside means convention, society, imprisonment and death, while the outside, what is "out there," means individuality, freedom and life. Claire's experiments with plants are her means of escaping place as a problem, her means of departure. It is undeniable that Claire's project is, borrowing Noe's words, "the modernist project of rejecting old forms and the feminist project of rejecting the old patriarchal social order of separate spheres and asserting the right of women to claim their own space for their own work as well as to define and speak for themselves" (2002: 159).

But as happened with the unconventional form Claire gave to her places, the shelters that became prisons, Claire's experiments with plants also fail, posing the vital question of whether the outside can indeed ever be reached. It seems Claire has achieved "otherness" with the Edge Vine, since "*the leaves of this vine are not the form that leaves have been. They are at once repellent and significant*" (230). But then Claire realizes that "it isn't — over the edge. It's running, back to —'all the girls.'... [*Looking somberly at it.*] You are out, but you are not alive" (246). The Edge Vine "cannot create" (246), thus, in a matter of time it will be trapped in form again. Notwithstanding, as its name presages, the plant just came to the edge, but it did not go any further. Claire's next experiment is her attempt to beat this limit, because she does not want to "die on the edge" (247). Glaspell creates an aura of mysticism around the Breath of Life that foreshadows a promising future for this plant. Unlike the Edge Vine, Breath of Life is not located center-stage, but in the inner room from which we can perceive "*the plant like caught motion glows as from a light within*" (259). With a magnificent use of light, Glaspell provides the plant with the leading importance it has for Claire and for the dramatic development of the play. When the plant is brought "out from its own place" (262), into the main room, Claire is congratulated on her achievement. The flower is "stronger, surer" and "more fragile" at the same time (262), and "a good deal of novelty" (263). It seems it has escaped from form, going beyond the limits of plants: "Then, it is out," says Claire (263). But again Claire's success becomes her own failure. She becomes rigid and utters,

> CLAIRE: [*And though speaking, she remains just as still.*]
> Breath of the uncaptured?
> You are a novelty.
> Out?
> You have been brought in.
> A thousand years from now, when you are but a form too long repeated,

Scene from *The Verge*, Act I. Rebecca Lingafelter as Claire Archer. Performance Lab 115 production, 2009. Director: Alice Reagan. Photograph © Sue Kessler (www.sue kessler.com).

> Perhaps the madness that gave you birth will burst again,
> And from the prison that is you will leap pent queernesses
> To make a form that hasn't been —
> To make a prison new.
> And this we call creation. [*Very low, her head not coming up.*]
> Go away! [263].

Claire's broken utterance verbalizes the impossibility of demolishing the geo-dichotomy between inside and outside in this play. Claire acknowledges the futility of her attempt to reach the outside through her plants because forms will always be repeated. Her Breath of Life becomes but a fixed form, it is "brought in." The artist's quest to find the untrapping form is an impossible one. As Nancy L. Nester points out, through Claire's quest what Glaspell reveals is that "there is no otherness. Otherness exists only in binary opposition to sameness, to which it is inextricably bound. Without repetition and constancy, other-ness or difference ceases to exist" (1997: 4). Although Claire is probably the strongest of Glaspell's female characters, all her attempts to reach outside, that is, outside the house, outside society, outside roles, prove a failure, thus giving way to her increasing feeling of victimage of location.

Having discussed the different geodichotomies Glaspell forces her characters to face, the next chapter focuses on the one aspect of dramatic geopathology every character has to go through: the spatial burden of the past. No matter whether these characters are isolated or not, whether they want to be outside or inside, or whether they want to consider their houses a prison or a shelter, all of them have a past. The extent to which these characters confront, promote or suffer from the spatial presence of their past will reveal their degree of geopathology.

4

The Burden of the Past
in Dramatic Geopathology

Time does not dim what is real.... The past does not lose its voice, but is there to speak to us [Glaspell 1942b: np].

Spatial representations of the past are relevant in this study because of the relationship between past and identity that they reveal. Doreen Massey has pointed out that the unearthing of heritages might be interpreted as a desire for fixity and for security of identity. "A 'sense of place,' of rootedness, can provide — in this form and on this interpretation — stability and a source of unproblematical identity," says Massey (1998: 151). Characters in plays, as people in real life, do not appear in a void, but are the fruits of heritage. Besides the influence that locations have on identity, to a great extent we are also who we are because of our past. On the one hand, as Massey believes, past helps to fix our identity, giving us "a sense of place." But on the other hand, past can become a problem for identity, especially when this heritage forces us to have an identity we do not want to maintain. "The past helps make the present," says Massey (1995: 187). Materially the past is alive in places through different means, such as photographs, books or monuments. And the past is also fixed in places through verbal references, such as the names of streets or villages. In theater the past is also identifiable both in material and verbal ways. Glaspell's homes, as has been said, are "material embodiments of, and links with, the past" (Ben-Zvi 2005: 334).

A very important aspect to be taken into account regarding the representation of the past is that, as Massey highlights, "the past of a place is open to a multiplicity of readings as is the present." Consequently, "the claims and counter-claims about the present character of a place depend in almost all cases on particular, rival, interpretations of its past" (1995: 184–185). Susan Glaspell herself was attracted by this idea of the changing and multiple meanings of the past. Indeed, in the fragment of a play she never finished, one of her characters says, "Never study history — they are always changing it about. History is not there to defend itself— if it could put up any defense — so they make it anything they want it to be. History depends entirely on the kind of person you are."[1] Decades before New-Historicism, Glaspell wanted to develop in a play the idea that history is a literary creation of those who write it.

This idea that the past can have different, and even rival interpretations, has a pivotal role in understanding the dramatic principle of victimage of location, since different types of geopathology can be born out of spatial representations of the past. On the one hand, some characters may see place as a problem because this place represents a past and an identity they do not want. "Root" is a key word to understand the power of the past in this concern. For Linda Ben-Zvi, "Glaspell saw roots as marks of fixity and stagnation, choking off the free growth of an individual, institution, or society" (2005: xii). However, roots are not always negative marks of fixity in Glaspell's works. In many of her plays, she dramatizes opposing poles: characters looking for their heritage to exploit it as a means of rooting their identity, and even struggling to maintain this past in their places, and characters who do not accept such inherited impositions.

Dramatic Re-negotiations
with the Pioneer Heritage

As seen in earlier chapters, due to her own origins, Glaspell was heavily influenced by her pioneer heritage. In *Close the Book* and *Inheritors*, she shows that this pioneer past constitutes a spatial burden for some characters, which even leads to important generational conflicts. In *Close the Book*, Glaspell portrays very straightforwardly the vivid quality of heritage in the present lives of her characters. It is not coincidence that the family surname is Root, a symbolic appeal to this family's close link to its past. *Close the Book* opens in the library room of the Roots, a family of "inheritors," in the sense that their roots spring from the most important social classes: soldiers and university men — a combination Glaspell also employs in *Inheritors*. The way the room is configured points to the status of this family:

> SCENE: The library of the Root home, the library of middle-western people who are an important family in their community, a university town, and who think of themselves as people of culture. It is a room which shows pride of family: on the rear wall are two large family portraits — one a Revolutionary soldier, the other a man of a later period. On the low book-cases, to both sides of door rear, and on the mantel, right, are miniatures and other old pic-

tures. There is old furniture — mahogany recently done over: an easy chair near the fireplace, a divan left. A Winged Victory presides over one of the book-cases, a Burne Jones is hung. It is a warmly lighted, cheerful room — books and flowers about [37].

The key words "culture" and "pride" appear in the description of the setting. This is a room the Roots have shaped to re-affirm their identity and to show off. The stage properties — lots of books, the Winged Victory and the Burne Jones — show the cultural interests of the family; the Roots have a special interest in past artistic forms. Traditional, not modern, art is present in the room. The Winged Victory is a Classical masterpiece. And the Burne Jones displays a "nostalgic cult of the past which found expression in the Pre-Raphaelite poets and painters" (Bablet 1981: 1–2). But the Roots' library not only shows love for the past regarding art, but also regarding their ancestors. Two portraits preside in the room. The portrait of "John Peyton of Valley Forge" relates to the social status that war gives to a family. And there is also a portrait of a man of a later period, which turns out to be a portrait of Richard Peyton, the founder of the town college. This portrait and the books crowding the library also stand for the family's heritage: the town college. Even before the founding of the college, the family had already been dedicated itself to teaching; they are descendants of "Gustave Phelps — one of the famous teachers of pioneer days" (38). The tradition of being university men has passed from generation to generation since pioneer times; at present, Uncle George is President of the Board of Regents, and Peyton Root is an instructor of English. The Roots' pride in their heritage is also evidenced by the lots of miniatures and old pictures of family members, as well as by the fact that the pieces of furniture are old. As if it were a museum, the configuration of the library tells the family history, constituting a stable container of the Roots' identity.

A stage prop breaks the idyllic atmosphere of this room as a sanctum of beloved heritage, and questions Jhansi's estrangement from the Roots' tradition. When a genealogy book of the Iowa Descendants of New England Families is brought into the room, the action of the play starts, provoking hilarious situations, as well as some serious thoughts about the shaping of identity.[2] The genealogy book appears as the Bible of heritage, the document that supports these characters' pride in their past and their status within society. Bessie brings this "*large book*" to testify that Jhansi is not the daughter of gypsies, but of very "respectable" people. Jhansi's father was "a milkman in the town of Sunny Center — an honorable and respected man." Her ancestors participated in the American Revolution, her mother taught in the Sunday School, and her parents' wedding took place in the Baptist Church (42–43). Moreover, Jhansi learns that her exotic name, which she considered the ultimate proof of her gypsy heritage, comes from a town in India where there was a missionary Jhansi's mother supported (43). Jhansi's heritage mirrors exactly all she despises: respectable and common people. The other characters, except for Peyton, agree on the importance that ancestors have to forge their identity, and so they recommend that Jhansi behave differently now that she knows her real origins. She is expected to be as respectable and as "within society" as her parents were, something Jhansi is not willing to accept:

> So *this* is what I was brought here for, is it? To have my character torn down — to ruin my reputation and threaten my integrity by seeking to muzzle me with a leg at Bull Run and set me down in the Baptist Sunday-School in a milk-wagon! I see the purpose of it all. I understand the hostile motive behind all this — but I tell you it's a *lie*. Something here [*Hand on heart.*] tells me I am not respectable! [43, emphasis in original].

However comic, Jhansi's words state her reluctance to accept that her heritage is the same that pervades the respectable house of the Roots. While Jhansi had dreamt of a gypsy covered wagon, her real heritage links her now to an Anglo-Saxon milk wagon, placing her inside the "respectable" circle of society.

A proxemic analysis of how Glaspell makes her characters pass around the genealogy book is enlightening to discuss the performance of heritage and identity. The book appears in the hands of Mrs. Byrd, one of Jhansi's recently found relatives. Mr. Byrd then shows it to Jhansi, so that she can see with her own eyes that she is the daughter of the Harrisons. Jhansi's rejection of "this story" (43) is suggested in her denial to even hold the book. On the contrary, Uncle George, who is very proud of his ancestors, takes it. He is eager to find more notable ancestors in the book because according to him, "Genealogy *is* interesting. One is democratic, of course, but when there is behind one what there is behind us, Senator, it enhances one's powers — responsibility — obligation" (44, emphasis in original). Furthermore, he recommends the book to Peyton and Jhansi "for study," to "think a little of those worthy men from whom you come" (44). At this point, the similarity between Uncle George and George Cram Cook surfaces clearly. Glaspell points out in *The Road to the Temple* that Cook "felt pride in these men from whom he came," and quotes him, "Male ancestors still tend to become tribal gods about whom marvelous stories descend, and it is part of piety to believe them" (Cook qtd. in Glaspell 2005: 34). Nevertheless, Glaspell provides a witty trick in *Close the Book* when the genealogy book reveals male ancestors who are far from being tribal gods. The book has some fine print describing unpleasant episodes. While Senator Byrd says, "It is in fine print because it is not important" (45), precisely this fine print solely interests Jhansi and Peyton, since they hope they will find "unrespectable" people in their pasts.

For obvious reasons, Jhansi "*seizes the book*" when she is told that her grandfather "burned down the neighbor's house because that neighbor had chased home his pigs" (45). That is, she turns to the book when she is told that the book contains an episode that could support the rebel identity she wants to maintain, an episode that makes her proudly feel that she is not respectable. Peyton also takes the book to examine the fine print, and discovers that one of Jhansi and the Byrds' relatives, Peter Byrd, was "unfaithful to the high office of treasurer of the Baxter County Cemetery Association," a grave robber (45). And college founder Richard Peyton's father, Stuart Peyton, sold alcohol and guns to Native Americans. Glaspell's point is that, by carefully choosing those episodes in their pasts that they prefer, the past is used to support the characters' present way of living, to enhance their feeling of power, their pride and position in society, or their will to be alien to society, as in Jhansi and Peyton's case.

In her more mature play, *Inheritors*, Glaspell returns to the past in space, and tests her characters' behavior regarding the role played by their heritage in the formation of their identities. Besides portraying her own romantic version of the old pioneer days, their ideals of community, pacifism, and equality, and how the present-days characters have betrayed their heritage, Glaspell employs some spatial elements to contrast further heritage vs. characters' manipulation of that heritage to suit their identity. As in *Close the Book*, heritage is spatialized through some important stage props: books and portraits. The first cornerstone of heritage Glaspell places onstage is Lincoln's portrait. It is not a coincidence that Glaspell chooses a portrait of the sixteenth president of the United States, because Lincoln was considered, and still is, "the original All-American" (Morris 2000: 4–5). In the purest Franklin style, Lincoln went from rags to riches, from the log cabin in Kentucky where he was born to the White House. Lincoln's portrait is a constant reminder of pioneer values, of the fight for freedom and democracy, and of the desire for the post–Civil War union. But Lincoln's portrait also hints at the image of the loss of innocence that the Civil War provoked, and at Lincoln's assassination by the Southerner and pro-slavery actor John Wilkes Booth at Ford's Theater on April 14, 1865. Thus, hinging on the implication of Lincoln's onstage portrait, Glaspell foreshadows that this heritage is difficult to maintain. The fact that Lincoln's portrait still hangs on the wall of the Morton farm in the subsequent acts, when the present characters have betrayed the pioneer ideas, becomes an ironic remark on the use of heritage.

Similarly, Glaspell places a portrait of Silas, the idyllic pioneer man in Act I, in the Morton library. After betraying Silas's dream of building a college open to everybody, a college "born of the fight for freedom" (205), in order to get money from the government, Felix Fejevary the Second and Senator

Lewis paradoxically agree they are sustaining pioneer ideals. As if paying homage to Silas, his portrait hangs among the stacks of books:

> SENATOR: And this old boy [*Turning to the portrait of SILAS MORTON.*] can look out on his old home — and watch the valley grow.
> FEJEVARY: Yes — that was my idea. His picture really should be in Memorial Hall, but I thought Uncle Silas would like to be up here among the books, and facing the old place. [*With a laugh.*] I confess to being a little sentimental [198].

Apparently, Silas's inheritors have taken into account his ideals and his preferences — his love for nature and books — to hang his portrait here. Nevertheless, at one point Glaspell underlines that Felix Fejevary the Second, who indeed was in Act I at the very birth of Silas's dream, is aware that he is not respecting that dream, nor is he living up to it. When Senator Lewis remarks, "Oh, our pioneer! If they could only see us now, and know what they did!" Felix is described "*silent; he does not look happy*" (196). Felix is aware that his pioneer ancestors would feel ashamed of how their ideals have been misappropriated. Silas's portrait is theatrically effective because it is due to its privileged location that, in a symbolic manner, Silas witnesses the onstage conversation between xenophobic and elitist Americans and the off-stage confrontation between the Hindu students, on one side, and Morton College students and the police, on the other. Therefore, in a metonymical sense, Silas witnesses how his college has betrayed his ideals of freedom, democracy, and equality.

In order to show the lie behind the onstage characters' alleged adherence to their heritage, Glaspell employs an interesting dramatic technique: she makes them discuss the same topic, only to show how different their perspectives are. In the opening act, Silas had found in Matthew Arnold the words to materialize his thoughts about life and education. Morton College was intended to bring "the best that has been thought and said in the world" (189). In sharp contrast, Glaspell suggests how far the present-time characters are from Silas's idealism in the way they handle Arnold's book. While holding Arnold's book in his hands, Horace affirms, "Matthew Arnold. My idea of nowhere to go for a laugh. When I wrote my theme on him last week he was so dry I had to go out and get a Morton Sundee" (199). And Doris and Fussie use this book to hide a love poem so that Eben Weeks finds it when he consults this book to write his essay. But worst of all is that with this poem, these girls want to laugh at Eben. A book on the importance of culture and of knowing "the best that has been said and thought in the world" becomes a mere vehicle for teenagers' jokes. Glaspell, however, not only employs Arnold's book to present the stupidity of puerile characters, but also the imbecility of the mature Senator Lewis, one of the one hundred percent Americans. Senator Lewis pursues "*Matthew Arnold with the conscious air of a half literate man reading a 'great book'*" (202). Although Morton College library is crowded with books, these have materialized into one of Silas's fears; books, instead of being used to make better people, are tools to merely show off and disguise "half" literacy: "It makes something of men — learning. A house that's full of books makes a different kind of people. Oh, of course, if the books aren't there just to show off," warns Silas Morton in Act I (187).

Glaspell constructs in Madeline a character aware of the dangers of the past when the good aspects of heritage are reshaped for the worse or kept in oblivion. Madeline is a victim of the place where she lives because she is supposed to behave in a given way out of the respect she owes to her ancestors' place. "If ever a girl had a background, Morton College is Madeline Fejevary Morton's background," says Fejevary (210). Madeline does not reject her background, but the fact that the ideals her ancestors defended, the ones presented in Act I, have become fossilized. Glaspell brilliantly exemplifies the fossilization of pioneers' ideals in *Inheritors* in the case of Ira. Afraid "of the challenge of modern life" (Waterman 1966: 77), Madeline's father sticks up for the past and is unable to evolve. A good example is found in the scene when, afraid that Madeline might be imprisoned, Ira claims: "There might be a fine, and they'd come down on me and take my land" (217). His sense of loyalty to the efforts his father and all the pioneers before him made to have this place leads Ira to assert, "Not for *anything*— you hear me?— would I mortgage this farm my father handed down to me" (215, emphasis in original). Ira's pride in material goods means Ira's victimage of location.

Completely opposed to her father's self-imposed duty to defend his material heritage, Glaspell evinces Madeline's rejection of her past in her denial to attend the celebrations on the fortieth anniversary of the founding of the college that carries her name. When recalled that she is the granddaughter of "the sainted pioneer," "the grand old man of the prairies," and the "man of vision," Madeline wittily remarks, "Wouldn't you hate to be the granddaughter of a phrase?" (201). This sharp reply summarizes Glaspell's standpoint about what happened to the old American ideals. They have been reduced to mere phrases, to nice quotations to show off. This issue is further emphasized when Ira agrees that all the good intentions of the past are only words:

> That's what the world is — all coming to nothing. My father used to sit there at the table and talk about the world — my father and her father. They thought 'twas all for something — that what you were went on into something more than you. That's the talk I always heard in this house. But it's just talk. The rare thing that came here was killed by the common thing that came here. Just happens — and happens cruel [224].

Nevertheless, Madeline's rejection of tradition is not as complete as could be extracted from her words, and eventually she emerges as a legitimate spiritual inheritor of the pioneers. In a later chapter, I shall discuss that Madeline understands the real meaning of the college manifesto, of her ancestors' beliefs, and that she is ready to fight for them as she escapes her own victimage of location.

The Spatial Burden
of the Pilgrim Fathers' Heritage

As Glaspell reworks the pioneer heritage in the plays set in the American Midwest, the portion of American history she revisits in the plays set in New England is significant regarding the spatial presence of the Pilgrim Fathers' heritage. In *The Verge*, given that Claire has endeavored to deviate from given forms, the presence of the past is felt more linguistically than visually. J. Ellen Gainor has identified the relevance of the New England setting: "As a locus of patriarchy, no place in America reverberates with more sense of 'fatherhood' than New England. The Puritan founding fathers, shapers of American morality and ethos, are palpable presences for Claire, representing all she wishes to escape" (1989: 87). As her sister reminds her, Claire has "great teachers and preachers behind," and so she is told to "live up to the men [she] come[s] from" (244–245). Claire's sister has found in her heritage the compass to direct her life and the life of Claire's daughter:

> ADELAIDE: There's something about being in that main body, having one's roots in the big common experiences, gives a calm which you have missed. That's why I want you to take Elizabeth, forget yourself, and —
> CLAIRE: I do want calm. But mine would have to be a calm I — worked my way to. A calm all prepared for me — would stink [251].

Claire rejects the kind of calm that her heritage provides, the calm of having a place, even if a good one, in society. The calm that comes from heritage, that calm "all prepared" for her, is another burden Claire wants to get rid of. Claire attacks her sister and their common heritage: "Well, isn't it about time somebody got loose from that? What I came from made you, so —... So — you being such a tower of strength, why need I too be imprisoned in what I came from?" and Adelaide responds, "It isn't being imprisoned. Right there is where you make your mistake, Claire. Who's in a tower — an unsuccessful tower? Not I" (249). Their argument displays the main features of how the past can be part of a character's geopathology. Adelaide affirms that Claire should be "what she was meant to be," that Claire should respect the traditional morality and ethos her Puritan ancestors established. The protagonist, on the contrary, shapes her identity in opposition to heritage, getting "loose from" heritage, a concept that shuts her in as in a perfect tower Adelaide, as Elizabeth, represents, and not in the "thwarted tower" Claire needs.

Glaspell also shows Claire's disgust at the entrapping concept she thinks heritage constitutes through her rejection of traditional art forms. While arguing with Adelaide about the role heritage should have in shaping one's identity, Claire has a book of William Blake's drawings in her hands. In his stark deviations from traditional art, Blake experimented with new forms and provided different angles from which to look at his work. Claire turns the book "*to see another way*" (248), symbolizing her urgency of looking at things from different angles and of finding new ways of expression. For obvious reasons, Adelaide prefers traditional art. She recommends to Claire, "You'd better look at the Sistine Madonna" (250). Regarding heritage, the meaning of the Sistine Madonna, painted by Raphael circa 1518, stands as an epitome of traditional painting, the kind of art Claire repudiates. Glaspell also suggests Claire's deviation from heritage relating to art through Claire's divorce from her first husband, whom she defines as "a stick-in-the-mud artist" (240), that is, as a painter who only created realistic portraits. In her quest to deviate from traditional art, Claire has chosen Dick, a modernist painter, as a lover.

While in *The Verge*, as in *Close the Book* and *Inheritors*, Glaspell argues that heritage can become a negative feature leading to her protagonists' victimage of location, in *The Comic Artist* heritage is spatialized in order to show a character's positive eagerness to come back to and to keep her roots. The set is described as follows: "*The house is two hundred years old.... For the most part the furniture is old American, but there has been no attempt at 'period' so the house has not the atmosphere of a museum*" (269–270). The "old American" pieces of furniture are a small and a larger table, a walnut horse-hair sofa, two or three Windsor armchairs, and a plain, full-length couch (270). The past here does not seem either a burden nor a matter of pride, but something to give a "sense of identity" and "security" to one's life (Noe 1981: 83). Moreover, since it has not "*the atmosphere of a museum*," this seems a nice place to live in. Eleanor consciously wanted to move here as a sharp contrast to the life she had in New York:

> ELEANOR: My people were here long ago. They built this house in seventeen hundred and something. I feel my great-grandfather in the old forgotten roads, on the beach.... He lingers in things he made or touched, in my own imagination.... He is in me. After long, home-sick wandering — in other countries, in New York — he has returned [13].

Eleanor articulates her return to her ancestors' house as her contribution to her great-grandfather's rest. For her, this place provides the peace she wants to grant her great-grandfather and the peace she wants for herself and her family after the bohemian life they led in New York. But moving to this old house was not enough, and Eleanor endeavors to get all the old things that were in the house before. "I like to go out and find the things that grew all through the time the land was alone. I like bringing them into the house and doing the same old things," she also says (294). In her conscious attempt to forge her identity, Eleanor buys the house where her distant ancestors had lived, and tries to get back all the belongings that once were in the house, regaining thus the identity the house once had. And then, hinting at the idea that identity is constituted through performative acts, Eleanor reinforces her link to her heritage, her identity, and her house, by repeating the same acts her ancestors allegedly performed there, "doing the same old things." And this is how she knows that "I belong here" (57).

Turning to Eleanor's love for old things, Glaspell employs two stage props to signify this character's attachment to heritage: a lantern and a jar. Karl and Eleanor talk about the lantern in the following terms:

> KARL: [*Sitting down and examining it.*] This is a curious old lantern.
> ELEANOR: An old ship's lantern. It was here in the barn. I think it belonged to my great-grandfather.
> KARL: Then it sent its light into some pretty stormy places, didn't it?
> ELEANOR: There does seem something valiant about the good old thing.
> KARL: [*Who is still leaning into the light of it, examining.*] It was good — your coming back to this old place [293].

This dialogue draws a relationship between the past and how it gives value to the present. The old lantern showed the way to the ship, in the same manner that Eleanor's return to the house, to her past, was aimed to give her life sense, to find her roots and to fix her identity. The lantern is also a metaphorical representation of Eleanor herself. She aims to send light to stormy places, that is, to guide Karl and Stephen in difficult moments. In the following scene Karl is lost outside, a little afraid of darkness, right until Eleanor shows him the way home with her lantern:

> KARL: It was nice to see your lantern, like a little circle of safety in the strange night. Or is it you, Eleanor?
> ELEANOR: Me?
> KARL: Makes that circle [293].

In this highly symbolic scene, Karl's loss of his husband role with Nina reflects in spatial terms in his fear of being lost and in darkness. Eleanor, who has apparently rooted her identity as wife and mother, and who seems to enjoy topophilia, appears with her lantern to symbolically save Karl. By basing herself upon her heritage, Eleanor makes "a little circle of safety."

Glaspell, however, complicates Eleanor's topophilia, for what was seen as Eleanor's positive quality, her love for her firm heritage, becomes the spark the displaced characters will use to symbolically destroy Eleanor's home. Glaspell symbolizes the destruction of Eleanor's past, as an attack on her identity, through the breaking of an old jar. When Stephen rejects Nina as a model and lover, Nina seizes Eleanor's jar and throws it at Stephen (291). The breaking of Eleanor's jar mirrors the destruction of her house and the shattering of her past. The jar is an old piece Eleanor cherished:

> STEPHEN: We'll get another.
> ELEANOR: You can't get another. It had always been here. It belonged here [292].

The conjunction of prop and place, that the jar belonged to here, is explicitly revealed. The old jar cannot be replaced because it had its vivid meaning, its sense of past. Invaders dismantle Eleanor's effort to keep the roots of her house and her family strongly fixed to the earth. Therefore, the past is a burden on Eleanor because she has to struggle against almost all the other characters to defend her belief in tradition, a burden that, as she says later, makes her feel "a little tired" (294).

Geopathic Crossroads: Place, Identity, and Tradition in Performative Acts

Tradition in Glaspell's plays is also understood in a broader sense beyond the Pioneer or the Pilgrim Fathers' ancestry. Indeed, social roles, which are strongly rooted in tradition, influence the arising of victimage of location. In some of her plays, Glaspell focuses on families that have an important role in society as guardians of heritage and tradition to disclose the powerful interplay among place, identity and tradition.

In his early analysis of *Alison's House,* Sievers claims, "the general theme is the return of the past" (1955: 71). This is noticeable in the configuration of the onstage library of the Stanhopes' homestead, where the past has never left. Indeed, this library seems to be frozen in the past. As in *Close the Book,* the intellectual and social status of the family materializes in books and portraits. There are volumes by Keats, Shelley, Spencer, and Shakespeare; and the portraits are "*of an older generation*" (312). The sense that the Stanhopes feel great pride in their past and tradition is shown as well in the kind of furnishings that crowds the room. While the play opens in the morning of the last day of the nineteenth century, "*The furnishings of the library are of a period earlier than this*" (312). Besides this visual assertion about the importance of tradition in this place, Glaspell verbalizes this idea through one of the characters. Louise refers to the house: "So roomy, and well built. And such *traditions*" (332, emphasis in original), and "The place has been in the family from the first" (334). Louise's words establish the close link between the Stanhopes as a family, their house, their heritage and their tradition; all apparently are "well built."

The set reminds one of *Close the Book*. However, while Glaspell treats the issue of heritage as a burden in a comic manner in *Close the Book*, this issue receives a more serious treatment in *Alison's House*, where respect for heritage and tradition triggers pain, sorrow and even death. Unlike *Close the Book*, where the library was traditional but cheerful, as suggested by the light design, in *Alison's House* the room is gloomy. Glaspell's use of lighting and color are determinant in this sense. In *Alison's House* the curtains covering the bay window on the rear wall are "*old plum-colored velvet*," and the room is carpeted in a tone deeper than the curtains (312). Certainly, the curtains point to the family economic status, since velvet is an expensive sort of fabric, and to its past, given that the curtains are old. But the opaqueness of velvet prompts negative connotations, which together with the dark carpeted floor shape an obscure atmosphere.

As the Stanhopes get ready to move out of the house, there is a certain disorder in this library too, a factor Chaudhuri also lists to detect dramatic geopathology. In *Alison's House*, throughout Acts I and II, the characters work together to "tear up" this room, packing books and the tea china. Significantly, as the characters dismember the room, Glaspell makes them waver between a feeling of happiness and relief for dismantling the house and a strange remorse for breaking up their past. For instance, whereas Eben feels that "everything should stay where it is" (326), as a reminder of their past, Stanhope understands that this is really pathological for Agatha and wants to release his sister from this burden. This idea appears again when the Hodges say they will redecorate the house, put in partitions, and so on:

> EBEN: They'll destroy it.
> STANHOPE: I want it destroyed.... I care for it so much I don't want — itself, to go to some one else [330].

Stanhope prefers to see the house destroyed rather than to see other people living in the house that represents his heritage. The Stanhopes' history is one of self-sacrifice to maintain their status in society. Accepting that the site of their identity may pass on to another family makes Stanhope question the futility of their efforts, and this is why the house has to be destroyed.

In *Chains of Dew*, Glaspell provides what is probably one of the main verbalizations of the geopathic crossroads among place, identity and tradition. In the following scene, Glaspell suggests that identity is utterly influenced by tradition and social environment, and steadily reaffirmed through performativity:

> DOTTY: Don't you think sometimes you are as you are — because you've *been* that way? [*Holds the doll at arm's length.*] And you've been that way — well because you are supposed to be that way. When you do certain things — bridge and dancing — then you're the kind of person who plays bridge and dances. But what sort of person would you be — if you did something else? ...it's an exciting idea — that you needn't be as you are [148, emphasis in original].

For Dotty it is evident that her identity is based on the repetition of her daily acts. Born to a wealthy and traditional family, married to Seymore, the vestry man, Dotty has been raised respecting traditions. She is now a traditional grown-up woman because, mainly, she does what traditional women of her status usually do. In Act II, she is seen performing the role of the dutiful wife; she behaves as if she were her husband's servant. She answers the phone and fetches Seymore a foot stool so that he is at ease, while, in a symbolic subjugation to Seymore, she sits in a lower chair. Besides home, the places she goes to, and which her husband and society approve, are the Monday luncheon club, the Wednesday, Thursday, Friday, Saturday, and Sunday bridge, dinner at Elmhurst, Edith's dinner, and the Verder's tea (143). Dotty's victimage of location is latent in her realization that she is caught in a traditional rhythm of life that does nothing but enhance her traditionalism.

In *Chains of Dew*, Seymore does his part in keeping Dotty tied to traditional places and performing only those acts which suit her social status. Above all, he wants his wife to stay as she is now, like a child he has to protect. He calls her Dotty Dimple, her childhood pet name, and talks about her in the following terms: "The things she grew up in. I — at no little personal sacrifice — have kept her happy in these things" (160). Seymore cannot accept his wife's interest in modern poetry because this would take her far from her traditional role. This is also the reason why Seymore is appalled by the arrival of his modern New York friends; they could show Dotty that there is another world, the "exciting" one Dotty thinks about in her dreams.

Glaspell also makes Mother experience the intersection among place, identity and tradition. The first time Mother appears onstage she seemingly represents a traditional woman. Some pieces of furniture and stage properties suggest her traditionalism. The sewing chair, the work table and the twin dolls stand for Mother's main occupation, reinforced by the fact that when she first appears she sits down in her chair and takes one of the dolls, ready to work. However, as the play develops, it is evident that this approach to Mother echoes the way in which Seymore has presented her in Act I and how he wants her to be, but that, as in the case of Dotty, has nothing to do with what these women really want to do and to be.

In keeping with Seymore's wish to retain Dotty in the things in which she grew up, he is also eager to accommodate Mother to what he thinks is the best situation for her: "Mother does live with us, and after her long faithful life I confess I do like to give her the kind of home she wants. She knows only those simple things in which she grew up — and old" (134). As with Dotty, Seymore has not bothered to consider what his Mother really wants, and he endeavors to keep her in "a peaceful resting place after her long life" (157). Nevertheless, Mother's open embrace of the modernity Nora brings to the house, the promotion of birth control in Bluff City, and the fact that Mother also has a try to see how a bob suits her, reveals how wrong Seymore is. Indeed, Kristina Hinz-Bode has identified a comic pun on Seymore's name: "see" "more" (2006b: 132). Seymore thinks he has some kind of superior wisdom, while the truth is that he should "see more," because he is unable to see the truth behind his mother and his wife. Seymore's catastrophic misinterpretation of his mother's dolls is very revealing. Seymore believes his mother's dolls represent the old lady's need to do something for others. But these dolls turn out to be Mother's witty rebellion, representative of what she thinks but dares not to say about the people she knows. Thus, this activity does not mirror the peaceful old lady making dolls for a church bazaar, but a silent and angry comment on people she cannot stand, as expanded in the final chapter.

The way both Mother and Dotty ally to rebel against tradition, by changing the configuration of the room, their own identities, and by performing different activities, is crucial. On the one hand, this shows that place, heritage and tradition can form a geopathic crossroad. On the other hand, this also shows that this geopathology can be avoided, at least momentarily, by behaving differently. When she faces modernity, Dotty realizes that "There are too many vital things in our lives to keep repeating tiresome things" (165), and so she changes her traditional performativity drastically. Dotty dismisses all her former friends, putting an end to the Monday luncheon club and the like; she accepts being the president of the birth control league in her area; and she has her hair bobbed. Mother, in turn, will help Nora display her birth control propaganda and make dolls for birth control as well.

A very interesting issue regarding the interplay among place, tradition, and performativity is that, through Dotty, Glaspell shows that Dotty's new identity and new performativity also require a place. As a matter of contrast to Dotty's lack of place, Glaspell presents onstage Seymore's place of his own. It is not a matter of coincidence that Seymore, the character who says that he has a problem with place, has a room of his own. In this manner, his discourse on his house being a prison for him loses strength again when he has a place where he can be himself freely, a privilege nobody else has in this play. Besides, Glaspell employs Seymore's studio to reflect upon gender politics in terms of space. Given that Seymore has a room of his own, Glaspell posits here the question of Dotty's necessity to have a room of her own, too. The new Dotty, the one all changed after Nora's arrival, also acknowledges her need for a place to work quietly. Dotty invites Nora and O'Brien to go upstairs to work on their speech for birth control: "Why don't we go upstairs? Where we won't be disturbed. [*Noting Seymore.*] Or — won't disturb.... Well, shall we stay here? [*Firmly.*] No. Let us go where we will be uninterrupted" (171). In her remarks about place, Dotty recognizes that she finds her work more or at least equally important to that of her husband, while earlier Seymore's work was her main concern.

Tradition vs. Modernity: Generation Conflicts Reflected Onstage

Generational conflict is a very precise configuration of the more general theme of family or tradition as a key factor in dramatic geopathology. And this conflict, indeed, is used by Glaspell to spatialize her most radical ideas about social and family roles vs. the struggle of the individual to be free from these ties. As pinpointed in Chapter 1, the generation conflict is a common theme many modern American playwrights employ as a device to set their plays in motion. The aim of this section is to place Glaspell within this tradition, reflecting on the way generational conflicts and dramatic geopathology relate in her plays. Moreover, the analysis of how the generation conflict is staged in Glaspell's plays will demonstrate that Glaspell's interest in this issue began very early, and that she exploited its dramatic possibilities in her early plays, and not exclusively in *The Comic Artist, Alison's House* and *Springs Eternal,* as has been said.[3]

A first interesting typology within generational conflicts enacted in space, and which thus contributes to dramatic geopathology, originates in the confrontation between two opposed kinds of women: the True Woman vs. the New Woman. Succinctly, the True Woman is characterized by domesticity and submissiveness. She defends traditional Victorian values, i.e., motherhood, women's subjugation to men, women's position inside the house and, by extension, within the moral frameworks established by society. Glaspell usually marks visually this kind of character with a traditional look, as are the cases of Mabel in *Suppressed Desires,* Clara Root in *Close the Book,* Aunt Isabel in *Inheritors,* Mrs. MacIntyre in *Chains of Dew,* Laura in *Bernice,* Adelaide in *The Verge,* Agatha and Louise in *Alison's House,* and Eleanor in *The Comic*

Artist. Moreover, Glaspell also places a character visually marked as a New Woman confronting these True Women.

A unitary definition of the New Woman or even an agreed date of birth of the "New Woman," which ranges from the end of the 19th century to the passage of the 19th Amendment in the United States, has not been reached. The one issue these women agreed on was, as Elizabeth Ammons has said, "a belief in female self-determination." But these women diverged on issues such as "awareness of racism, class bias, oppression of women by women, the draw-backs of sexual revolution for women, and the danger of individualism as a prime human value" (1991: 95). While Glaspell does not cover all these models of the New Woman in her plays, and she usually presents the white and Anglo-Saxon model, Glaspell's New Women vary greatly in her plays. The main aspect that unites Glaspell's New Women characters is their opposition to True Women and male characters who defend Victorianism. Writing for the *Weekly Outlook* in 1896, Glaspell set her own definition of the New Woman, a definition which deserves being quoted in full:

> First ... you must be ... clever; you need not be pretty, but you must be bright, vivacious, interesting. You are not expected to spend your life buried in an encyclopedia or a treatise on the Origin of Man, but ... be able to talk with intelligence and wit on anything from the penal laws of Russia to the latest production in the farce comedy line. You must have sufficient resources within yourself not to be afflicted with *ennui* every time there is no man in sight, and when the man does come into view, you must stand ready to cope with him on his own grounds rather than docilely and demurely wait for him to fill your ears with pretty nothings [qtd. in Ben-Zvi 2005: 33].

Many of these features underline Glaspell's dramaturgy. Glaspell's New Woman character is often talkative, learned, intelligent, and what is most significant, unafraid of men or men's territories: "You must be ready to cope with him on his own grounds," says Glaspell. Besides the features seen above, Glaspell's New Woman also follows the paradigm Lois Rudnick has provided; for this scholar, the New Woman is "a conflicted figure" because Victorianism still casts a heavy burden on this kind of woman, but she could be defined as "having the attributes of independence, self-definition, physical adeptness, and mental acuity, qualities that allowed her to work, play, study, volunteer, and socialize with equal aplomb" (1991: 73).

The generational conflict Glaspell dramatizes in some of her plays regarding exclusively her female characters establishes opposed sets of characters, New Women, vs. their antagonists, True Women. There are some clear cases of confrontation: in *Suppressed Desires*, in order to avoid the sanatorium, Mabel wants to occupy Henrietta's place in Steve's life, that is, she wants to become his wife. Clara Root in *Close the Book* cannot accept that the modern outsider Jhansi is inside her house, her family and her social circle. Aunt Isabel in *Inheritors* tries to convince Madeline to stay within the family, society, and her heritage. In *Chains of Dew*, Mrs. MacIntyre attempts to defend Dotty's traditional house by verbally expelling the New Woman Nora from Bluff City. Laura confronts Margaret in *Bernice* because Margaret is an independent New Woman; she is single, childless, and free to move, and according to Laura this disqualifies her as a real woman. Adelaide reproaches Claire with the same crimes in *The Verge*, urging her to return to her heritage and to her roles of dutiful wife and loving mother. Agatha and Louise in *Alison's House* cannot accept Elsa's liberty, going away with a married man, and then they do not want her inside the house; and finally, Eleanor appears in sharp contrast to cheeky Nina in *The Comic Artist*, who has appeared to break the tranquility of Eleanor's house.

Nonetheless, Glaspell's opposition between New Woman vs. True Woman is not simplistic. Two kinds of New Woman have been identified in Glaspell's *oeuvre*: "strong, independent women who forswear lovers and family for self-actualization or principle" and "comic characters who interrogate radical notions and unconventional ideas about women" (Noe 2002: 153). For instance, regarding comic characters, Jhansi in *Close the Book*, though claiming her outsider status, finally remains inside the Roots' house and within society. And the stronger New Women characters in Glaspell's plays, such as Claire in *The Verge* and Madeline in *Inheritors*, go through a painful, lonely, and long spatial confrontation also due to the generational conflict. Since Claire epitomizes the attack on the idea of female virtue, her battle against Victorianism is a solitary and brave enterprise. This might be the reason why members of Heterodoxy, the Greenwich Village radical feminist club, applauded Claire so heartedly: "It seemed to me, while these women were talking about *The Verge*, that I was in church, that they were worshipping at some holy shrine; their voices and their eyes were full of religious excitement" (Dufour qt. in Hapgood 1939: 377).

Claire, "the antithesis of the True Woman" (Noe 2002: 158), violates all the norms of femininity. A very interesting issue regarding Claire as a New Woman is that she is not young. And, curiously, the youngest female character in the play, Claire's daughter, Elizabeth, is a True Woman as much as her aunt Adelaide. Though Ben-Zvi calls Elizabeth a New Woman (2006: 294), maybe because of her youth, an analysis of how Glaspell describes her reveals the opposite. Indeed, through Elizabeth, Glaspell shows the fall of the New Woman. As Deborah Kolb says, the Progressive Era (1890–1920) is characterized by the rise and fall of the New Woman. After the 19th Amendment was passed in 1920, "the professional feminist movement began an unmistakable decline, and not until the 1960s did a strong revival begin" (1975: 149).

In her analysis of feminism in Greenwich Village from 1910 to 1920, June Sochen highlights the value of Crystal Eastman, Henrietta Rodman, Ida Rauh, Neith Boyce, and Susan Glaspell, and calls the readers' attention towards the fact that these feminists had foreseen the failure of their movement. These women saw that the problem of feminist agitation was that a great part of its supporters thought that gaining the vote would be enough to ameliorate women's situation in every realm. This limited scope provoked a paralysis regarding other improvements in women's situation that feminists were requesting. In this manner, all the agitation of the feminist movement before 1920, which not only called for the vote but also for a real cultural revolution, became minimized. After 1920, "none of the existing women's organizations carried on the feminist campaign. Most women's organizations in the twenties refused to discuss abortion, birth control, or liberalized divorce laws" (1972: 146). Borrowing Ann Jones's words, "After a century of struggle, women came back to square one" (1980: 260).

Besides struggling to keep Adelaide and the traditionalism she represents out of her places, Claire also has to confront her daughter, representative of the demise of the New Woman concept. Elizabeth represents what Claire hates in a woman: submission to the location where tradition has put her. Glaspell shows this through a few questions Elizabeth answers. When asked about her studies, she says she studies "the things one studies." And in her free time, Elizabeth also does "the things one does. Tennis and skating and dancing" (244). But Elizabeth is unable to explain what she studies or does. She is not even able to explain why she is glad she is an American: "[*Laughing.*] Why — mother. Of course one is glad one is an American. All the girls —" (244). She just follows the current of "all the girls." As seen in Chapter 2, although Elizabeth is somehow free to move — she has been to Europe — her memories of the trip do not make us think of a New Woman. She summarizes her trip as "awfully amusing" (244) and adds nothing else. Probably, this trip mirrors the kind of trip her aunt Adelaide, who has raised her, wants Claire to take: "Go to Paris and get yourself some awfully good-looking clothes — and have one grand fling at the gay world. You really love that, Claire, and you've been awfully dull lately" (251). Elizabeth is all appearance. The stage direction describes her as "*the creditable young American — well-built, poised, 'cultivated,' so sound an expression of the usual as to be able to meet the world with assurance — assurance which training has made rather graceful. She is about seventeen — and mature. You feel solid things behind her*" (243). But as soon as she is questioned, her solid appearance falls down. She is the product of what she has been taught, but she is empty inside. Elizabeth is a victim of place and tradition as they have made an empty, "usual," person out of her.

Madeline in *Inheritors* also takes her stance in the generational conflict by opposing True Women's ideals, traditional male characters, and uncommitted young female characters. The main representatives of the older values in this play are Felix Fejevary the Second and Ira Morton, who for very different reasons defend Victorian values. Felix Fejevary, as has been said, for financial reasons, and Ira because he is trapped in the past. Madeline, as Claire, is alone in her struggle to defend her beliefs and make Morton College the place it was meant to be. Unlike Madeline, the other young characters onstage do not defend the modern outlook. Horace is closer to his father's generation in his belief to keep America as a place devoid of immigrant characters. Emil, a descendant of immigrants himself, is fully accommodated now to his position, and thus he does not help Madeline, either.

Glaspell shows the possibility that young women who are still traditional can be shaped into New Women through the process Madeline undergoes in *Inheritors*. Marcia Noe has described Madeline in the following terms: "the quintessential New Woman: bright, well-educated, lively, independent-minded, high-principled, and non-conforming. But there is a side of her that is more Society Girl than New Woman" (2002: 155). Madeline, as Noe puts it, moves from the tennis court, the symbol of her traditional and bourgeois place in society, to the court yard, the place that symbolizes her rebellion against what her place has become. Madeline, like Jhansi in *Close the Book*, is a girl that takes advantage of the fact that women are allowed to attend colleges; they avidly read and reflect upon what they read. Madeline's first appearance onstage is in a tennis outfit, ready for a match, symbolic of her status as a Society Girl. But the moment Madeline makes use of the tennis racket to hit the police in order to defend the Hindu students, she begins to change. Her political ideas for free speech are not something to merely read about and discuss, but a serious matter that requires her physical involvement too.

While Glaspell shows hope for women in the change Madeline experiences, she also warns about the more traditional young girls who, as does Elizabeth in *The Verge*, embody the fall of the New Woman after 1920. Doris and Fussie's first appearance onstage already reveals them as frivolous characters: "*Two girls, convulsed with the giggles, come tumbling in*" (198). Glaspell seems to be criticizing here the fact that when women are allowed to attend college, many of them do not take advantage of the possibilities this institution offers, and probably they only attend college to find a good husband and become housewives. These girls damage the identity a library has for the New Woman, and they completely destroy this identity as a site of learning when Doris and Fussie dance in the library. They are far from being mature college girls and New Women, and closer to the concept of the flapper, more interested in liberation regarding clothes and behavior than in political and social power. For

Scene from *Inheritors*, Act II. Margaret L. Robinson as Madeline Morton Fejevary. Metropolitan Playhouse production, 2005. Director: Yvonne Opffer Conybeare. Lighting design: Alexander Senchak. Set design: Ryan Scott. Photograph © Michelle DeBlasi.

Doris and Fussie, dancing in the library is something risky, even liberal, while the truth is that their actions are simply worthless for women's struggle in America. These girls' lack of interest in any intellectual activity is demonstrated in a line that echoes Elizabeth's response in *The Verge*. When asked about her favorite studies, Fussie replies, "I like all of them" (201). And their hobbies are also tennis and dancing. Glaspell employs the same theatrical technique, their inability to think by themselves, to portray the place women lose due to the decay in the women's rights movement after 1920, and that they constituted indeed a hindrance women had to overcome to regain their places in society.

Glaspell creates a similar young female character, only caring for her looks and for fun, in Nina in *The Comic Artist*. Again, the generational conflict, together with the portrait of a decayed New Woman, is used to break the meaning of a place. Raised in New York and Paris, and a woman who enjoys the Myth of Mobility, Nina has, nonetheless, not taken any advantage of the possibilities these bohemian cities could offer her. Her main interest is looking pretty and making men fall at her feet. Glaspell visualizes this point through her use of costume. Nina has a fur coat, which her mother, Luella, who can be considered a fallen New Woman too, makes her try on: "Isn't she ravishing in fur?" Nina answers, "Some day I'll have a sable" (283). Nothing is good enough for Nina; her hunger for material things is never satisfied. Furthermore, the places Nina usually goes to are also the places one goes to show off, such as the country club: "Nina liked it so much. She is wonderful — the kick she gets out of dressing up and going off to tea at some swell place" (287). Nina's main reasons to move to New York are to buy smart clothes and to dress up to go to nice places. Importantly, Nina does not have a job, but she depends totally on Karl's financial support. He is the one that pays for her clothes, her furs, and her trips. Nina has learnt from her mother how to take advantage of men: "Men are selfish, and it's a woman's job to get what she wants from them by finding out what they want and keeping it from them" (300).

Luella had also learnt from her mother how to use her beauty to get what she wants from men, and she is teaching her youngest daughter Alice as well. Thinking about the money Luella needs from her latest ex-husband, she admits, "the money you can spend for clothes, and the right teachers and doctors!" (276). Clothes, education, and health — in this order — constitute the basis of Luella's scheme. No wonder Luella rejoices at the thought that Alice will "make the men stand around" (276). In this manner, Luella's later comment, "Now I want to be independent of men, that's why I've come to you" (276) sounds extremely ironic and paradoxical. She claims she wants to be independent of men, a lie revealed as she comes to Stephen to ask him for money and connections to start a business in New York. Her dream shop is intended to sell those things that may make women more attractive to men — scarves, frocks, and bracelets. All the women in Luella's family seem doomed to become fallen New Women; all of them, from Luella's mother to her youngest child Alice, have been educated to be so. And hence, Luella and Nina come to Eleanor's place to engage in a conflict between a True Woman, Eleanor, and themselves, who are modern in looks and atypical regarding traditional behavior, but lacking the moral consistency of the New Woman who wants to make a living for herself.

Regarding the generational conflict between women in Glaspell's writings, Linda Ben-Zvi believes that, "Central to her work is the idea that if women are to progress and find their voices, they must finally overcome or ignore those loving, but constricted, figures who stand more threateningly in their way: *their mothers*" (2005: 28, emphasis added). Ben-Zvi's assertion about the need Glaspell's female characters have to overcome their mothers in order to become independent and fulfilled women rightfully applies to most of Glaspell's fiction, but only to some of her plays. Nina must get away from what her mother taught her in *The Comic Artist* if she is to be a New Woman; similarly, Clara's stricture in *Close the Book* is not a good example for her daughter-in-law, as Jhansi reacts against what Clara represents through-out the play; and we can assume that Claire's mother in *The Verge* resembles Adelaide and that probably she was another "Flower of New England." How-ever, in many of Glaspell's plays, mothers and grandmothers have a lot to teach younger female characters about how to have one's own place. In *Inheritors*, Madeline has the example of her mother to aid outsiders. Elizabeth, in *The Verge*, instead of escaping her mother, would gain independence if she followed Claire's model of independence from given rules. And then Glaspell offers the range of grandmother characters whom her modern female characters should follow. Mother in *Chains of Dew* and Grandmother in *Close the Book* are more willing to accept modernity and the outlook of the New Woman than other characters in these plays, and Grandmother Morton in *Inheritors* is a symbol of exceptional strength.

In her portrait of the New Woman's struggle against tradition, Glaspell sometimes makes other characters, male or female, join her heroine in order to fight the Victorian values that imprison them. This is the case of *Alison's House*. For scholars such as J. Ellen Gainor and Karen Laughlin, the main conflict of generation stands for "essentially opposing the traditional, Victorian values of Alison's brother and her sister Agatha, to the modern outlook of Father Stanhope's children, Eben, Ted, and Elsa, as well as his young secretary, Ann" (Laughlin 1995: 221). Moreover, it is also true that Glaspell questions here the value of patriarchy and its relation to stultifying, moral, given roles for men and women alike. But as seen in other of Glaspell's plays, the conflict cannot be reduced to such an easy matter of age. For instance, Louise, who belongs to a generation in between, respects the given order and struggles so that this given order is maintained. And Ted, the youngest character in the play, is presented as an individualistic and self-centered young man who is not interested in any defense of new values, but solely in his personal profit.

Glaspell completely abandons gender issues in order to concentrate fully on the clash between generations in her last play, *Springs Eternal*. I agree with Hinz-Bode's belief that the main conflict happens between two males, Owen and Jumbo, reproducing the more traditional opposition between father and son, a generational conflict "concentrated on the contrast between isolation and connection" (2006b: 216), a set of binaries related to place, the geodi-chotomy between physical isolation and community. Glaspell makes use of the main theme of the play, war, to set the ground for the generational conflict, which is divided into two sides: isolationists and interventionists. Although the issue of war is treated in depth in the following chapter, at this point I would like to highlight some important facts about the generation conflict in this play. In *Springs Eternal*, the older generation feels responsible for the war. Owen regrets, "I feel I brought on the war.... I mean my generation, and particularly those people in it who were supposed to be thinking things out" (364). Surprisingly, and in spite of their responsibility, the older generation in this play spends time in isolation, but they still force the youngest character, Jumbo, to join the Army and fight for their country. Thus, the generational conflict in this play is built upon the fact that the older generation chooses isolation for themselves, while they force interventionism upon the younger characters. Only two characters of the older generation, Margaret and Mrs. Soames, defend Jumbo's right to stay at home: "A man has a right to be the thing which in an honest heart he is. He doesn't *have* to be — what Hitler or his own dear father tells him to be!" (393, emphasis in original). Like Madeline in *Inheritors*, Jumbo will also be forced to leave his house, the place where he is not accepted because of his ideas, as I discuss in the following chapter.

5

Imagery of Death in Dramatic Geopathlogy

The presence of death is palpable in almost every play by Susan Glaspell. Her drama is crowded with corpses. Corpses appear onstage or in a near off-stage place in *The Outside*, *Alison's House*, *The Verge* and *The Comic Artist*. In *Bernice*, there is a corpse in an adjoining room, while the farm in *Trifles* is the place where John Wright died before the play opens. Moreover, in other plays, such as *Chains of Dew*, Glaspell describes places by connecting them to death imagery. Consequently, death has a leading role in the geography of her plays, and this chapter examines to what extent death determines self and space.

Home as Grave

In a general statement she does not develop sufficiently, Chaudhuri claims that images of burial are common to geopathic dramatic homes. Chaudhuri briefly mentions the disastrous link between two prominent figures in the discourse of geopathology: home and burial (2000: 75). The scarce references to this issue later on in her book mainly relate to the buried child figure, but burial is never construed as a separate figure on its own. There is a certain consistency, however, in Glaspell's creation of onstage places which could indeed be seen as metaphorical graves, and which add to a geopathic atmosphere. The abundance of images of graves in Glaspell's plays locates her work within the tradition of women writers that Sandra Gilbert and Susan Gubar analyze in their *The Madwoman in the Attic* (1979). As Gilbert and Gubar claim, the grave image in women's literature usually means "enclosure without any possibility of escape" (1979: 94). In the plays analyzed in this chapter, Glaspell does not portray actual images of burial, but the places created onstage can be considered places of burial in themselves, metaphors of graves. The means Glaspell employs to suggest the burial atmosphere in her fictional places vary. In *Trifles*, the onstage farm can be regarded as a metaphorical grave because it is set in a low, tomb-like site. In other plays, the corpses that appear onstage, in a near offstage place, or in verbal references suggest the grave-like atmosphere of the place.

In *The Outside*, both the interior setting of the old life-saving station and the localized offstage fictional place, the Outside, represent images of death. The station is described as "a buried house" (61), and the Outside the title refers to constitutes an image of burial, as is clear from the first description that Glaspell provides of the location of the old life-saving station. Through a big sliding door opening at rear onstage, one can perceive the dunes and the woods:

> At one point the line where woods and dunes meet stands out clearly and there are indicated the rude things, vines, bushes, which form the outer uneven rim of the woods — the only things that grow in the sand. At another point a sand-hill is menacing the woods. This old life-saving station is at a point where the sea curves, so through the open door the sea is also seen.... At right of the big sliding door is a drift of sand and the top of the buried beach grass is seen on this [59].

Glaspell describes this landscape as a natural place of burial: the sand buries the woods, the sea provokes deaths and threatens to swallow, to bury, the old life-saving station.

Glaspell also makes the old life-saving station a place of burial by placing a corpse onstage. *The Outside* opens with the actual death of a sailor. As the curtain rises, there is a corpse in a room adjoining the center of the stage, where the main action takes place, and it is partly seen at some moments. This corpse shows that the place where Mrs. Patrick now lives is a place of death, and suggests visually the dead-in-life state of the female characters. Glaspell enhances the association between Mrs. Patrick and death the moment the dead sailor seems to offer his hand to her: "*One arm of the man [the Captain] is working with is raised, and the hand reaches through the doorway*" (60) in the direction of Mrs. Patrick. The atmosphere of death is also created verbally through the male characters' conversation. Given that many wrecks have taken place close to the old life-saving station, Captain, Bradford and Tony recall that many men have died here: "Lord, the things that happened *here*. There've been dead ones carried through that door. [*Pointing to the outside door.*] Lord — the ones *I've* carried" (60, emphasis in original). The image of all these dead sailors, reinforced by the actual corpse the audience can partially see onstage, is extrapolated to Mrs. Patrick and Allie Mayo. The male characters even compare these women to the sea: "But the sea is friendly as a kitten alongside the women that live here" (60).

Significantly within the discourse of dramatic geopathology, it seems

Scene from *The Outside*. Lisa Armytage as Allie Mayo. Orange Tree Theatre production, 2008. Director: Svetlana Dimcovic. Photograph © Robert Day.

hardly possible to live a happy life in a place surrounded by images of death. The male characters agree, "The sand has put this place on the blink all right" (60) and they cannot understand why Mrs. Patrick has taken this menaced and abandoned place to live. But Allie, who also lost her husband, perfectly understands her. After losing her husband to the North Sea, Allie detached herself from social life and decided not to say "an unnecessary word" (62). In keeping with Glaspell's mastery of body language as an instrument of expression better than spoken language, Allie reproduces with her body her own metaphorical death in this ice metaphor: "The ice that caught Jim — caught me. [*A moment as if held in ice.*]" (62). The very first description of Allie can also be read in terms of burial: "*ALLIE MAYO has appeared outside the wide door which gives on to the dunes, a bleak woman, who at first seems little more than a part of the sand before which she stands*" (61). Allie is described as part of the sand which buries and menaces the woods.

Mrs. Patrick is also a "buried" woman in a metaphorical sense. That Mrs. Patrick wants to be detached, "buried," is shown in the fact that she has taken Allie, a woman known in town for not saying an unnecessary word, as her sole companion. Furthermore, Mrs. Patrick has what I call a geoempathetic feeling regarding the image of burial this natural landscape creates. That is, she rejoices in the enterprise of the sand-hills, which bury the grass fighting to see the light. There is a clear parallel between this image and Mrs. Patrick's wish: "Everything that can hurt me. I want buried — buried deep" (64). Mrs. Patrick hates Spring, the season that makes her *feel* that on the Outside, life, not only burial, is possible. At one point she even unconsciously contributes to the natural burial that takes place outside: *"She pushes the sand by the door down on the half buried grass — though not as if knowing what she is doing"* (63). Mrs. Patrick is here burying the only blades of grass that remind her of life, contributing to the natural image of burial, and at the same time her own wish to be buried is evidenced.

Glaspell underlines Mrs. Patrick's longing for death when, contemplating the burial of the woods with which she identifies, and as she reflects upon this landscape, Mrs. Patrick lifts *"sand and let[s] it drift through her hand"* (64). Visually, this is her sinister rejoicing in death, to which Allie replies:

> ALLIE MAYO: I know where you're going! [*MRS PATRICK turns but not as if she wants to.*] What you'll try to do. Over there. [*Pointing to the line of woods.*] Bury it. The life in you — watching the sand bury the woods.... Meeting the Outside. [*Moving nearer; speaking more personally.*] I know why you came here. To this house that had been given up; on this shore where only savers of life try to live. I know what holds you on these dunes, and draws you over here [63–64].

Allie Mayo understands what Mrs. Patrick is doing on the Outside because that is exactly what she has been doing since her husband died. Devoid of their traditional role in life, they have given in to their personification of loss and death in the landscape before them. Thus, in *The Outside*, place is a problem for characters, since its deadly configuration enlarges their own feeling of burial in life, and Allie and Mrs. Patrick are geopathic characters who have consciously chosen this geopathic place to live in.

In *Alison's House*, the Stanhope homestead in Iowa is so suffocated by nature that it resembles a grave. The Mississippi menaces the house: "seems like she'd wash this place away 'fore we could get dead and buried" (328). As Hodges further says, "The place ain't healthy" and "Seems like the river had something against this place. Right here on this bend's where she washes in more and more" (328–329). The Mississippi threatens to bury the Stanhope house, in the same way that the trees help to suffocate it. The trees "make the place gloomy" to an extent that this is "a place nobody can see" (328). And Eben makes an explicit connection between the house and Alison's burial in these terms: "When I got the first glimpse of the place through the trees I had a feeling of the whole century being piled on top of [Alison], that she couldn't get out from under" (321). In Eben's words, the house is Alison's own metaphorical grave. This is not only the place where she died, but also the place where she was secluded and dead in life, a similar case to that of her sister, Agatha. The library setting further resembles a kind of grave to the audience. The portraits of all those dead ancestors seem to be the company of the onstage characters trapped in this house, and the darkness of this room, as seen previously, also contributes to the creation of a grave-like atmosphere.

The spatial configuration of the Standishes' house is not, however, as gloomy as Alison's is in *Alison's House*, probably because the prevailing tone in *Chains of Dew* is comic. The setting of this play is a richly furnished and comfortable room, used for social meetings. However, in dramatic geopathology even the nicest of places can be graves if they keep their dwellers dead in life. The metaphorical conception of the house as a cemetery in *Chains of Dew* gains force once Seymore reads aloud one of his poems:

> She's in her coffin — she's in her grave,
> Outside her coffin, she was not brave.
> What did she have, when she had life?
> She had long hair — a good sound life.
> What has she now that she is dead?
> She has long hair — outside her head.
> So what is death — and what is life?
> To one who's but — a long-haired wife? [149].

In the fashion of the British "Graveyard Poets," who initiated the gothic aesthetics of bodily corruptions, Seymore has written a very mediocre poem on a dead woman whose hair, following *post-mortem* processes, goes on growing. While inspiring himself, Seymore muses that a woman is glorified by her hair, and, significantly, that her hair has nothing to do with her volition or her aliveness; this woman's hair keeps on growing even when she is dead. The significance of the poem and of her husband's explanation is that they make Dotty realize that her house is her grave. The only feature of the protagonist in Seymore's poem is that she had long hair, symbolic of the fact that she did nothing in life. Dotty, who also has long hair, feels she is like this woman in the poem, and even more when Seymore brandishes Angelica, the long-haired doll that Mother had modeled after Dotty. For Dotty, her coffin and her grave are her house, the place from where she does not dare to depart, unless to go to other places where her husband lets her go. Following the discourse of the poem, Dotty realizes that all she has in life is long hair, the symbol of the respectful, dutiful, and quiet wife she is. This acknowledgment will trigger the events that take place later in the play, regarding Dotty's struggle to get away from her identity as a long-haired wife and the subjugation to the patriarchal power this image of the dead long-haired wife stands for.

The Buried Child

According to Chaudhuri, the literary figure of the buried child is a privileged device of the modern American drama. The buried child, a casualty of problematic places, appears in modern American drama to confront the myth of home and family. This image, nevertheless, not only refers to to a dead child character, but also to the images of the unseen child, which may also refer to a denied or unborn child character (Chaudhuri 2000: 110). Unlike the physical muddy remains of Sam Shepard's *Buried Child*, Glaspell never presents onstage a dead child. Glaspell, however, utilizes her dramatic skills to present the absent characters with great success and variety. The death, disappearance, or non-existence of the delicate figure of the baby certainly has a powerful dramatic effect on the audience, provoking thoughts about the reasons behind the absence or disappearance of this kind of character. For, as Chaudhuri has also noted, the buried child as an image functions as the secret in realist drama: "the buried child underwrites a drama of secrecy and revelation, of deeply hidden meaning and inevitable disclosure" (2000: 281, n. 14).

Glaspell consistently works on the buried child image in three of her plays: *Trifles*, *The Verge* and *Chains of Dew*. These three plays answer to three different versions of the motif of the buried child. In *Trifles*, the unborn child has a vital importance for understanding the geopathology inherent in the play. *The Verge* focuses on the dead child, while *Chains of Dew* deals with birth control. The different versions of the buried child motif could seem opposed, but they answer to Glaspell's personal situation and her social consciousness. Barbara Ozieblo and Linda Ben-Zvi have observed that Glaspell's childless condition obsessed her throughout all her life.[1] After her miscarriage in 1914, a fibroid tumor was detected in her uterus. The tumor was removed, but the operation left Glaspell unable to have children. "I always wanted children but couldn't have any of my own," confided Susan to one of her friends (qtd. in Ben-Zvi 2005: 376). But as a feminist, Glaspell was well aware of the fact that a child requires a nice home, hence her participation in the women's movement and her defense of women's right to decide whether to be mothers or not. Glaspell's thwarted wish to be a mother is evident in what Glaspell considered the best pose for a woman:

> the best pose for a woman is when she is a mother and holding a baby in her lap. In focusing on the baby — wanting to hold her forward so the baby looks good — the mother herself looks beautiful. In the transcendent act of love and self-effacement she becomes the object of adoration [Sundgaard qtd. in Ozieblo 2000: 263].

This description resembles enormously the pose of the Sistine Madonna, a pose that Glaspell attacks in two of her plays, *Chains of Dew* and *The Verge*, for establishing the constraining maternal role usually attached to women. I think that although there is no doubt that Glaspell always wanted to be a mother, she understood that having a baby was a personal decision every woman had to be free to make or not. This is the reason why the different versions of the buried child motif appear in her plays with different purposes. The female characters she depicts in her plays are all different, and their positions towards motherhood also vary.

In "'Murder She Wrote': The Genesis of Susan Glaspell's *Trifles*," Ben-Zvi highlights how the fact that Margaret Hossack, the real Minnie Wright, had given birth to a child before marriage was determinant at her trial. Using Glaspell's reports on the Hossack trial, Ben-Zvi argues that County Attorney Clammer used this bombshell to provide the jury with the impression that Mrs. Hossack "was a woman who could not to be trusted" (1992: 151). The double standard was exercised to sustain that, as Mrs. Hossack had done something improper for a woman — being pregnant before marriage — she could as well have killed her husband. Consequently, in her version of Hossack murder case, Glaspell provides children with a leading importance in the dramatic development of the play, and even more important is the image of the buried child. In *Trifles*, this image is closely linked to the pioneer experience. The hostile environment of the isolated Midwest farm where the play is set seems crucial to the most fragile characters. Mrs. Hale and Mrs. Peters talk about the stillness of the prairie environment in these terms:

> Mrs Hale: [*Her own feeling not interrupted.*] If there'd been years and years of nothing, then a bird to sing to you, it would be awful — still, after the bird was still.
> Mrs Peters: [*Something within her speaking.*] I know what stillness is. When we homesteaded in Dakota, and my first baby died — after he was two years old, and me with no other then.... I know what stillness is. [*Pulling herself back.*] The law has got to punish the crime, Mrs. Hale [33].

In Mrs. Peters's words, the isolated and isolating pioneer life makes infantile death a common casualty. While it is true that the reason why Mrs. Peters's baby died is unknown, she makes the connection between stillness and death. The Peterses "homesteaded" in Dakota as the Wrights live in a farmhouse in Iowa, miles apart from other farmhouses, as usually happened in the process of colonization. The pioneer Grandmother Morton of *Inheritors* also regrets this relationship between physical isolation and children's death: "Well, I don't know how children ever get raised. But we raise more of 'em than we used to. I buried three — first ten years I was here. Needn't 'a happened — if we'd known what we know now, and if we hadn't been alone" (190). It is not only that the feeling of isolation and stillness is enlarged by being childless, but what Glaspell also denounces in *Trifles* and *Inheritors* is that many children died in pioneer times because the organization of the land deterred assistance.

In *Trifles*, Glaspell broadens the figure of the buried child with the figure of the unborn child. It is significant to notice that in the Hossack case Margaret had nine children; five were with her at the farm when the murder occurred,[2] while her dramatic counterpart, Minnie, is childless. This is a determining factor in the analysis of victimage of location in this play. All Minnie had was the "stillness" Mrs. Hale and Mrs. Peters lamented on earlier. About children, Mrs. Hale claims, "Not having children makes less work — but it makes a quiet house, and Wright out all day, and no company when he did come in" (31). It is clear, both women agree, that a child would have brought joy and company to Minnie's life, because Mrs. Hale and Mrs. Peters have experienced themselves how lonely one can feel on their isolated farms without the company of children. In *Bernice*, Glaspell comes back to this issue of how a childless house is quite probably a sad house. Right after commenting on Bernice's life with her solitary father, Craig suggests his relief about Bernice's childless condition:

CRAIG: Well, Bernice isn't leaving any children to — be without her. I suppose now it's just as well we lost our boy before we ever had him. But she would have made a wonderful mother, wouldn't she, Margaret?
MARGARET: Oh, yes! [103].

There is not any more information about the causes of Bernice's miscarriage, but Margaret's exclamation leads to the assumption that it is not only that Bernice would have been a wonderful mother, but also that she really wanted to be one. Having lost her baby, Bernice lived in this isolated house, with a father that had decided to live apart from the world, surrounded by lonely woods, and with her husband absent on his multiple trips to Europe and New York.

As in *Bernice*, in *Trifles*, the reason why the Wrights never had a child remains unknown. Nevertheless, the unborn child is used in *Trifles* to justify the murder of John Wright. In the eyes of Mrs. Hale and Mrs. Peters, one of the reasons why Minnie killed John was that he never gave her a child that could help her overcome her geopathic loneliness. Mrs. Hale and Mrs. Peters present John as an unloving and "hard man. Just to pass the time of day with him —[*Shivers.*] Like a raw wind that gets to the bone" (32). The way the murder is committed in *Trifles* is closely related to Minnie Wright's childless condition. The murder takes place off stage in bed. The crime scene can be analyzed in realistic terms. That is, taking into account that there is an implied possibility that John was a battering husband, and that he was stronger than Minnie, this could have led her to kill her husband while he was sleeping, and thus defenseless. A more metaphorical interpretation of the reasons why probably this murder takes place in bed is also possible. In her analysis of women's death in Classical literature, Nicole Loraux describes bed as a symbolical place to die: bed is "the scene of the pleasure that the institution of marriage tolerates if it is not excessive and, above all, the place of procreation" (1991: 24). As the Wrights' bed has nothing to do with marital love or passion, and less with the verification of procreation, in the case that Minnie had killed her husband, the mechanics of her murder could be interpreted as a symbolic retribution for not having been given a child to be with her during her long, lonely days.

In *The Verge*, Glaspell employs the image of the buried child to reflect upon the kind of world children are brought into. Pages and pages have been written on Claire's mistreatment of her daughter, making her appear as an "unloving mother" (Noe 2002: 158). However, little has been said about Claire's dead son, David, and her deep love for him. The first time Claire mentions David, she makes the shocking comment that she is "glad he didn't live" (252). Later on, when Claire explains her point, she reveals her great love for him, a love that makes her see his death as preferable to the life he would have had: "The man unborn, he too, would fly. And so — I always loved him. He was movement — and wonder. In his short life were many flights.... But, yes, I am glad. He would always have tried to move and too much would hold him. Wonder would die — and he'd laugh at soaring. [*Looking down, sidewise*]" (255). Claire's buried child was like her; he could not stand conforming to the rules of the Earth. David was a baby that liked flying and movement, escaping from the place he was supposed to occupy. As Tamsen Wolff states, Claire "loved her son because he displayed mobility" (2003: 210). Her baby, Claire acknowledges, would have suffered, as she does, the constraining impositions of society. Thus, with his death, David was released from an almost sure victimage of location.

A third variation on the figure of the buried child appears in *Chains of Dew*, where Glaspell explores women's rejection of compulsory motherhood, and shows her belief in women's freedom to decide whether to have children or not. This unborn child differs from the ones in *Trifles* and *Bernice* because in this case there is neither a miscarriage, nor a husband who does not fulfill a woman's motherly need. Glaspell joins here a very important movement: the birth control campaign. Margaret Sanger was its main crusader in the United States, and the campaign brought together many Greenwich Village celebrities, such as Emma Goldman, Elizabeth Gurley Flynn, and Mary Ware Dennett, who politically demonstrated their belief in the importance of voluntary motherhood, demanding the spread of contraceptives. These women were also supported by men, such as Max Eastman, Floyd Dell and Hutchins Hapgood, although the real extent of their commitment is still a controversial matter.[3] The women of the Provincetown Players, most of them members of Heterodoxy and the Liberal Club, took part in the struggle for birth control through their writings.

In *Bernice*, Glaspell presents the topic of birth control briefly. Margaret, the New Woman of the play, has no child because she has neither the time nor the place a baby requires for its proper development. Margaret, who is too busy with her commitment to social causes, cannot enjoy motherhood. This is her decision and her sacrifice. Nora in *Chains of Dew* incarnates a similar stance. She wants to be a mother, but this will happen only when circumstances are fair, or as she says, when she "can get around to it" (154). With Margaret's and Nora's brief comments on motherhood, Glaspell introduces the topic she develops more extensively in *Chains of Dew*, namely that the unborn child is sometimes preferable to having a child when the mother has not the place or the time to take proper care of it. The born child and a healthy place should come together, otherwise the outcome will be victimage of location.

Many critics have seen Glaspell's *Chains of Dew* as a mere mockery of the birth control movement. For instance, the headline of the *New York Herald* review of this play was "Susan Glaspell's 'Chains of Dew' Is Sharp Satire. Provincetown Players' Production Attacks Bobbed Hair and Birth Control" (1922: 10). Many critics of Glaspell's day, as well as more recent ones, have been misled by the secondary title of the play, "A Comedy in Three Acts." Certainly, *Chains of Dew* is a comedy, but it also "give[s] one something to think about" (Rathbun qt. in Gainor 2001: 193). Glaspell brings to surface the seriousness of the unborn child in the physical configuration of Nora's workplace, her birth control office, which confronts the audience with the reality of compulsory motherhood. On the wall of Nora's office, there is a poster representing two houses. One shows a mother with nine children and the other a mother with two children, saying "*in no uncertain terms that it is more desirable to have two children than nine.*" There is also an excess family exhibit, like a scale stage set representing "*a forlorn kitchen in which a mother struggles with seven children*" (127). In Nora's words to O'Brien, these materials stand for the respect children deserve: "The demonstration is to demonstrate the stupidity of the law. The cruelty. The vulgarity. The brainlessness. [*With growing excitement, personally directed against the young man.*] Do you wish to give birth to seven children you cannot feed? Have you no respect for children? A child has a right to be wanted" (131).

Glaspell also employs the figure of the unborn child to show that the defense of birth control is not an easy matter in a society that grants women a primary place as mothers. To depict this confrontation, Glaspell establishes a dialectics between stage properties that embody two points of view: Nora's posters and family exhibit and a portrait of the Sistine Madonna. When Act II opens in the library of the Stanhopes, the room is presided by a picture of the Sistine Madonna, hanging on the rear wall, center stage. The Sistine

Madonna, which is a strong symbol of idealized motherhood, has always "exercised an immediate influence on the destiny of the sex," as Margaret Fuller wrote in *Woman in the Nineteenth Century* (1999: 27), and marks the lives of Dotty and Mother. The unborn child image has no place in Seymore's house, for women must be Madonnas. Thus, though Glaspell suggested that the best pose for a woman is to resemble a Sistine Madonna, she does not present the Sistine Madonna in a positive light here. Her female protagonists resist being considered "objects of adoration," and oppose the idea of bringing children into a world which cannot take proper care of them.

Although at the beginning of *Chains of Dew* Dotty and Mother are traditional female characters, their contribution to the development of the unborn child image happens early in the play. In the very first glimpse we have of the Sistine Madonna in *Chains of Dew* it is already a weakening symbol, since the Sistine Madonna "*appears to be attempting to lower herself*" (144). The Madonna is "loose at one end" (144) because Dotty has been trying to take it down:

> SEYMORE: My dear Dot, you know perfectly well I want you to have the Madonna hanging here. Since you like Madonnas — by all means let her bless our home. [*He is all the while making her secure, Dotty steadying.*]
> DOTTY: I'm not crazy about her. But I didn't know what else to put up [144].

This dialogue reveals the determinism of motherhood in spatial terms. Seymore wants the Sistine Madonna to "bless" the house, and thus right after this dialogue, he returns the Madonna to its place. Meanwhile, Dotty has already attempted on her own to liberate space from the immediate influence of the Sistine Madonna. As she says, she is not crazy about it. Actually, a bit later she emphatically affirms, "I'm *off* Madonnas" (163, emphasis in original). When Nora brings all her information about birth control, Dotty will be able to materialize her uncertainties, and she will know what to put up on the wall instead of the Madonna: the birth control posters.

Glaspell also gives strength to the image of the unborn child through birth control as Mother, who should be the most traditional character, has a say on this topic. Given her advanced age, it is surprising that Mother is so promptly and eagerly committed to the birth control campaign. But it is precisely because she has given birth to many children that she knows of the difficulties of providing them with a place to be properly raised in. Visually, Glaspell puts this idea on stage as Mother helps Nora to set up the excess family exhibit. Significantly, there are seven children, the same number of children she has. Read as a proxemic sign, Mother indicates that if she had had the opportunity, she would not have had so many children. Indeed, she gives seven hundred dollars for birth control, something that disturbs Seymore.

As he says, "that's one way of wishing me out of existence." But as his mother wisely replies, "You never had seven" (169). Mother's argument, springing from her own experience, is maybe the most convincing and serious one regarding birth control. Echoing Nora's standpoint to become a mother when she has time, as well as Margaret's concern in *Bernice* and even Claire's in *The Verge*, Mother proposes a new hymn for birth control, saying, "Don't call them from heaven/ Till earth has a home" (167). The hymn sounds comical if one imagines a birth control hymn being chanted in a church. But Mother's point that children should only come to life as long as they have a home is totally serious and perfectly summarizes Glaspell's use of the image of the unborn child in close connection with dramatic geopathology.

Places of War

Wars occupy an important place in Glaspell's work. In many of her short stories, novels and plays war is treated not only as a historical background, but also as a literary device to set in motion the development of characters and plot. In novels such as *Judd Rankin's Daughter* (1945) and short stories such as "The Escape" (1920), Glaspell depicts boys who come back from wars suffering from physical and psychological wounds. Nevertheless, Glaspell's position on war is unfixed. Linda Ben-Zvi has pointed out that Glaspell "was not a pacifist. She simply believed that America was not best served by its intervention, particularly since it deflected attention from pressing issues at home such as suffrage, child care, and labor rights; and it caused the government to stifle debate and trample free speech in the name of patriotism" (2005: 189). Nevertheless, Ben-Zvi's standpoint seems to refer merely to the World Wars. But Glaspell also deals with American wars in her plays. Moreover, it could be said that Glaspell changed her position towards war with World War II. Indeed, in a later article, Ben-Zvi affirms that in many of her works Glaspell "expresses her pacifism, a position she held until America's entry into the Second World War, which she strongly supported" (2006: 280).

Consequently, in the same manner that Glaspell seems to have a dual position regarding wars, this duality is reflected in her works. This is clearly seen in the contrast between *Inheritors*, a play clearly influenced by Transcendentalism, where Glaspell denounces any armed conflict, and her later *Springs Eternal*, where she defends the United States' duty to participate in World War II. The reason behind Glaspell's interventionist position in this case has a clear spatial dimension: the United States was physically threatened after Pearl Harbor. Jasper Deeter's Hedgerow Theatre had been producing *Inheritors* for years. Five days after Pearl Harbor, Glaspell sent him a letter urging him to stop producing her anti-war play until the war ended:

Scene from *Chains of Dew*. Helen Ryan as Mother. Orange Tree Theatre production, 2008. Director: Kate Saxon. Photograph © Robert Day.

> I think our country [is] in greater danger than ever before in its history — that all we hold dear, all worth living for, is threatened. The light might go out — and for generations to come. I would not have words of mine — even though unjustly, for those words were not spoken of *this* time — give support to those who oppose this war which has been forced upon us [Glaspell qtd. in Ben-Zvi 2005: 380, emphasis in original].

J. Ellen Gainor has observed that another reason that could have led Glaspell to support intervention in World War II is that she, as many other intellectuals, felt she had failed younger generations (2001: 253), a point overtly developed in *Springs Eternal*.

It is interesting to note that in her early *Close the Book*, Glaspell suggests the status of wars as icons of pride, implying that participating in wars have always helped families to have a distinguished *place* in society. In this play, the Roots have a prominent position in the community because they are descendants of John Peyton, who fought with George Washington in the Battle of Valley Forge, a battle that represents the bitter hardship of the 1777–78 winter encampment in the American Revolution. The portrait of Peyton dressed as a revolutionary soldier that hangs on the wall symbolizes the importance he has within the family. The Roots' ancestors also participated in another of the great American wars: the American Civil War. Peter Byrd was "one of those dare-devils whose leg was shot under him at Bull Run" (43).

As Doranne Jacobson has pointed out, Bull Run was part of "the litany of disastrous encounters [that] still brings tears of emotion to citizens of both the North and South" (1995: 52).

In *Inheritors*, Glaspell shows more specifically the role armed conflicts had in establishing the orders of territoriality. Several wars are brought onstage: the American Revolution, the Civil War, the Black Hawk War, World War I, the Hungarian Revolution and the contemporary conflict in India under British rule. All these conflicts serve Glaspell to question the purpose, heroism and outcome of war. Regarding geopathology, Glaspell shows in this play how wars are conflicts for space. Thus, place is used dramatically as a problem because the fight for its occupation leads to death. The Black Hawk War (1832) played a vital role in the distribution of the Mississippi land that, as Glaspell emphasized, once belonged to the Sacs, who, furthermore, were willing to share it with the white colonizers. But the whites wanted the whole land for them, and thus the confrontations began. "Didn't want to give up their land — but I've noticed something of the same nature in white folks" (182), says Grandmother Morton. Many years later, Silas Morton admits all the wrongs done to the Sacs, and feels he cannot be the absolute owner of this land: "I love land — this land. I suppose that's why I never have the feeling that I own it" (188). "To look out at the hill sometimes makes me ashamed" (187). Indeed, in the first typewritten draft of *Inheritors*, Glaspell makes Silas's remorse about how they treated Native Americans much more obvious. Owning the hill causes him disgust: "There's our crime," he says,[4] a statement that, though erased from the final version of the play, survived implicitly in some of Silas's utterances. Silas is a geopathic character in this concern because, contrary to the Roots in *Close the Book*, he cannot enjoy the place he has, given that to own this land, many Native Americans and whites alike died. In order to "assuage his guilt about taking land away from the Indians" (Noe 1983: 42), Silas reaches a symbolic treaty in spatial terms: "I got to give it back — their hill. I give it back to joy — a better joy — joy o' aspiration.... Then maybe I can lie under the same sod with the red boys and not be ashamed" (193). Grandmother Morton sees the problem that would arise in giving this land when Silas should provide for his own children. To solve his victimage of location, Silas has to convince the other characters that materialism, embodied in the ownership of the hill, is less important than idealism. "Isn't it providing for them to give them a better world to live in?" wonders Silas (192). With his act of giving up his land, Silas shows that there are more important things in life than owning a piece of land. He wants to show that giving back the hill means reconciling with the Native Americans, making the world a fairer and better place for everybody.

In *Inheritors*, Glaspell also tackles the fight for space through the celebrations of the Fourth of July, the day the play opens on. Glaspell presents the American Revolution onstage as Silas and Felix come from the parade wearing their army uniforms and carrying their muskets. While Grandmother Morton regrets that "nothing draw men together like killing other men" (183), and despite the men's common eagerness and delight in talking about past wars, the pioneers Glaspell presents onstage do not want to talk about it. They are not uncritically proud of the fight for space in which they participated. Silas says in this concern, "The war? Well, we did do that. But all that makes me want to talk about what's to come — what 'twas all for. Great things are to come" (188). Through Silas, Glaspell makes her point that war for freedom was necessary, but what matters now is to achieve a peaceful future.

Although the pioneer characters in the first act of *Inheritors* seem to have solved the problem of place, the peaceful future these pioneers dream of becomes a vain hope in the subsequent acts. World War I has taken place, leaving thousand of corpses behind and prompting the American urge to keep its space isolated from the rest of the world. Morton College, built on Silas's hill as a symbol of reconciliation, paradoxically supported the war in order to meet government approval for financial reasons. Trying to gain Senator Lewis's favor, Fejevary the Second proudly claims, "Morton College did her part in winning the war" (194). Morton College students became strike breakers during the Steel Mill strike, and they enroll in the reserve Officers' Training Corps as an extra curricular activity. The college also applauds youths who died in the Great War, such as Fred, Silas's grandson and Madeline's brother. The excuse for participation in World War I was, in President Wilson's words, to "make the world safe for democracy" (224), a motto several characters employ as a learned verbal excuse. Only Madeline openly denounces the nonsense of war. She has serious doubts about her brother's reasons for joining the army: "He wanted a trip. [*Answering his exclamation.*] Why, he *said* so. Heavens, Fred didn't make speeches about himself. Wanted to see Paris — poor kid, he never did see Paris. Wanted to be with a lot of fellows — knock the Kaiser's block off— end war, get a French girl. It was all mixed up — the way things are" (212, emphasis in original). In Madeline's words, participating in the war was Fred's way to get away from the Midwest, his enactment of the Myth of Mobility, and his desire to be part of a community, but it had nothing to do with democracy *per se*.

The last armed conflict Glaspell presents in *Inheritors* is a contemporary conflict in India, which Glaspell employs to reveal a problem with place in this American Midwest area. When the Hindu characters state publicly that they want India free from British rule, the most violent side of those Americans proud to call themselves "democratic" shows. These American characters ignore the fact that the Hindu students are defending the same principle of

independence that America defended in its Revolution, the principle celebrated each Fourth of July. Moreover, these mistreated characters remind the
audience of Felix Fejevary the First, who had fought in the Hungarian revolution of 1848 to release Hungary from Austrian rule. But Fejevary's grandson,
Horace, and Senator Lewis do not appreciate these alien characters' rebellion.
The Hindu students are considered "dirty anarchist[s]" and "revolutionists"
(202, 198), and are expelled from Morton College as an anticipation of the
deportation they will experience under the Sedition Act. Horace appears happy
about their forthcoming deportation and death, since "when they get him —
[*Movement as of pulling a rope*.] They hang there" (197). Glaspell uses the
conflict in India as part of dramatic geopathology to show that Morton College
is in itself a problematic place because it fails to recognize the fairness in the
Hindus' claim. What was fair for the United States and prompted the American Revolution is here dismissed as an anarchist revolution.

In *Springs Eternal*, Glaspell goes back to the theme of war, where it is
the main device to set the play in motion. Probably prompted by the crudity
of World War II, in this play Glaspell does not subtly suggest the imagery of
death inherent to wars; she describes war in detail. Dr. Bill Parks, who is in
New York recovering from a tour of duty in Africa, tells,

> All over the world. Think of them. In holes. Crawling on their bellies. The
> mud. Mud's not fun. You get awful sick of mud. Jammed together up in the
> air — jammed on the sea and under the sea. It's cold. It's hot. It's not the way
> you want it. Things bite you. There aren't any girls and that's not the way you
> want it. But there they are — all over the world. And his heart is breaking —
> because he has lost his faith in life. Let us pray [360].

The description of these soldiers, trapped in holes, in the mud, dying in far
off places, is very interesting regarding victimage of location. Significantly,
Glaspell reworks here images that usually appear in her *oeuvre* with positive
qualities. Air and sea typically symbolize freedom. But in the quotation above,
Glaspell turns the air and the sea into death domains. Glaspell uses Bill's
description of this unlocalized offstage place of war to set a sharp contrast to
the onstage fictional place, the pleasant library where the characters carry on
with their useless lives, and therefore to reveal that this war could have been
avoided somehow, but it was the paralyzed Americans who let their boys go
to war. Glaspell puts this idea straightforwardly when Bill says, "Listen, my
nutty friends. You know something? Now I know why we had a war. People
are like you. *You* are the people. You don't *care*. You go in a huddle about your
gains and losses — ... what *are* we fighting for? Fellows are dying and you're
chewing the rag about your silly little lives" (371, emphasis in original). Therefore, one of the most important dramatic effects of images of wars regarding
geopathology is that they provoke a sense of paralysis in the onstage characters.

Glaspell had already used this theme in *Bernice*. World War I had proved the difficulties that the world presented for the peaceful coexistence of all its inhabitants. One of the consequences that World War I had for the United States was the establishment of a policy of isolation. To protect its space, the country had to close its boundaries. Glaspell symbolizes the isolationist policy the United States adopted in Father's card game: solitaire, a game that symbolically only needs one player. When this play opens, "*FATHER is seen sitting at a long table at the side of the stairway, playing solitaire. At the back of the cards, open books are propped against the wall, and papers on which he has been writing*" (94). The connection among the solitaire game, the books, the papers which Father is working on, and war, is made evident a bit later: "What can the old do about war? I had my vision of life. If that had been followed there'd have been no war. But in a world that won't have visions — why not study Sanscrit while such a world is being made over — into another such world" (95). Detached from a world which does not share his "vision," from a world that suffers from an utter blindness that only leads to wars and deaths, Father cannot find anything else to do to spend his time than studying Sanskrit and playing solitaire.

Studying Sanskrit has many implications. Hinz-Bode believes that Glaspell employs Sanskrit to suggest the futility of war: "Bernice's father studies Sanscrit in a withdrawal from the hopelessness engendered by World War I" (2006b: 103). But studying this language has further connotations. Sanskrit is the antique Indo Iranian language in which the sacred Hindu Brahman texts were written. As Glaspell did in several of her works, and probably influenced by Cook's love for Greece and the Classical times, she is here making a call to the antique times of great creations, in contrast to the present times of massive destruction. Moreover, the study of Sanskrit seems important here because it opens up (for Father in this case) a vast philosophical and literary knowledge which could help to solve or endure, at least spiritually, the present conflict. But taking into account that Father's work on Sanskrit is quite passive, given his defeatist position towards war, maybe the most relevant feature of Sanskrit is that it is a dead language, and unless something livelier is done with it, it will never contribute to make the world a better place. Paralyzed, Father's only hope for Sanskrit is that one day it will be useful. As he asserts, the world needs "being made over — into another such a world" (95), a vision which will never materialize if everybody keeps on playing "solitaire."

Glaspell represents Owen's paralysis in space in *Springs Eternal* by using the same stage properties she used for Father in *Bernice*. Putting these two plays together, it is significant to note Glaspell's remark that, contrary to Father's hope that the world could be made over during and after World War I, the world of *Springs Eternal* is still the same during World War II. Like

Father in *Bernice*, Owen focuses on dead languages and games as means to "take [his] mind off" World War II (373). Working "in the old place" "on the good old ancient languages" is his "refuge in time of storm" (362). Owen puts into words what Father in *Bernice* never articulated verbally, namely, that working on old languages is a shelter to avoid facing what is happening in the "modern" world, and that this is why he stays "in the old place," the place that keeps him secure from outside events. Through Owen's words, Glaspell reunites here many of the tropes and themes of dramatic geopathology: the need to have a shelter, the rejection of the outside, and the support found in past and tradition.

In Owen's case, the contrast between his present hobby and what he did in the past is greater than in Father's case. Owen was a writer, hence aware of the power of modern and "living" languages. Indeed, his main work, entitled *World of Tomorrow*, is a book that made youths volunteer for the war. But Owen has decided to "[abandon] tomorrow and [go] back to yesterday" (364). In this manner, throughout Acts I and II, Owen is messing around with books and papers on the table and taking down notes for his study of dead languages, an enterprise that he hopes "will deafen me to a living language" (373). But unlike *Bernice*, where the absent protagonist found her father's obsession with Sanskrit "amusing," in *Springs Eternal* Glaspell creates a character, Mrs. Soames, whose own son is in the Pacific, to contest Owen's negative resolution. This woman reproaches Owen for this attitude and poses a vital question for the solution of war, and this is what the use of writing or reading about dead languages is. Owen's response suggests the uselessness of his task, since, as he says, only those old and tired, as himself, might be potential readers of his work. But Owen is not as old as Father in *Bernice*, for whom, according to Mrs. Soames, working on old languages is all right. Owen had proved he can write in living languages pieces of literature to awake people's feelings, so this is why Mrs. Soames cannot understand Owen's neglectedness.

Like Father in *Bernice*, Owen had a vision. But dreams blinded the dreamers, and these dreams and visions prevented him, and others who like him are representative of Glaspell's generation, from realizing that another war was approaching. Owen feels that his generation "brought on the war" while they "were supposed to be thinking things out." And he adds, "We betrayed you," "We should be executed" (364). In this manner, Owen believes that the best he can do is to shut up and do nothing about the war. Nevertheless, Owen suggests, as could also be interpreted in Father's case in *Bernice*, that dead languages have some good things to offer. Owen is right to assert that dead languages are by far more alive than crosswords and checkers, or more alive than Father's solitaire game in *Bernice*. Dead languages are not completely dead because they bring knowledge from the past, they make "men come to life," and they emphasize, borrowing Gainor's words, "the connection between ideas and the history of the language used to convey them" (2001: 260). But, on the whole, Father and Owen are similar characters in their detachment from the world and in their defeatist behavior.

In *Springs Eternal*, it is not only Owen who rejoices in paralysis. His ex-wife, Harry, also justifies paralysis while World War II is going on. Her claim is that "it is our duty to go on with our lives, so that which the boys are fighting for will be right here for them when they come back" (394). Consequently, Harry spends her days writing her worthless memoirs under the title "I Wear Pink," recalling her unsubstantial childhood trauma of wearing a dress of this color when she wanted to wear a blue one. But as advanced earlier, it is relevant for dramatic geopathology that these boys should not come back to the same place they left. They should not come back to a stage space whose key stage properties are useless notes on dead languages and silly memoirs, puzzles and checkers. It is the complacency of this place that made these boys go to war. The absent soldier characters must come back to a better place, to a place, a "here," where those characters who stayed will have been working to prevent any further confrontations for space. There is victimage of location because during war, the "here" goes on with idle contemplation while "out there" soldiers are losing their lives.

An interesting dramatic device Glaspell uses to explore the confrontation between the paralyzed life "back here," and the war taking place "over there," is her characters' position towards conscientious objection.[5] In *Springs Eternal*, characters do not deny the necessity of war, but they regret the situation in the Pacific: "A terrible place for an American boy to be — all jungles and Japs.... And so far from home" (364). Thus, when they learn that Fred Soames has been caught, they are conscious of the mortal consequences and impact that war has on the people they love. Paradoxically, all of them, except Margaret and Mrs. Soames, still think of Jumbo as a "coward" for being a conscientious objector. As the government moves Jumbo from one state to another, from camp to camp, Stewie chases him because he hates "conscience objectors" (398). And when Jumbo appears onstage, he is utterly ostracized by his family.

Most members of his family make a geopathic character out of Jumbo as they turn their home into a hostile place for him. The apparently homely library room where the play is set is ready to capture a victim of location. Very early in the play, Margaret had suggested this idea: "While a peace-pipe is being smoked in one corner of the room, knives are being sharpened at this fireplace" (357), and "I fear this house isn't going to be much of a refuge in the next few days" (362). Jumbo comes back to a home that is not a shelter, and where knives have been sharpened against him. Owen cannot be in the same room as Jumbo is, he regrets "bringing him into the world," and mocks him by calling him "Jumbo," instead of using his real name, Harold (378). Even more, Glaspell shows spatially the effect of the offstage war on the stage when Jumbo dares to make minor changes in Owen's library (390). He has rearranged his father's books to make room for his painting. As Hinz-Bode says, "Owen — in a rage over his son's 'cowardly' decision to become conscientious objector — storms into the room" and tears Jumbo's picture, what can be interpreted as Owen's attempt to show that he does not allow any different position towards war (2006b: 213). Harry, Jumbo's mother, continuously tells him to go to war, and Dottie, who apparently loves him, will not talk to him until he fulfills his patriotic duty. When Jumbo announces that he has renounced his objection and that he is departing that very night, he is accepted and applauded. Nevertheless, the reasons Jumbo has for joining the war have nothing to do with killing enemies. Naïvely enough, he hopes he will not need to kill anybody. He feels encouraged to do it because of his family, and also because he wants to feel he is part of the world. In other words, he enlists so that his home can really be his *home*, and so that the world accepts him as an integrating part. Jumbo's decision echoes Glaspell's belief at that time that "the war makes a difference and it is better to be part of the time, where you feel one of the crowd" (qtd. in Ben-Zvi 2005: 382). Glaspell shows how Jumbo understands that he has to help to solve the problem with the struggle for place if he wants to live in a blossoming expression of *topophilia*.

A key aspect to understanding the role of images of war within the dramatic discourse of geopathology is that war times should be employed to radically change places that had proved problematic, to start over again, and to work on place-improvement. Indeed, Glaspell's conception of war as a means to improve the world conforms to the ideology behind Modernism.[6] In *The Verge*, Claire explicitly refers to World War I as "a stunning chance!" and regrets,

> But fast as we could — scuttled right back to the trim little thing we'd been shocked out of.... And it was — a stunning chance! Mankind massed to kill. We have failed. We are through. We will destroy. Break this up — it can't go farther. In the air above — in the sea below — it is to kill! All we had thought we were — we aren't. We were shut in with what wasn't so. Is there one ounce of energy has not gone to this killing? Is there one love not torn in two? Throw it in! Now? Ready? Break up. Push. Harder. Break up. And then — and then! — But we didn't say — "And then —" The spirit didn't take the tip [240].

World War I destroyed the world physically, and so was its ideological schema. This is why Claire so euphorically uses the words "destroy," "break," "Push. Harder. Break up." Claire rejoices in the image of the complete destruction of such a problematic world, since the world could only be reborn after its complete destruction. "Mankind massed to kill" means that humankind had reached its limit, and also that conflicts for space would always take place unless the world were reorganized from top to bottom. As Madeline says in *Inheritors*, "The war must have been a godsend to people who were in danger of getting on to themselves" (221). Wars demonstrate that there is no use in creating shelters, since the problems of the outside will transcend any boundaries. Unlike Harry in *The Verge*, who celebrates "our good sense" (240), which mainly means coming back to the old things, "the trim little thing we'd been shocked out of," Claire is the only one to realize that this coming back to old things will be but the starting point for new conflicts, as subsequent wars demonstrate. As has been observed, most of the characters in Glaspell's *The Verge* "have learned nothing from the war and have attempted to carry on with business as usual, almost as if the violence of the war were a spoiled dish that could be discarded, allowing us to return to the same meal at the same table" (Wainscott 1997: 28).

Through the role Glaspell bestows on images of wars in her works, the whole world can be regarded as an enormous geopathic place if wars cannot be avoided. In *Springs Eternal*, Glaspell explicitly voices through one of her characters that "something is wrong with the world" (400), and that it has to be re-done all over. Jumbo expresses this idea in one of his paintings:

> JUMBO: You see this color breaking through the gray sky?
> OWEN: Yes — yes — I see it.
> JUMBO: Just put your fingers on the color — cover it — and I'll show you.
> HARRY: Is this important?
> OWEN: [*Trying to do as Jumbo has told him.*] Yes.
> JUMBO: Now you can see the sky is too dark. I thought it would be good for the sunflowers — but it just buried the shed.
> OWEN: [*Eager to understand.*] Y-es —
> JUMBO: Now take your fingers off. There! Don't you see? Even though it isn't right yet you can see how it was all coming together!
> OWEN: All — coming together [395–396].

At first Owen thinks that his son's art is a waste of time in the face of war, another proof of his son's cowardice, but later he recognizes that Jumbo's canvas constitutes a metaphor of the world. In Jumbo's explanation of his painting, one can see his dream that the world be repaired and no more struggles for space take place. The world, like the sky in Jumbo's painting, was too dark and lost. Then war, embodied in "the color breaking through the sky," shattering the uniformity of the gray sky, took place. But although this color is something disruptive, as war is, it makes "all coming together." Echoing Claire in *The Verge*, war is an opportunity for unity. As Hinz-Bode comments on Jumbo's painting, "each element of the painting stands in relation to all its other elements, and if one thing is changed in order to 'correct' a certain relation, other connections are inevitably influenced" (2006b: 213). The world should unite and fix it so that there is no need of any other war. Jumbo's idea for his next painting, the one he dreams of completing when he comes back from war, stands for this hope. He describes it as follows: "I want to do my horses. [*Anxiously.*] I hope I don't forget. [*As if making notes for himself.*] Very tired — last strength of the day. Rough ground —*pulling*. *Really* pulling. Quite dark below — where *they* are — earth darkening — and wide luminous sky" (396, emphasis in original). Darkness and roughness once again represent the collapsed state of the world. But in the world of his canvas, Jumbo imagines his horses pulling hard for the promise of a wide luminous sky. He hopes his father will become one of these pulling horses that will find the way to make the world better once the war is over. When Jumbo announces that he is joining the army, he wants to reach the compromise that they "fix it so there won't be any more wars" (400). He is joining the army, but he wants those staying at home to contribute to the solution of the world problem with place that has provoked this war.

Haunted Rooms

Most critics agree that one of Glaspell's greatest dramatic achievements is her absent protagonist, who is embodied and very present in spatial terms. For instance, Arthur Watermann believes "Glaspell's most effective and most characteristic dramatic technique was centering a play around an off-stage character," since "somehow this generates a peculiar tension, like a hushed whisper that grows stronger as the play progresses" (1966: 88). Glaspell employs this technique mainly in three of her plays: Minnie Wright is the absent protagonist in *Trifles*; Bernice in the namesake play; and Alison in *Alison's House*. Though these characters are never seen — Minnie is in jail, and Bernice and Alison are dead — their presence is felt onstage in the spaces they inhabited. In this respect, Jackie Czerepinski believes that "absence has a gravitational force, drawing the other characters to the physical and psychic spaces left by the protagonists" (1995: 149). In relation to space, Glaspell constructs haunted spaces, that is, fictional homes where the presence of the absent characters suggests their own victimage of location, and where their presence becomes an integrating element for the development of geopathology in the present characters as well.

One of Glaspell's most typical devices to make the absent character present relates to the character's stage properties and pieces of furniture. In *Trifles*,

Mrs. Hale and Mrs. Peters are able to reconstruct Minnie's life and feelings
through the configuration of her disordered room. A reconstruction is apparently easy for them, given that they share the same chores. As seen previously,
Mrs. Hale and Mrs. Peters feel Minnie in the rocking chair, in the canary, in
the broken cage, in her quilt, and in her unfinished work: the bread, the dirty
towels, the disordered pans, and the broken jars of preserves. It is at this point
that Mrs. Hale and Mrs. Peters can be seen as geopathic characters. As they
go "through a process of identification" with Minnie (Mustazza 1989: 495),
Mrs. Hale and Mrs. Peters constantly draw parallels between Minnie's life
and their own. Then, besides Minnie's alleged geopathology, what is actually
shown onstage is Mrs. Hale's and Mrs. Peters's own victimage of location.
This is the reason why Mrs. Hale and Mrs. Peters defend Minnie and Minnie's
place so earnestly; they are defending themselves through Minnie's case. The
scene where the women talk about Minnie's preserves plainly exemplifies how
Glaspell maintains Minnie's presence through a stage property to reveal the
onstage female characters' victimage of location:

> MRS. PETERS: [*To the other woman.*] Oh, her fruit; it did freeze. [*To the
> LAWYER.*] She worried about that when it turned so cold. She said the fire'd
> go out and her jars would break....
> MRS. HALE: It's a shame about her fruit. I wonder if it's all gone. [*Gets up
> on the chair and looks.*] I think there's some here that's all right, Mrs. Peters.
> Yes — here; [*Holding it toward the window.*] this is cherries, too. [*Looking
> again.*] I declare I believe that's the only one. [*Gets down, bottle in her hand.
> Goes to the sink and wipes it off on the outside.*] She'll feel awful bad after all her
> hard work in the hot weather. I remember the afternoon I put up my cherries
> last summer [28–29].

What begins as a comment on how bad Minnie will feel when she learns about
her spoiled preserves turns into a reflection upon Mrs. Hale and Mrs. Peters's
hard work and gender politics. Preserves are not only important for Minnie,
but for any pioneer woman, because the sustenance of the farm in these far
places depended heavily on the provision of food. In this manner, the reasons
why Minnie's preserves are lost are subtly questioned by the other two women.
Obviously, the cold weather has spoiled them, but as Mrs. Hale and Mrs.
Peters see it, and as they make the audience see it, the appalling outside
climate is but one reason; the broken stove is perhaps the most important reason. According to the distribution of work on the farm, mending the broken
stove was supposed to be Mr. Wright's task. Had the stove worked properly,
that is, had John mended it, Minnie's preserves would have been safe. The
importance of this stove is more explicit in the story "A Jury of Her Peers,"
where Mrs. Hale indeed says, "The law is the law, and a bad stove is a bad
stove" (1917: np). In this manner, she justifies Minnie's alleged murder of her

husband as well as their, i.e., Mrs. Hale and Mrs. Peters's, illegal behavior when they take clues from the crime scene at the end of the play. As Mrs. Hale's words imply, if the law is made by men and to protect men, and men are going to condemn Minnie, women have to find their own way to defend themselves.

Minnie's presence at the farm is further emphasized when some of her belongings are brought onstage. As Minnie had requested, the two other women take a pair of shoes, an apron, a petticoat, a skirt, and a dress, which the women examine in detail, leading them to conclude that "Wright was close" (29). They conclude so because Minnie's clothes are "shabby" (29), in contrast to the pretty clothes Mrs. Hale remembered that Minnie used to wear. In the way Mrs. Hale and Mrs. Peters reconstruct Minnie's physical appearance, Minnie is pictured as a trapped character, trapped in a poor and isolated place from where she could not escape, in contrast to the lively white and blue outfit she wore when she was single and could move outside the farm to attend the mass.

In the same way that Glaspell suggests the problems Mrs. Hale and Mrs. Peters could have with their places through the preserves, Mrs. Hale's and Mrs. Peters's empathy for what they see as Minnie's situation also applies to her clothes. The importance they give to Minnie's clothing reveals their own concern for how they dress, for this represents the place they occupy in society. As Glenda Riley observes, "The way women dress reflects what their society thinks about their position and roles in life" (1981: 73). Mrs. Hale, in the quotations above, makes a clear connection among three points: Minnie was different when she was single; she used to dress nicely, and colorfully; and, finally, she draws a relationship between dressing in pretty colors and being lively. It seems that once a woman marries, her taste for fine dresses is killed by wearing the dark clothes of the dutiful farmer's wife. It is significant that Mrs. Hale, a farmer's wife too, also appears on stage in a similar costume to the ones she despises, and probably sometimes she has to dress shabbily. The fact that she claims, "You don't enjoy things when you feel shabby" (29) reinforces the point that Mrs. Hale, by using the second person singular pronoun, admits that she also feels shabby in her old clothes. Visually, Mrs. Hale's costume marks her as inferior to Mrs. Peters, since her coat is plainly described, without any adjective, unlike Mrs. Peters's "*fur tippet*" (30). This visual difference separates both women regarding their social and economic status in a very realistic way. Hence, while Mrs. Hale's and Mrs. Peters's recreation of Minnie's life is meant to shape Minnie as a geopathic character, they also suggest their own geopathology, and even more in the case of Mrs. Hale, given that her socio-economic status is closer to Minnie's.

In *Trifles*, the onstage home stands for the metaphorical death-in-life state of Minnie, and how her liveliness had been killed off by her husband

Scene from *Trifles*. Helen Ryan as Mrs. Peters and Nancy Crane as Mrs. Hale. Orange Tree Theatre production, 2008. Director: Helen Leblique. Photograph © Robert Day.

and the farm. The homes in *Bernice* and *Alison's House*, however, do indeed embody the dead and absent characters who inhabited these places. If in *Trifles* Glaspell uses the presence of Minnie at the farm to hint at the problems Mrs. Hale and Mrs. Peters could have with their own places, in *Bernice* and *Alison's House*, the onstage characters' victimage of location comes from their confrontation with the presence of the dead absent characters in the rooms they have to inhabit.

When *Bernice* opens, the absent protagonist has been dead for a day. The first stage direction already establishes the powerful link between the onstage place and the deceased protagonist: "*You feel yourself in the house of a woman you would like to know, a woman of sure and beautiful instincts, who lives simply*" (94). The pillows are on the seats under the window where Bernice used to sit to contemplate the woods, her high vase is still at the window, her chest, containing her beautiful little cigarette box, is on the mantelpiece, and her tea table is exactly where she had it. The connection between Bernice and her belongings is clear:

> FATHER: Bernice made this house. [*Looking around.*] Everything is Bernice. [*A pause.*] Change something, Abbie! [*With growing excitement.*] Put something in a different place. [*He takes a pillow from the seat under the window, holds it irresolutely a moment, puts it on the floor at the side of the fireplace. On the other*

side he moves a high vase from the window. Then helplessly.] Well, I don't know.
You can't get Bernice out of this room. The tea-table! Come, Abbie, quick!
We will take this *out* of the room. [*Together, ABBIE reluctant, they move into
the passage-way leading out from the living-room. The FATHER comes back and
sees the chair, now without its table. He goes as if to move it, but cannot do this*]
[94, emphasis in original].

Bernice is felt in the room, and she has a great power over the other characters.
Father tries to remove his daughter's presence from the room by changing the
spatial configuration of the place. As Waterman says, "she influences the
actions of all the characters who gather at her home" (1966: 74). Indeed, the
rest of the play spins around the onstage characters' attempt to reconcile themselves with the idea they have of Bernice, a reconciliation also carried out in
spatial terms.

   Bernice's presence is felt in Craig's first entry onstage. Craig's proxemic
signs reveal his own feelings towards Bernice. At first, he *"holds back as if to
enter this house is something he can scarcely make himself do; he does not look
around the room"* (96). He is even afraid of looking around, and several times
takes *"a few stumbling steps toward the room where Bernice is"* (97).Craig's
reluctance to enter the house and Bernice's room is construed as his denial.
Bernice has died without giving him the chance to subjugate her. Craig, like
his sister Laura, cannot comprehend that Bernice stayed alone while he was
traveling and sharing his time with other women. Paradoxically, her staying
at home made these two other characters see her as an unnatural woman: a
wife who did not react against her husband's infidelities. It is only when Craig
is told that Bernice has committed suicide that he begins his reconciliation
with the place that embodies his wife. This suicide relocates Bernice in the
role Craig wanted for her, the wounded wife who, unable to have Craig for
herself, put an end to her own life. It is only then that *"he goes to the door,
bows against it, all sorrow and need"* (107).

   The exact location where Bernice's presence is most strongly felt is, of
course, the room where her corpse is. Bernice is "In there. Alone. Still" (101).
This offstage room has a connection with the onstage space through its door.
And, as has been said, "the door becomes a projection of Bernice in death —
an object approached with conflicting emotions, shrunk from yet reached for"
(Gainor 2001: 102). Glaspell employs this room and this door to visualize the
changing attitudes the other characters display regarding victimage of location.
That is, at some points they get over Bernice's death, and are able thus to
cope with her metaphysical presence, and at other points, their inability to
stand Bernice's death and presence in the house reflects precisely upon this
door and this room. Throughout the play, when characters talk or think about
Bernice, they usually look at the door that separates them from the corpse.

Glaspell also uses proxemics to reveal Bernice's father's victimage of location due to the spatial remembrance of his daughter in the house. For Father, the room where Bernice's corpse rests is a constant reminder of the reality he cannot stand. Before there is any verbal indication that Bernice's corpse is in the adjoining room, Father's gestures tell us so. He *"looks old and broken as he faces the closed door"* (94), and complains, "I wish they'd left Bernice upstairs, Abbie, in her own room. Now *there*— so near the living-room — right off the living-room" (94, emphasis in original). Bernice, now dead, is right off the *living*-room, an ironic remark on the thin line between life and death.

Margaret's relationship with this room is a bit more complex, and Glaspell again works brilliantly on her character's movements to reveal this character's spatial relationship with the house. As she arrives at the house, Margaret rushes to this room to see her friend, implying that she is the only character who is brave enough from the very beginning to face Bernice's death. She says to Craig, "I came here to see *her*. Not to sit here talking to you.... I want to see Bernice!" The stage direction informs us, *"Crying she goes blindly toward the closed door, and to Bernice"* (98, emphasis in original). The effect of seeing Bernice is so painful, that the house becomes a geopathic location for her, so after seeing her friend, Margaret needs to get out of the house.

The reasons behind Margaret's victimage of location vary throughout the play. At one point she will not stay in the house precisely because she cannot conjoin the identity this house always had, that of the tranquil and happy Bernice, with the idea that Bernice was evil when she made Abbie promise to tell Craig that she had killed herself. Whereas earlier Margaret could not be inside the house to avoid the sorrow the memories of her friend brought, now she cannot be in the house because it represents an evil side of her friend she did not know. As she says, "Oh, no — no — no. I can *never* go in there. I — I never *was*— in there" (108, emphasis in original), and "I must go away. I can't stay. I can't stay here" (109). As she did with Craig, Glaspell shows Margaret's hesitations about what to believe about Bernice in her relation with the door that separates Bernice from the living room. At one point Margaret *"puts out her hands, but she does not even touch the door and when she cannot do this she covers her face and, head bent, stands there before the closed door"* (111). Margaret is only reconciled with the room once she interprets Bernice's lie in a different way. Towards the end of the play Craig confides to Margaret that Bernice's suicide has made him realize how much she loved him, and that this has made a new man out of him:

> CRAIG: Now — of course it is another world.... and Bernice's world gets to
> me. Don't you *see*, Margaret?
> MARGARET: Perhaps — I do. [*She looks at the closed door; looks back to him. Waits.*] O-h. [*Waits again, and it grows in her.*] Perhaps I do. [*Turns and*

very slowly goes to the closed door, opens it, goes in] [113, emphasis in original].

Margaret deduces that Bernice's lie was her means of making Craig feel a better man, giving him power to be a better writer too. Margaret reinserts Bernice's lie within the image she had of her dear friend, and from now on, Margaret is willing to enter the room, a spatial reconciliation with the place the protagonist inhabits.

Glaspell uses a similar dramatic technique in *Alison's House*. As in *Bernice*, the absent protagonist is quite vivid in spatial terms, marking a special relationship between the onstage characters and the rooms that represent her. The first obvious remark that makes one consider the power Alison exerts on this place is that the house, although she has been long dead when the play opens, is still considered hers, as the title of the play announces. Alison is present in the library in Acts I and II through her books and documents, in the stage properties that the other characters are selecting and packing to move. For instance, the way Elsa handles Alison's books is as tender as the feeling she has for her aunt. When the fire puts the books at risk, Elsa "[*Looks around the room. Softly.*] Don't burn. Don't. [*After another moment, having looked from one thing to another, she goes to the books, runs her hand over them. Stands there. But at the noise of something falling upstairs, she becomes frightened, suddenly takes an armful of books*]" (322–323). In Elsa's relation with the books, Alison comes alive. Elsa needs to save the books along with her aunt's memory and symbolic presence. Indeed, Glaspell considered books to be extensions of one's soul:

> Two people do not really live together until their books become one library. You have known just how to classify your own — books you have had, some of them since you were eleven years old. Strange now to have them adapting themselves to the books of someone else — these two life-histories becoming one, two pasts uniting [2005: 191].

For Glaspell books are the bearers of one's taste and past. They are symbols of one's own that melt with their partner's books and adjust themselves when their lives come together. Glaspell further employed this idea to embody Alison in the following scene, where Stanhope reads aloud Emerson's poem "The House":

> "There is no architect
> Can build as the muse can;
> She is skilful to select
> Materials for her plan;
> Slow and warily to choose
> Rafters of immortal pine,
> [*He glances up to the beamed ceiling above.*]

Or cedar incorruptible,
Worthy her design."
Some other things, and then —[*Looking ahead.*]
"She lays her beams in music,
In music every one,
To the cadence of the whirling world
Which dances round the sun.
That so they shall not be displaced
By lapses or by wars,
But for the love of happy souls
Outlive the newest stars" [337–338].

Scholars have concentrated on how this poem foreshadows the idea that Alison outlives the house with her poems.[7] Moreover, Glaspell's aim with this long quotation from Emerson's poem is to suggest that Alison is the onstage characters' support. Mapping this poem against the image the onstage characters have of Alison, Alison appears as the beams of the house. She is also like the muse that inspires and supports those around her. She, as the beams, was strong enough to reject her lover, to fake a happy life and stay in the house to maintain the family social status "for the love of the happy souls." But as discussed earlier, Alison, the symbolic beams of the house and the family, hid geopathological woodworms only revealed in her secret poems.

Besides being a victim of location herself, the discovery of Alison's unhappy life has a tremendous effect on the other characters, an effect that is carried out in spatial terms too. It is interesting to note that in *Alison's House* one can find the only instance in Glaspell's plays in which a bedroom, a place considered the keeper of one's most hidden secrets, is shown. Agatha's ultimate defense of Alison's room with her own life and Knowles's assertion that "Alison Stanhope's room — holds something" (316) prompt a curiosity Glaspell eventually satisfies; the final act takes place in Alison's room. This room, kept as Alison had it, is a sanctuary. In fact, as Ann looks around the room, she claims, "Alison's room. As if— as if she might be going to bed here" (341). As the curtain rises, the room is dimly seen to provide a mysterious atmosphere, as if this room were indeed inhabited. The clock that "told the hours for Alison" (344) is stopped, a symbol of the paralysis and entrapment her family has endured since Alison disappeared. There is a picture of Alison in a gold, oval frame hanging over the desk. Importantly, this is the very first time Alison's physical appearance is seen, a luxury Glaspell never provides to any of her other absent characters either, and which contributes to make Alison's presence more vivid.

Glaspell suggests the characters' uncanny entry into Alison's room in the way they move, which also enhances the absent protagonist's presence in her room. Elsa "*waits a moment by the door, as if to be asked to enter*" (341), and once inside, she moves extremely slowly across the room. As Mrs. Hale does in *Trifles*, Elsa feels unable to sit in the absent character's chair. Stanhope enters the room in a similar way. He *"opens the door. Stands there a moment before closing it. Continues to stand near the door."* Feeling Alison's presence, Stanhope says, "I wish I could talk with Alison" (345), and the other characters in the room keep silent for a while, thinking about what they would like to say to Alison, too.

It is through this configuration of the room that the present characters will come to understand Alison's entrapment; they will understand her victimage of location, and will be affected by what Alison had to do for them. The key moment of revelation takes place when Alison's secret is discovered, a secret Glaspell grants spatial relevance. In *The Poetics of Space*, Gaston Bachelard dedicates a whole chapter to what he considers "images of secrecy," namely, chests, caskets, closets, keyholes, and drawers. For Bachelard, "the casket contains the things that are *unforgettable*, unforgettable for us, but also unforgettable for those to whom we are going to give our treasures. Here the past, the present and a future are condensed. Thus the casket is memory of what is immemorial" (1994: 84, emphasis in original). Alison's unpublished poems constitute an image of secrecy too, and when the portfolio is opened, something similar to what happens to Bachelard's chest occurs. These poems reveal Alison's past, while they link this past to the present of the onstage characters as well as to their future. As in a set of Matryoshka dolls, the first time the poems were seen they were inside a portfolio in Agatha's bag. And now that the characters are in Alison's room, her poems are inside one of the drawers of Alison's desk. When all these metaphorical doors are opened, Agatha's bag, and later the drawer and the portfolio, what Bachelard might call "the dimension of intimacy" opens (1994: 85), and what is inside gains full relevance. Alison's poems, as the secret in realistic drama, are what the room "holds," what characters entering the room felt about the room. What the poems tell promises a change in the dramatic development of the play.

The family reunion to read Alison's poem becomes a ritual that brings Alison more back to life than ever. Glaspell locates Elsa at the table, apart from the rest of characters, who sit in chairs apart, and she occupies the front space of the stage, spatially granting an enormous importance to the revelation that is going to take place. Then, *"she unfastens one side, takes out a slender package of old papers, tied with a thread."* As Glaspell says, Elsa is *"feeling"* Alison's paper (347). Glaspell increases the tension as Elsa has trouble trying to untie the knot, and she finally has to break it. Elsa gives different packages of Alison's poems to Eben and Stanhope, so that they all share this moment of recognition, of meeting the real Alison, "Alison — at her best" (347). After they have silently read the poems, they struggle over what to do with them.

Scene from *Alison's House*. Grainne Keenan as Elsa Stanhope. Orange Tree Theatre production, 2009. Director: Jo Combes. Photograph © Robert Day.

Glaspell dramatizes her characters' renegotiation with Alison's identity and her presence in the house and in her poems, in the different positions they hold as what to do with the poems. Ted, the young character eager to know more secrets about Alison, secrets that will pave the way for his college studies, "*with a swift movement he puts some of the papers in his pocket, reaches for others.*" Stanhope, representative of the older generation, and who indeed told Alison to stay at home, prefers keeping the poems in the house. Glaspell shows this by making Stanhope spring at Ted, menacingly saying, "Drop them! Drop them or I'll kill you!" (350). When Ted snatches for more poems, Eben, who also wants to protect Alison, "*seizes him,*" and they fight until Elsa separates them (350).

The physical and dialectic confrontations among these characters stand for the different perspectives from where they want to remember Alison. For instance, Elsa, considering the poems she has just read, concludes that Alison would be "glad I have my love. In spite of— all the rest. Knowing what it is to be alone, I think she would be glad I am not alone" (351). Elsa agrees with this new identity of Alison as a dead-in-life woman who would be glad her niece did not stay trapped inside the walls of the house and its respectability. Stanhope, on the contrary, highlights Alison's submission to the rules, and adopts Agatha's mission to protect his sister. For him, it is more important to "think of others," of family and of "our little town" (352). Regardless of their position, the truth is that these characters have just discovered that Alison was forced to stay and that, contrary to what they had always thought, she led a sorrowful life. Knowles quotes again a fragment from Emerson's poem, now uttered emphasizing that the words "*have a great mission*" (352). The mission is that the onstage characters have to adjust themselves to what Alison really constituted. They cannot keep her as the "beams," the support of the family, because they are now aware that she was not who they thought. The final chapter considers these characters' departure from their geopathic location and the way they will help Alison to escape posthumously from her own entrapment in the house and given roles. This is the "great mission" Glaspell's geopathic characters share.

6

Dramatic Principles of Departure

Departure has been identified as "an overriding mission and desire" many characters in modern drama share to escape their victimage of location (Chaudhuri 2000: 56). While home-leaving is a very common dramatic device in plot convention, it is not an easy and common resolution in realistic drama. If one of the cornerstones of Realism is to maintain the given power, departure is most often just "an impossible ideal" (2000: 62). Obviously, there are blatant exceptions, among which Ibsen's Nora is a superb example. Against all expectations in realistic conventions, Nora puts an end to geopathology by stepping outside of the place that encapsulated her problems. Her departure, far from being a quiet and secretive one, is performed with the most infamous slamming of doors ever heard or seen in a play before. Nora's act, however, did not become the norm of Realism. In Glaspell's theater some characters abandon the stage, thus escaping their victimage of location *à la* Nora. Her amalgam of Realism and modernisms is what allows Glaspell to make her characters deviate from the constraining social orders that in purely realistic drama confer an inescapable spatial determinism on her characters. But what appears as a most interesting case are other principles of departure, different from actually leaving the stage space that suffocates the geopathic character.

The appropriateness of the term heroism of departure needs revisiting. While Chaudhuri merely considers the physical implication of departure, I advocate understanding it in broader senses, most importantly regarding changes in identity. In many dramatic instances, characters depart from an identity imposed on them and choose freely what they want to be or to do, and this change in identity usually reflects upon the physical space, which I understand as another kind of departure. Furthermore, heroism is generally used to refer to brave and courageous acts. But very often the characters that "depart" can hardly be called heroes or heroines in the traditional sense. Many of Glaspell's characters employ what Jane Wolff, referring to literature, calls "guerrilla tactics," i.e., little strategies of resistance that many women writers employ to subvert the established patriarchal power (1990: 82). Therefore, though "guerrilla tactics" might not be regarded as fair game, they cover a practical goal. And although they are not heroic, these tactics enable characters to come to terms with the places they inhabit, escaping thus their geopathology.

Judith Butler has pointed out that "the possibilities of gender transformation are to be found precisely in the arbitrary relation between such [performative] acts, in the possibility of a failure to repeat, a deformity, or a parodic repetition that exposes the phantasmatic effect of abiding identity as a politically tenuous construction" (1999: 179). That is, there might be a moment when the subject fails to repeat the same act, the act that gave the subject a gender identity, in the same place. Or when the subject willingly stops repeating that act in that place. Some of Glaspell's female characters depart from given roles in this way. It is significant that Butler stresses this point:

> If subversion is possible, it will be a subversion from within the terms of the law, through the possibilities that emerge when the law turns against itself and spawns unexpected permutations of itself. The culturally constructed body will then be liberated, neither to its "natural" past, nor to its original pleasures, but to an open future of cultural possibilities [1999: 119].

Gender transformations, according to Butler, can only occur within the limits of law. Most of Glaspell's female characters' departures take place within the limits of law. Nevertheless, some other characters perform acts to liberate themselves that go straight against the law and the integrity of other characters, as in the case of violence. These departures cannot be called heroic acts. Consequently, the term "principles of departure" is more suitable to cover the spectrum of heroism of departure, as well as other principles that allow characters to get away from the suffocating places they are trapped in, and to find new spaces for themselves.

Physical Departure from Fictional Locations

Some of Glaspell's characters follow Chaudhuri's pattern of heroism of departure: they leave the stage space in their attempt to beat their victimage of location. Elsa in *Alison's House* seems to be the only one to closely follow this path, leaving the house that trapped her to live her life with her lover. If scholars have long wondered what happens to Ibsen's Nora once she slams the door, Glaspell makes Elsa return home to talk about the aftermath of her courageous resolution. Elsa experiences a failed homecoming; she is abjectly displaced. But although Elsa won over her victimage of location, she has not managed to be happy far from "home," a fact that complicates the question of her "heroic" act. Elsa describes her departure in the following terms: "I wasn't brave. I was trapped. I didn't think it was right — but I couldn't help myself. And Bill. When you love, you want to give your man — everything in the world.... Our love is a flame — burning fiercely — in sorrow" (343). All the younger girls, as Ann tells her, find in Elsa an example to follow; she is the girl who "was trapped" and bravely went away. On the contrary, Elsa suggests that maybe her departure might not be completely worth it. She and Bill have to live a life of isolation, separated from their families and the places they love. "He misses the business, and his friends, and the children. I can see him missing them," regrets Elsa. They are, as she admits, "Happy, and unhappy" (339). Their sorrow is their payback for taking the courageous decision to depart from trapping places.

Other characters in Glaspell's plays that abandon their homes to overcome their sense of ill-placement are Minnie in *Trifles* and Madeline in *Inheritors*, and as happens with Elsa in *Alison's House*, the aftermaths of their departures are also problematic. Both leave their houses to go to jail, so they move from one imprisoning space to another. But, on the whole, Minnie has got rid of a place that oppressed her, according to Mrs. Hale and Mrs. Peters. With an apparently paradoxical epigram, "I'd rather be a locked up American than a free American" (145), Madeline asserts that she prefers being in prison, defending the principles she believes in, rather than staying in the prison of her house and society, and accepting the rules under which she cannot live. Madeline "decides that she prefers being a free spirit in prison than being fettered to hypocrisy the rest of her life" (Rathburn 1921: np). However, as will be seen later, Minnie's and Madeline's departures from their homes open up a different field of heroism in more symbolic terms.

Chaudhuri has pinpointed that some characters in modern drama see "death as liberation" (2000: 250), erecting death as a principle of departure. As seen, Agatha's death in *Alison's House* is the only means this character has to escape her victimage of location. Bernice's case of physical departure through death is especially noteworthy. Although the protagonist has died of natural causes, the aftermath of her demise turns her into a tragic heroine. Most critics have seen in Bernice's command to Abbie to make Craig believe she has committed suicide a proof of her moral superiority and immense love.[1] While in life Bernice was never the wife Craig desired, her faked suicide is construed as a compensation for her deviation from the ideal wife role she had never performed. Nonetheless, in the same way that previously I discussed how Bernice did not live a happy life, and that she was already dead when her physical death occurred, I share the standpoint of other scholars whose interpretation of Bernice's faked suicide sets her apart from her insertion in the role her husband wanted for her. As Sharon Friedman has said, "her intentions are obscure" (2006: 47). Friedman draws a very significant parallel between *Woman's Honor* and *Bernice*. In *Woman's Honor*, the Scornful One claims, "A life that somebody has died for is practically a ruined life. For how are you going to think of it as anything but — a life that somebody has died for?" (72). Was Bernice's mock suicide a gift of love or an act of revenge?

Glaspell suggests Bernice's real intention with the lie about her death, which is her principle of departure. Abbie recalls how Bernice asked her to lie: "'Oh, Abbie, do this last thing for me! After all there has been, I have a *right* to do it. If my life is going — let me have *this* much from it!'" (107, emphasis in original). Glaspell makes Bernice say that she has the "*right*," so this is not the duty of the perfect wife that Bernice had rejected in life. On the contrary, Bernice feels she has the right to avenge herself "after all there has been," after all her sorrow, stillness, and entrapment.

Bernice is a play about the protagonist's self-revenge for her victimage of location. While it seems Craig is stupid enough to see in his wife's suicide a proof of love, the spectator cannot but share Margaret's first impression, namely, that Bernice goes too far with her lie. Even though Margaret abandons her idea when she sees Craig utterly happy, convinced that he finally had Bernice, when Bernice's mock suicide is mapped against the Scornful One's comment above, Bernice's obscure, and real, intention surfaces. Bernice is determined to ruin Craig's life forever. From now on, Craig's life is "a life that somebody has died for." Indeed, Bernice consciously worked on her death as she saw it approaching. Knowing that the doctor could not make it on time, she prepared her death in such a way that she would get transcendence and greatness once she had died, illuminating and controlling her husband's life. As Christine Dymkowsky has affirmed, "By using her death to convince Craig that he had the power over her he yearned for, Bernice, from her remote position, exercises a liberating power of her own" (1988: 97). Bernice *liberates* herself; she gets loose from her victimage of location by making use of her death to exert her power over the other characters.

Making Others Depart

Only in a few cases does Glaspell use the physical departure of her victims of location as a solution to geopathology. Some other characters overcome their victimage of location by making other characters depart, that is, by literally expelling from the stage space those other characters that had contributed to the creation of a geopathic atmosphere. Seymore in *Chains of Dew* is representative of this principle. When Seymore cannot stand what is happening in his house, and with the phoney excuse that he does everything for Dotty and his mother, he expels Nora, Leon, and O'Brien from his house in order to recover control. And this is Eleanor's unfulfilled wish in *The Comic Artist*, that Luella and Nina leave her house. *The Comic Artist* has two different endings, and none of them provides Eleanor with a principle of departure. In the published version, Nina threatens to kill herself when she and Stephen are discovered embracing. Karl runs after her and drowns. In the Broadway production ending, Karl rebels against his brother and sister-in-law, turns into a patriarchal husband and orders Nina to pack. It seems that the couple is now closer than ever. Stephen and Eleanor, nevertheless, are left with the death of their marriage. As Eleanor had feared, her house is not her house anymore.[2]

The most extreme example that can be found in Glaspell's plays regarding a character's expulsion as a solution to geopathology is killing that character. The trope of "death as liberation" suggested by Chaudhuri is here enlarged to refer to other cases where other characters' demise helps the protagonists to break away from ill-placement. In *Trifles*, Mrs. Hale and Mrs. Peters see in Minnie's alleged murder of her husband her means of releasing herself from the suffocating farm. This is a dramatic device Glaspell also uses in *The Verge*. Tom's death at the hands of Claire is one of the most controversial issues in the play, as can be observed in the amount of criticism and different interpretations that Claire's final act has given way to. While Tom has been Claire's ally throughout the play, she strangles him close to the end. Tom's death is described as a strange mixture of love and death. The scene begins as if Claire were embracing Tom or about to kiss him, only to suffocate him in the end. Though in *The Verge* the strangulation is partially performed onstage, unlike in *Trifles*, the reasons are not clear. Most critics have seen in Claire's violent act a murder only explained in terms of madness.[3] Nevertheless, this interpretation solely responds to a realistic reading of Tom's death, and sets aside the modernist implications of the play. A reading alien to the realistic optics reveals that this is the most extreme proxemic sign used to disclose Claire's need to escape from forms molded for her. Through this death Claire departs from her given place and becomes a goddess, the superwoman she has longed for. She had failed in her goddess's project when her plants, the Edge Vine — which symbolically had the shape of the cross to mean Claire's intention to save humanity, to show everybody that other forms are possible — and the Breath of Life, only took her to the edge. If she cannot be a creator, she has to be a destructor. And Tom collaborates in her new principle of departure. Her soul mate, who had admitted that he would stop his existence "for Claire — if it were the way to help her" (241), accepts his mission so that Claire can finally escape from conventionality. She feels she has "Saved-myself"

Scene from *The Verge*, Act III. Rebecca Lingafelter as Claire Archer. Performance Lab 115 production, 2009. Director: Alice Reagan. Photograph © Sue Kessler (www.sue kessler.com).

(266). After killing Tom, Claire sings a religious hymn, an act most critics understand as Claire's final submission to the Protestant church and thus to patriarchy. For instance, Hinz-Bode believes that Claire's use of the hymn to express herself "entails the inevitability of woman's renewed imprisonment" (2006b: 165). This hymn, however, is another means Claire employs to manifest her final salvation and her ultimate escape from the structures that have victimized her. In the manner in which Claire chants "Nearer my God to Thee" she reveals her final victory. She is so near to God that she has occupied His place. As God in the Bible also puts His people in lethal situations, Claire has tested Tom's fidelity. Claire had advanced, "If one ever does get out, I suppose it is — quite unexpectedly, and perhaps — a bit terribly" (234). To get out of family, society, the burden of her heritage, and place in itself, all the factors of Claire's victimage of location, Claire does something unexpected and terrible: killing Tom.

Subversions of Power Geometry

Glaspell consistently questions the rules that govern places in terms of power. In some of her plays, her characters' principle of departure is enacted as a subversion of the rules of power geometry. In these cases, those characters usually disempowered overcome their victimage of location by assuming their right to power. This is the main principle of departure in *Trifles*. As seen, the onstage farm is representative of ill-placement for Mrs. Hale and Mrs. Peters, and though at the end of the play they seemingly escape this victimage of location, since they abandon the farm physically, they leave only to go to their farms, that is, to their own ill-placements. Due to the process of identification Mrs. Hale and Mrs. Peters experience with what they think was Minnie's problem, the two female characters manage to depart from their victimage of location. In spite of the fact that several critics have seen in the end of *Trifles* a subjugation of women to the rules of patriarchy, the truth is that the women depart from the rules of patriarchy by subverting power geometry in silence.

In the first place, Mrs. Hale and Mrs. Peters become members of a jury of her peers they were not entitled to form at that time. As Ann Jones says, "The laws that deprived women of rights and made them dependent upon men made them subject to tyranny" (1980: 116). Patricia Bryan has extensively argued that Glaspell's plot is meant to evidence the biases of men that judged women at the time (1997). In *Trifles*, it is obvious that Glaspell highlights the necessity of a jury of her peers, and she does so by guiding audience and readers as her female characters subvert power geometry, as they disclose the stories that could not be heard in a courtroom. Male power is clearly identified as the men in the play, representative of the prosecution at a real trial, have already decided "that Mrs. Wright is guilty, and now they have to make this objectively viable" (Wright 2002: 239–240), a fact that proves the unfairness of the legal system and women's powerlessness. Contesting this unfairness, Mrs. Hale and Mrs. Peters turn the onstage kitchen into a fictional court; they present before the audience those important issues which could never be discussed in depth at a trial at that time, i.e., hard work, isolation, wife beating, childless marriage, and so forth, issues that, as seen throughout this study, constitute factors making up these characters' victimage of location.

Besides Glaspell's contribution to legal discussions, what really should be given importance is that with *Trifles* Glaspell calls for women's political and social empowerment and rebellion against the mere definition of women as pure and dutiful mothers, wives, daughters, and sisters. Susan Koprince notes that in depicting Minnie Wright's gloomy homestead, Glaspell "criticizes a social system that promotes a stultifying cult of domesticity, that silences and disenfranchises women, and that quashes their desire for self-fulfillment" (2006: 77). That is, Glaspell is making a call for rebellion against the victimage of location many women suffer because society only allows them to occupy one place, that of the angel of the house.

Moreover, far from being passive True Women, with *Trifles* Glaspell presents onstage that these women do have power. As powerlessness has been defined as one of the faces of oppression, featured by "the lack of that 'authority, status, and sense of self' which would permit a person to be listened to with respect" (Harvey 1993: 56), Mrs. Hale and Mrs. Peters demonstrate that they have more power than the men in the play, or even themselves, think. Mrs. Hale and Mrs. Peters begin to revolt against the frustrating tyranny of patriarchal power the very moment that they start playing at being detectives. This new role allows Mrs. Hale and Mrs. Peters to "perceive to be more sinned against than sinning" (Stein 1987: 255). Instead of behaving as the passive and naïve women their men think they are, they disobey the rules of the authority and blur the alleged evidence of Minnie's crime. Ironically, Mrs. Hale's and Mrs. Peters's rebellious behavior takes place in what has been traditionally accepted as the female space: the kitchen.

The last sentence of the play is worth analyzing in this regard, for it represents the final enactment that Mrs. Hale and Mrs. Peters subvert power geometry. After being asked several times about the quilting technique, Mrs. Hale answers back: "[*Her hand against her pocket.*] We call it — knot it, Mr. Henderson" (34). Critics have long debated about the meaning of this sentence, and most of them agree that it stands for the union of women, the fulcrum of subversion of power geometry. At the same time, this final sentence makes a reference both to the knot around John Wright's neck and to "not" as a negation of what these women think they know about Minnie's life but which they will never tell.[4] Certainly, Glaspell gives great importance to women's union to start their subversion of power geometry, and the terms "female bonding" and "sisterhood," commonly used to refer to women's union, have been discussed in relation to Glaspell's works to some extent. Veronica Makowsky, like many other earlier Glaspell scholars and feminists, uses the terms "female" and "sisterly solidarity" to refer to women's bonding in the face of male oppression (1993: 62). Sisterhood has been understood as "the natural and pre-existing relationship that women — especially those pursuing economic reform and revolution — must rediscover" (Stretch 2006: 226). However, I prefer the term "women's coalition" instead of sisterhood or mere female bonding when talking about Glaspell's work.[5] As seen in *Trifles*, and accounting for their status, Mrs. Hale and Mrs. Peters belong to two worlds, so after the rebellion they carry out together at the Wrights' farm, they separate. Moreover, the extent to which Glaspell saw sisterhoods as completely positive organisms must not be taken for granted.[6]

Besides the importance of female coalition for victimage of location, and how this is symbolized in the final sentence of the play, "We call it — knot it," I believe that this ending can be read more radically as far as power geometry is concerned. The fact that Mrs. Hale presses her hand against her pocket, where the dead canary is, is a symbolical act. On the one hand, it symbolizes Mrs. Hale's disobedience. She is hiding a piece of evidence similar to those searched for by men — one that suggests anger. On the other hand, as Mrs. Hale presses her hand against her pocket, this might be seen in proxemical terms as an act of anger and repression, an image similar to the macho one of clenching a fist instead of punching someone. In this reading, Mrs. Hale is threatening Mr. Henderson and the other men. This is reinforced by the "knot it" as a kind of verbal threat. The fact that this is the last line of the play is significant and makes this ending be open to wider interpretations different from the traditional ones, usually limited to the issue of "women's bonding." Furthermore, I believe that this reading demonstrates these women's possible potential for murder, their "retaliatory violence" (Fetterley 1986: 153) within the system that oppresses them.

Glaspell also suggests Mrs. Hale and Mrs. Peters's gradual awareness of their power through the way they talk. At the beginning both women speak very little, their sentences are usually crowded with silences and hesitations, and they seem to rely more on what the men say and think than on their own ideas. For instance:

> MRS PETERS: Mr. Peters says it looks bad for her. Mr. Henderson is awful sarcastic in a speech and he'll make fun of her sayin' she didn't wake up.... They say it was such a — funny way to kill a man, rigging it all up like that.
> MRS HALE: That was just what Mr. Hale said. There was a gun in the house. He says that's what he can't understand.
> MRS PETERS: Mr. Henderson said coming out that what was needed for the case was a motive; something to show anger, or — sudden feeling [29–30].

In this scene, everything these women say is a repetition of the men's points of view. But as Mrs. Hale and Mrs. Peters become more self-confident, more conscious of their own power, their utterances change enormously. Later in the play, instead of simply echoing what they heard the men say, Mrs. Hale and Mrs. Peters begin their utterances with "I think" (32), "I knew" (33), "I know" (33), "I guess" (34), and so on. Both women begin to recognize their power as thinking and acting subjects, and consequently they start using the pronoun "I" more and more often. Their new awareness of their own power is also what leads them to a communal union in the final "we" in "We call it — knot it."

Mrs. Hale and Mrs. Peters's evolutionary subversion of power geometry is also revealed in the kind of women they represent. Mrs. Hale is closer to the New Woman from the very beginning, willing to defend Minnie. In contrast, Mrs. Peters is a True Woman. The development of Mrs. Peters is very meaningful in this regard. At the beginning, her only sign of identity is linked to her husband's job. She is the sheriff's wife, and as such she defends the men by saying that it is their duty to snoop around the kitchen (29). Mrs. Peters is entirely dedicated to fulfilling what her husband orders, that is, to collecting the belongings Minnie had requested. She also excuses the men's laugh at "trifles" because, "Of course they've got awful important things on their minds" (30). That is, as the sheriff's wife she has learned to say that women's things are trifles as well, and to believe that men's things are much more important. Nevertheless, she adopts a new identity that makes her rebel against her husband through her lie and the deletion of clues. Once she comes closer to Mrs. Hale and Minnie's situation, and once they are on the same side, Mrs. Peters ignores that "a sheriff's wife is married to the law" (34), and when the County Attorney discovers that there was a bird at the farm and asks about it, Mrs. Peters consciously supports Mrs. Hale's lie that a cat got it. And later she participates in the deletion of the evidence they have found, which they think could be used against Mrs. Wright. In this manner, Mrs. Peters rejects her identity as the sheriff's wife in order to adopt her new identity as a woman conscious of other women's problems as well as her own.

In this manner, triggered by Minnie's alleged murder, by the end of the play both pioneer women are potential New Women that reject patriarchal rules and imposed identities. "These women experience their own *anagnorisis*, challenging and rejecting male-defined norms, including such concepts as woman's honor, abstract justice, and the male's right to dominate and control," says Sally Burke (1996: 63–64). At the end of the play, the case of Mrs. Hale and Mrs. Peters has contributed to the dramatic discourse of geopathology in two ways. On the one hand, they solve what they think is Minnie's geopathology by, first, understanding how Minnie's home was one of the main factors that could have led to her alleged murder of her husband, and second, by liberating her from the offstage prison where she is. Since they have removed all the evidence from the kitchen, the male characters will not be able to find Minnie guilty. On the other hand, Mrs. Hale and Mrs. Peters overcome their own geopathology as they come back to their homes with changed identities. By understanding the rules of power geometry, they have departed from their roles of dutiful and subjugated wives to assume their new power.

Reshaping Home Physically

Not every solution Glaspell offers her characters to escape from places that constrain them are as extreme as Minnie's and Claire's. Indeed, one of the most recurrent principles to overcome geopathology found in Glaspell's dramaturgy is something as simple as redecoration. Many of Glaspell's characters are victims of location because the places they are forced to inhabit impose upon them an identity or role they reject. Therefore, a possible means of departure from ill-placement is provided by changing the spatial configuration of the room these characters are placed in so that these locations match their identities. About changes in space Henri Lefèbvre says, "A mere change of position, or a change in a place's surroundings, is enough to precipitate an object's passage into the light: what was covert becomes overt, what was cryptic becomes limpidly clear" (1991: 183). That is, redecoration is a powerful ideological tool, and although it can be regarded as simple and naïve at first sight, it can be charged with impressive meanings. "To change life we must first change space," says Lefèbvre (1991: 190), a statement many of Glaspell's characters turn into action. For the present analysis, then, a semiotic approach is vital, since usually "objects on the stage tend to merge into the background, and they become meaningful only when handled, looked at, or referred to" (McAuley 2000: 91). Once the stage property is moved, reshaped or brought on or taken out from the stage space, its meaning goes even beyond the symbolical quality it could have earlier, and a whole spectrum of significance opens before our eyes.

The first case in Glaspell's plays that exemplifies redecoration as a means of changing life, and thus of ending geopathology, is found in *Suppressed Desires*. As seen earlier, with this play Glaspell and Cook present onstage the struggle for space of a bohemian couple. And Henrietta is the first character in Glaspell's plays that tries to change her identity and her home. Besides telling Mabel, who wanted to occupy Henrietta's place as Steve's wife, to go away (making another character depart), the solution that Henrietta and Steve find to solve the invasion that psychoanalysis had carried out in their studio apartment consists of getting rid of all the volumes on this topic. To Steve's question, "Will you clear off my work-table so the Journal of Morbid Psychology doesn't stare me in the face when I'm trying to plan a house?" Henrietta replies, "I'll *burn* the Journal of Morbid Psychology!" (23, emphasis in original). With his question, Steve brings to the front two key elements of geopathology in this play: the house and the elements disturbing its peace, the psychology books. It is not merely that his work as an architect is disturbed by Henrietta's books, but what Steve's petition reveals clearly is that his wife's interests have disturbed his work and his house.

Henrietta's decision to burn the books pleases Steve and prompts the happy reconciliation at the end of the play. Critics have seen in this reconciliation Henrietta's punishment for having moved into the male realm of public discourse and her subjugation to patriarchal power.[7] Henrietta seemingly goes back to her place as wife, giving up her battle for the living room. However, in spite of the happy ending that has led many scholars to question the seriousness of this play, the ending is not closed, and Steve's newly-regained control over the apartment will not last. On the contrary, it seems rather improbable that on the basis of where the characters live and Henrietta's commitment to the feminist cause, the couple will live happily, and traditionally, ever after. All throughout the play, the Washington Arch in New York's Washington Square has been seen through the window of their apartment as a constant reminder of the fact that Henrietta and Steve live in a bohemian atmosphere, and that they will not escape from the influence of bohemianism unless they move out of this area. Moreover, Henrietta is a member of the Liberal Club. Both conditions make their apartment an obvious target for new influences on Henrietta that will invade the place that Steve wants to keep. Henrietta's compromise to burn her books does not mean she is going to become a True Woman. Indeed, all she says is that she will get rid of her psychoanalysis books, but she will not quit the Liberal Club. In tune with the features of this female character, one can easily imagine Henrietta bringing home some new craze, such as birth control, that will make her work passionately, and probably invade again Steve's work place with her books.

In *Bernice*, characters also try to reconcile identity and space by changing the decoration of the room. Characters first change the configuration of the room to avoid the memories of Bernice that the place bears, especially in the case of Father and Craig. Their final reconciliation with her death will also be evidenced through their reconciliation with the place as Bernice had it. As one critic says: "The superficial changes that the characters make in Bernice's room in an attempt to distance themselves from their loss are rescinded at the end of the play: the room is given 'back to Bernice'" (Czerepinski 1995: 149). Craig, supported by the alleged immense love that his wife had for him, is eager to maintain everything as Bernice had it, so that he can maintain this new identity of his wife that suits what he wants to believe, i.e., that she committed suicide for him. Close to the end of the play, Craig decides to rearrange Bernice's things *"until [the room] is as it used to be"* (114).

Craig not only leaves things as Bernice had them, but he also endeavors to rearrange the room as she would like it to be. That is, Craig's performative acts come to enact the actions his wife would do. Craig goes out to pick up some red and yellow branches, the ones Bernice used to pick up and put in a vase at this time of the year, and he arranges them as Bernice used to do it. Then Glaspell makes Bernice completely invade her room when Margaret, who comes out of Bernice's room, leaves the door open. As Father says: "You have given the room back to Bernice!" (144). Instead of considering that there is "death in the next room" (101), they now see life, the life they feel Bernice taught them to live.

The solution that these characters find in *Bernice* to cope with the presence of the absent character on the stage space is to ally with it. When they all understand that Bernice's death does not mean the end of life, but the continuation of all she had taught them, regardless of what kind of woman they think she was or of what Bernice's real intention with her lie was, they are able to cope with her physical absence and her metaphysical presence. The door to the room where her corpse has been throughout the play, which was first closed, is from now on left open. Moreover, as they acknowledge that Bernice will always be with them, Glaspell creates a wonderful gesture to symbolize all this and to close the play: Margaret "*closes her hand, uncloses it in a slight gesture of freeing what she would not harm*" (114). Using her body to signify what she cannot say with words, Margaret expresses her idea that Bernice's love was meant to be perceived by all around. Thus, with all these final redecorations and with Margaret's gesture, Glaspell shows that her characters get over their victimage of location. The onstage characters accept Bernice's death and her metaphysical presence, and Bernice, who had won over geopathology with her death, will have the command over the house and its dwellers forever as everything is physically as she left it, a constant reminder of her power.

The play where Glaspell works more clearly on redecoration as her characters' means of escaping "place as a problem" is *Chains of Dew*. The traditional configuration of the library of the Standishes changes the moment Nora arrives from New York and her birth control posters and leaflets invade the room. The way the Sistine Madonna is handled reveals Dotty's means of escaping ill-placement. When Dotty discovers the poster of the mother with nine children and the mother with two, she is happy that "at last we have something to take the place of Sistine Madonna! [*Takes a chair to the Madonna*]" (162). Now that she knows how she wants the room to look, she does not ask Seymore about hanging the posters. Departing from the subjugated wife role, Dotty's identity begins to change here at the same time that she is redecorating the room.

The idea that traditions are difficult to get rid of physically is symbolized in this scene in the difficulties O'Brien and Dotty have trying to put the Sistine Madonna away. Meaningfully, they cannot reach to get it down (162). This difficulty also denotes that the change of identity that Dotty is beginning to experience will be hard to accomplish. On the whole, geopathology, with its physical and psychological dimensions, is not an easy disorder to get rid of. The strength required to overcome geopathology, even through apparently simplistic redecoration, is revealed as Dotty needs a stick and a hammer to fulfill her goal. Once armed, and with the motto "down with the Madonna!" "*They get it down*" (163). She then "*begins to pound,*" hammering the wall to put up the poster of the mother with nine children. In a symbolic way Dotty is hammering the walls that imprison her, the walls of respectability and moral

Scene from *Chains of Dew*. David Annen as Seymore Standish, Helen Ryan as Mother, and Katie McGuiness as Dotty. Orange Tree Theatre production, 2008. Director: Kate Saxon. Photograph © Robert Day.

codes she is so sick of: "Wall? Who cares about the *wall*? [*Nailing down the words with the hammer*]" she wonders (163, emphasis in original).

Dotty also changes herself physically to reflect her new identity as the first president of the first birth control league of the Mississippi Valley. Dotty had already suggested she wanted to have her hair bobbed when Seymore was cutting Angelica's hair. Having Nora as a pattern, Mother bobs Dotty's hair. Dotty's shocking appearance in Act II, scene 2 is described in terms of her hair and the enormous change it provokes: "*Her hair is bobbed. It is extraordinarily becoming. She is young and gay and irresistible. The DOTTY that never had a chance is gleaming there*" (160). Her hair becomes the emblem of her new identity:

> DOTTY: Well, here I am. How do you like me? [*She gives her head a shake, fluffing out her bob.*]
> SEYMORE: [*In the terrible voice of the outraged male.*] Who cut my wife's hair? [*Turning upon NORA.*] You come here, come into my house, breaking up my life, cutting my — cutting my — What do you mean cutting my wife's hair?...
> MOTHER: [*Very casually.*] I cut Dotty's hair.
> SEYMORE: [*Unable to believe it.*] You? You? So — even my mother. *Even my mother* [160–161, emphasis in original].

The revolution that Seymore began unconsciously in Act II, scene 1, when he cut the doll's hair, is blossoming now. Seymore's emphasis on using the possessive "my" to refer to the house, to Dotty, and even to Dotty's hair, highlights that he is taking all these changes as a direct attack on him and his property. He is what had been foreseen from the beginning: despite his modernist discourses about freedom, he is a true supporter of patriarchy. The fact that the women come together for the small matter of Dotty's bobbed hair is significant, related to women's struggle about ill-placement, and in more general terms about women's movement, a wink at women's union, as in *Trifles*, for suffrage and birth control.

Significantly, as Dotty's geopathology and her departure from it emerge, Seymore's faked victimage of location becomes evident. Previously Dotty had behaved as her husband's servant. But the new Dotty has her new worries: writing an essay on birth control and making calls to gain supporters. This is more than Seymore can bear: "*He gives up writing and is thinking over more than he can bear*" (163). Although Seymore complains about the chains that tie him to Bluff City, this is a prison he likes, and therefore, it is when his prison is reshaped and totally changed that he has an actual problem with place. Mother, recognizing Seymore's self-inflected geopathology, realizes that her son is suffering from these spatial changes and that he cannot live without his chains. He cannot be happy either in Bluff City or New York because this unhappiness is what keeps him alive and safe. Moving from the Midwest to the East and changing his identity accordingly allows Seymore to avoid any confrontation in these places. This is the reason why the reunion of his two worlds makes Seymore totally unable to bear his very house. Moreover, as his two worlds have come together, he has lost the leading roles he had in both. His New York friends find the Standish women pleasant and intelligent and vice versa, leaving Seymore metaphorically out of place.

The dramatic solution Glaspell constructs for Seymore's geopathology comes in two phases. First, by expelling the "invaders," his New York friends, and second, through redecoration. Dotty and Mother ally to make Seymore think they prefer to go back to the way things were before Nora's arrival, and that he is still the needed guide of their lives. This reversal, nevertheless, does not signify Dotty and Mother's submission to patriarchal rules. Most critics agree that Dotty's tears at the end of the play prove that this is Dotty's painful sacrifice for her husband, that she has to give up her ambition so that Seymore can be happy. As Hinz-Bode claims, "Dotty cannot control her tears at the thought of her lost new life while Seymore restores his world to normalcy" (2006b: 129). And Gardiner notes that Dotty's "sobs signify a plaintive mourning wail for the sacrifice of Diantha," her real self (2006: 195).

But there are some factors in the play that make Dotty's sacrifice unlikely, and thus, her sobs might be read differently. One of the reasons why Dotty's sacrifice seems improbable is that "there is nothing in Seymore's depiction of character that renders his wife's dramatic sacrifice convincing in the end" (Hinz-Bode 2006a: 213). And as Ozieblo believes, Dotty's sobbing "could easily antagonize a thinking audience; it could also reduce Diantha to a sentimental heroine who unthinkingly obeys the Zarathustan precept 'Let woman be a plaything, pure and fine like a precious stone'" (2006b: 22). And these features, certainly, do not fit into the coherence of Dotty as a character. Glaspell has shown that Dotty seeks empowerment and that she is quite a strong character once she has found her identity. If Dotty surrendered, she would be the first of Glaspell's protagonists that gives in so easily to the rules of patriarchy, and that, after tasting power, accepts being re-imprisoned within the four walls of her house. Dotty, I think, behaves as a well-trained melodrama actress, pretending she is sobbing, so that Seymore can save her: "Please, stop crying, Dotty. I will make things just what they were before" (176). To please Seymore, little by little the room recuperates its former shape. Before going, Nora removes the family exhibit, and the Sistine Madonna is inevitably to be back, "just as if nothing had ever happened" (176). In a very symbolical scene, Seymore is taking down the poster and hanging the Madonna while Mother and Dotty are simply witnessing how things are going back to their former shape. Dotty even promises to let her hair, the symbol of the traditional and subservient wife Seymore needs, grow.

However, this scene uncovers a seed of hope for Dotty and Mother, a seed that reveals that, to some extent, they will never be the subjugated women they were earlier, and that they can escape from their victimage of location through their new awareness of the power of place. While Seymore regrets that Dotty had made holes in the wall when she drove the nails in so energetically, Dotty shows "*malicious satisfaction*" with the physical reality that there will always be holes in the wall that will reflect her real self (177). The Madonna can cover up the stratum of the new things that invaded the house and which Dotty and Mother enjoyed, but the holes will be the reminder of their real selves. Surfaces are not important, but rather what is underneath, and this applies both to physical appearance and to the decoration of the room. And the compromise Dotty extracts from Seymore that she will go with him when he goes to New York supports this point. Accepting to accompany Seymore to New York as "Dotty Dimple" (177), in her role of docile wife, is a promise Dotty does not have to respect. Thus, the solution for Dotty's geopathology at the end of the play comes from her newly acquired awareness that she is superior to her husband and from the promise to go to New York, which will physically allow her to depart from the house that does not fit in her identity any longer.

Beyond the physical presence of holes in the wall as a means of departure in the case of Dotty in *Chains of Dew*, Glaspell also uses this technique, though a bit differently, in *The Verge* and in *Close the Book*. The "*innumerable pricks and slits*" of the metal lantern reflected on the wall of Claire's tower support visually Claire's wish to throw darts through the circle of respectability that she uses to refer to society, a solution to Claire's geopathology that is insufficient. However, a mere verbal reference to crevices is enough to solve Jhansi and Peyton's ill-placement in *Close the Book*. Given that Jhansi and Peyton's main problem with the onstage place is that this place is heavily loaded with Puritan traditions and symbols of respectability that they do not accept as part of their identity, the genealogy book is seemingly a symbol of tradition that will oppress Peyton and Jhansi even more. But this book offers these characters the solution for their geopathology, and this solution is formulated under the metaphor of crevices:

> PEYTON: Jhansi, I don't know that we need to leave society. There seems little — crevices in these walls of respectability.
>
> JHANSI: And whenever we feel a bit stifled we can always find air through our family trees! [46].

Those notorious ancestors Peyton and Jhansi find in the book are referred to as "crevices in these walls of respectability," and they will be the ones that enable Jhansi and Peyton to stay in the house. Jhansi and Peyton, who are not but comic characters, quickly abandon their idea of taking the open road and surviving on berries and nuts for the secure place that society offers them, as long as they can find support in the "disrespectful" pasts the outcasts of their families created.

Departure through Art

Art is another means that Glaspell uses to relieve her characters of oppressing houses. Several scholars have focused on the role of the woman artist in Glaspell's works, especially in *Trifles* and *The Verge*. For instance, Veronica Makowsky has pointed out that Minnie in *Trifles* is representative of the female modernist artist and that her erratic stitches are her new art form (1999: 93). And Claire is the female modernist "trying to break through boundaries of artistic and social conventions" (Duneer 2006: 45). The relevance of art in terms of the spatial determinism that the female protagonists experience is also a key principle of departure in *Chains of Dew* and *Alison's House*.

Mother's dolls in *Chains of Dew* constitute an important attempt in Glaspell's plays to show art as a medium to express oneself and to escape from the reality of the place where a character is forced to live. In this regard, the connection between *Chains of Dew* and Ibsen's *A Doll's House* requires special attention. As Ben-Zvi has pointed out, Ibsen's Nora had become "a very popular figure in 1915 Greenwich Village circles" (2005: 158). Besides the most obvious link between both plays — having a Nora onstage — I believe that Glaspell reworks Ibsen's metaphor of dolls. In *A Doll's House*, Nora is considered a doll trapped by the obligations that her home, her husband's domain, assigns to her. Glaspell, however, not only uses the doll's house as a metaphor for the creation and solidification of women's identity as their husbands' dolls, but male characters also respond to a similar pattern. At the end of the play, Seymore is a doll, a token to play with. Moreover, the physical dolls that appear in *Chains of Dew* stand for art, a kind of art the male characters in the play cannot understand.

Glaspell highlights the importance of these dolls by giving them a central location. Among the usual props that can be found in a living room, one is surprised to see three dolls. There is a pair of twin dolls, described as "*dolls that say things about people*," and there is another doll, "*only half stuffed*" (143). Seymore, representative of what patriarchy refuses to see, thinks that making dolls is his mother's way to pass the time and to do something for others: "She makes them for the church, you know. They sell them at the bazaar.... mother just has to go on doing things for people — she's got the habit" (157). But, as advanced earlier, the uncanny truth is that Mother employs these dolls to express her anger at the dull people around her: "After you've lived with respectability for seventy years it helps to make a stiff neck and a smile that doesn't know how silly the neck is. These dolls have kept me out of lots of trouble. Tell me [*Taking up the incompleted doll*] do you think this doll looks at all like Seymore?" (159).

The contemporary concept that identities are constantly changing is reflected in the changes enacted on the dolls. Mother adjusts the twin dolls as the other characters' identities also change. One of the dolls, appropriately called Angelica, stands for the dutiful Dotty. Physically, they both have long hair, knotted at the back. The half-stuffed doll is Seymore. As with the other dolls, Seymore does not realize that this doll stands for him, and instead he refers to it as follows: "Now look at that happy doll mother is making" (173). It is not only that Mother is not making a "happy" doll, but the truth is also that she is not making it, but emptying it. That the doll is only half-stuffed at this point highlights the complexity of Seymore's character. He has a divided identity. He is trapped between being a poet longing for freedom and his self-imposed burdens as a family and traditional man. And his mother is very rough with the doll, as rough as she wants to be with her son. Towards the end of the play, Mother is mending the doll that looks like Seymore, but suddenly she *"gives an exasperated sit-up to the doll,"* and *"rips the doll's head and begins to let the sawdust out"* (172–173). She empties the doll's head because she realizes that her son is collapsing in the face of the latter events. Nora interrupts her:

> NORA: [*Noting the somewhat depleted head.*] Are you unmaking Seymore?
> MOTHER: I mustn't — unmake Seymore. It really couldn't be done. He'd become — [*Pours out the rest of the sawdust, holds up the rag that was once a head.*] Would you like to see him — like that?
> NORA: Not permanently.
> MOTHER: Then you'd better go away.
> NORA: I make him like that? — [*Pointing to the rag.*]
> [*Seymore's mother nods*] [173].

Seymore, dispossessed of his role as the martyr of the family, has been reduced to a rag. His wife and mother are no longer the weak women he has to protect. His mother uses the rag, flapping it repeatedly in the final act, to convince Dotty that for the love she has for her husband, she must sacrifice herself and go back to her old role, or at least pretend to go back. This sudden turn at the end of the play has given Glaspell the label "traditional." However, besides the holes in the wall discussed previously, the play ends with some images contrary to this view. When Mother energetically re-stuffs the head of the Seymore doll, Glaspell shows that, eventually, Seymore is the only doll character. Mother and Dotty are the ones that take care of him and know how to control him, and not the other way around, as he believes. Mother's art safely saves her from ill-placement as it goes unnoticed by the male characters in the play. It is through the dolls that Dotty and Mother come to an agreement regarding what to do with Seymore: to re-stuff him, to make him believe that they need him in order to survive.

In *Alison's House*, art also saves Alison from her imprisonment during her lifetime, and art will release her and the other members of the family. Given that Alison talked about her imprisonment, her geopathology, in her poems, the final solution for Alison's entrapment involves publishing these secret poems, making her words as free as she would have loved to be. At this point, the comparison between Alison Stanhope and Seymore Standish is revealing regarding Glaspell's main denouncement against gender politics. Like Virginia Woolf in *A Room of One's Own* and Judith Shakespeare's story, Glaspell criticizes gender politics regarding female artists and the place they have in literature. Seymore and Alison are both poets. But Seymore lives a life of privilege based on his gender. Only two poems of his are read in the play and they are not very good, but in spite of his mediocrity, his work is published and well-known. On the other hand, Alison, who is indeed a great poetess, lives a life of reclusion and her poems are not published while she is alive.

The publishing of Alison's poems is not only important for her merit as a writer, but also because these poems make her free. As Gardiner says, "Alison remained chained and walled, but beyond the story her words may finally break the chains of affection and slip the walls as she was never able to do" (2006: 196). The publication of these poems, importantly, will also liberate Eben, Stanhope and Elsa forever, since they refuse to live under social pressure. That is, they acknowledge that the geopathic conditions of society circles cannot trap them any longer. Indeed, the key matter is the liberation of the present characters, since what Alison really wanted regarding her poems cannot be ascertained. I agree with Hinz-Bode's question: "Might the protection of her privacy, then, and of her decision to respect the social institution of marriage along with another woman's feelings, not have been what Alison Stanhope truly wanted?" (2006b: 190). The final moments in the last act become a dialectical and physical struggle to assure to whom the poems belong and what to do with them. Eben and Ann agree that Alison's poems, regardless of what they might reveal about her, belong to the world. But to overcome what society could think of the family is not trouble-free for Stanhope. During the final moments of the play, Stanhope keeps putting on more wood in the fireplace, ready to burn the poems to keep the family secret, resembling Agatha's unfulfilled wish. But later Stanhope is convinced that these poems do not belong to him, so it is not up to him to decide what to do with them. Though it is Elsa who eventually keeps the poems, since "Alison said it — for women" (352), the characters agree that Alison said it for them all, for all the characters that feel as trapped as she felt in one way or another. The characters argue:

ELSA: I feel Alison wrote those poems for me.
STANHOPE: I feel she wrote them for me.
ELSA: And there will be those in the future to say, She wrote them for me.
STANHOPE: I feel — something right, something that all the time had to be, in you and me, here alone in her room, giving back to her century what she felt and did not say.
ELSA: But she did say [353].

Blocking her father's way towards the fire, Elsa also reproduces with the movement of her body the same images that inspired Alison: "The bird that sang thirty years ago. [*Her hands go out, as birds.*] The flower that bent in the wind. [*She bends, as in the wind*]" (353). The image of freedom incarnated in the bird, as in *Trifles*, and the images of nature so recurrent in Glaspell's plays combine here again to remind Stanhope of the liberty Alison did not enjoy and which they can provide her with by letting her poems "depart." As the clock strikes twelve, Stanhope says: "She loved to make her little gifts. If she can make one more, from her century to yours, then she isn't gone. Anything else is — too lonely. [*He holds the poems out to her.*] For Elsa — From Alison" (353). In the final moment, Stanhope realizes he has to let the truth be known about Alison, to make her be remembered as she was.

Alison is reconnected to life as her clock, which has not told the hour since her death, works again. Making use of a little obvious device, the clock strikes the beginning of the new century as the curtain begins to fall. The new century also marks the beginning of a new life for the Stanhopes as well as Alison's release. Symbolized in the release of her poems from the house, Alison gets away from the house. And her family also escapes geopathology as they sell the estate, physically leaving the house, as they accept and effect Alison's release. The final movement that all the characters in this play will make locates them outside the walls of the house, the oppression the concept of their family had constituted for them, and outside the rules of society.

Departure through Nature

In straight conjunction with the image Elsa creates at the end of *Alison's House*, her body moving as a flower at the mercy of the wind, there stands another of Glaspell's favorite fields through which she reconciles her characters with space: her characters' experimentation with nature. Experimentation with nature was an image that marveled Susan Glaspell. Her own grandfather, Silas Glaspell, experimented quite successfully with plants, the reason why many critics have seen in Glaspell's ancestor a possible model for both Ira Morton in *Inheritors* and Claire in *The Verge*.[8] Glaspell's husband was also interested in experimenting with nature. Cook had his greenhouse, where he worked with plants, as Claire does in *The Verge*. Moreover, nature has always enjoyed a primary role in American literature. Concretely, the Transcendentalist writers who Glaspell admired deeply, such as Henry David Thoreau, Ralph Waldo Emerson and Walt Whitman, wrote extensively about nature. As Transcendentalist writers saw it, the American landscape offered a unique possibility for the complete union between nature and soul. As some scholars have highlighted, one of the most important influences on Glaspell's work and life was her devotion to Monism, a stream of thought that in America found its source in American Transcendentalism.[9] Indeed, as Floyd Dell recalls in his autobiography, the Davenport Monist Society brought together Dell, Cook and Glaspell in the early 1910s (1969: 31, 170). In the words of Cook, "this earthly life has risen from soil to plant, from plant to animal, from water to air, from unconsciousness to consciousness, from mindlessness to mind, and from mind — whither" (qtd. in Glaspell 2005: 164). In *The People*, Glaspell offers her own vision of Monist philosophy, displaying outstanding imagery derived from the American landscape. This excerpt deserves being quoted in full:

We are living now. We shall not be living long. No one can tell us we shall live again. This is our little while. This is our chance. And we take it like a child who comes from a dark room to which he must return — comes from one sunny afternoon to a lovely hillside, and finding a hole, crawls in there till after the sun is set. I want the child to know the sun is shining upon flowers in the grass. I want him to know before he has to go back to the room that is dark. I wish I had pipes to call him to the hilltop of beautiful distances. I myself could see farther if he were seeing at all. Perhaps I can tell *you*: you who have dreamed and dreaming know, and knowing care. Move! Move from the things that hold you. If you move, others will move. Come! Now. Before the sun goes down [53, emphasis in original].

This Monist possibility of the conjunction of nature and soul is remarkable in the present study on dramatic geopathology. The American landscape seems to offer a possibility for the soul of a trapped geopathic character to join the open and lively nature outside the walls of their houses.

As argued, in *Inheritors* there is a strong bond between identity and land, in the sense that there is a powerful link between the characters' places and their heritage. Silas solved his problem with place by sharing the hill, and hence through nature. But for his son, Ira, the remaining land that belongs to the family has given way to his geopathic condition. He has been presented as a character totally obsessed with the land, symbolized in his pathological experimentation with corn. Towards the end of the play, Madeline claims:

> MADELINE: The world is all a — moving field. [*Her hands move, voice too is of a moving field.*] Nothing is to itself. If America thinks so — America is like father. I don't feel alone anymore. The wind has come through — wind rich from lives now gone. Grandfather Fejevary, gift from a field far off. Silas Morton. No, not alone any more.... Yes, I'm leaving grandfather's college — then maybe I can one day lie under the same sod with him, and not be ashamed. Though I must tell you [*A little laugh.*] under the sod is my idea of no place to be. I want to be a long time — where the wind blows.
> AUNT ISABEL: [*Who is trying not to cry.*] I'm afraid it won't blow in prison, dear.
> MADELINE: I don't know. Might be the only place it would blow [225].

Madeline appropriates the image of her father's experimentation with corn to talk about the whole world. While for her father the wind was a negative element — the wind robbed him of his seeds to share them with his neighbors — Madeline sees in the wind not just a positive thing, but actually the main ingredient in the world she dreams. Her own hands and voice are described in terms of movement. The wind does not respect human barriers, and it respects neither walls nor houses. The wind is free. According to Madeline, the whole world should be an open field.

In visual terms, it is significant that the image Madeline appropriates from her father had been used first by her grandfather, Silas, with the same positive meaning. Silas muses, "Ain't it queer how things blow from mind to mind — like seeds. Lord A'mighty — you don't know where they'll take hold" (190). Grandmother Morton also contributed to this image of seeds in Act I. It is not a coincidence that she gave the Native Americans cookies "with seeds" (186) and that she provided Delia Fejevary with her best "purple pansy seeds" (188). The seeds carry an essential physical and symbolic meaning. They are used to unite the WASP Mortons with Native Americans and with the Hungarian immigrants in the cross-pollinating field that America is. At the end of the play, Madeline decides to go to court with Emil Johnson, the Swede neighbor, and accepts imprisonment, a penalty she could avoid if she accepted her uncle's connections. But she feels that she is doing right and not alone. The final moment of the play describes Madeline as a free seed herself:

> From the closet MADELINE takes her hat and wrap. Putting them on, she sees the tennis racket on the table. She goes to it, takes it up, holds it a moment, then takes it to the closet, puts it carefully away. Closes the door behind it. A moment she stands there in the room, as if listening to something. Then she leaves that house [226].

This superb ending symbolizes Madeline's victory over her geopathology. Madeline first takes the symbol of her bourgeois class, her tennis racket, which had had a violent use, too. Madeline puts it back in the closet, an act that suggests that she is for peace and joins Silas and Fejevary the First in their anti-war and anti-violence position. Finally, the wind gains leading importance as Madeline acutely listens to it, making the audience fully aware of its significance. As if carried or enchanted by the wind she is listening to, Madeline leaves the stage and becomes her father's corn: "It gives itself away all the time — the best corn a gift to other corn. What you are — that doesn't stay with you. Then — [Not with assurance, but feeling her way.] be the most you can be, so life will be more because you were" (225). Madeline decides to "throw [herself] to the winds," giving the wind "something to carry"[10] (225). As seen in this principle of departure, with her throwing herself to the winds, Madeline shows that identity is movable and that it cannot be walled in.

In *The Outside*, Glaspell also employs nature to solve victimage of location. Mrs. Patrick and Allie had reaffirmed and projected on the outside landscape their wish to be buried in life. But this same landscape will bring them back to life. Some scholars have seen in the male characters the dramatic element that makes the female characters come back to life. "[T]he appearance of life-savers acts as a catalyst," says C. W. E. Bigsby (1983: 27), and according to Hinz-Bode, "Allie's decision to follow the Captain's example and fight for life against all odds is drawn out to full awareness precisely when one of the men confronts her straight out with the question why she would want to work for a woman who apparently '[wants] folks to die'" (2006b: 90). However, I believe that the women come back to life by themselves, and above all, due to Allie's effort and her reading of the Outside. Interestingly, in the setting there is a clue that, regardless of the appearance of the male characters, bears a seed of hope in spatial terms. The stage direction reads, "*At the ceiling is seen a part of the frame work from which the boat once swung*" (59). This framework is the reminiscence that in this place people were once saved, a symbolic foreshadowing of what is going to happen.

Allie is the first of the two female characters to read the Outside in a different and positive way. A split character herself, Allie is described as "part of the sand" (61), and in her one can also suspect "*the peculiar intensity of twisted things which grow in unfavoring places*" (61). Allie is like a blade of grass, a clear Whitmanesque reference. She is not only buried in the sand, but she also "grows." Instead of just seeing the physical and symbolic burial of the grass at the mercy of the sand, Allie emphasizes the struggle that takes place, that "*They* fight too. The woods!" (63, emphasis in original). Unlike Allie Mayo, who believes that life is in the struggle, Mrs. Patrick stands for the derelict side. She cannot see the wonder of the stiff grass trying to grow. The woods, as she says, "lose" (63). Unable to make Mrs. Patrick share her vision of the struggle in life, Allie adopts a new tactic. She becomes physically the Outside, a part of the landscape. She "*slowly raises her arm, bends it to make the form of the Cape. Touches the outside of her bent arm,*" and says: "The Outside. But an arm that bends to make a harbor — where men are safe" (63). Glaspell identifies Allie with the clearest image of life in the dunes, namely, the harbor when sailors return safely.

Allie attempts to liberate Mrs. Patrick from the prison of dead images projected on the Outside, and offers instead this other image of shelter she finds on the Outside too. Once again, Mrs. Patrick reads this image as a symbol of failure. She says to Allie: "You're like this Cape. A line of land way out to sea — land not life" (64), to which Allie responds, "A harbor far at sea. [*Raises her arm, curves it in as if around something she loves.*] Land that encloses and gives shelter from storm" (64). Besides metaphorically metamorphosing into the landscape, Allie's body constitutes a powerful image in another regard. As her movement forms an embrace of love, Allie offers Mrs. Patrick the point of support the abandoned woman needs: the female connection, the reconciliation with the community Mrs. Patrick had rejected. Women's coalition, which works so obviously in *Trifles*, *Chains of Dew* and *Bernice*, is also a means of negotiating the power of place in *The Outside*. As in the cases of Mrs. Hale and Mrs. Peters, Dotty and Mother, and Abbie and Margaret, Mrs. Patrick and Allie do not ally because "they like it," but their union is a form of survival in a hostile environment.

In *The Outside*, it is also remarkable that in contrast to the image of death and failure, as the men can be seen taking the corpse of the drowned sailor out of the station at the end of the play, Allie erects herself a real life-saver. While the men were grouped together to fulfill a goal, Allie and Mrs. Patrick will in the end become allied with promising success. The play ends with a "symbolic resurrection," as J. Ellen Gainor rightly claims (2001: 78), when Mrs. Patrick repeats the phrase "Meeting the Outside!" The first time she says it mockingly, but she eventually accepts the challenge to meet the outside and embrace "*the wonder of life*" (65). Both women are now ready to see the landscape in a different way, to see the life that there is in the struggle. They have overcome, thus, the malignity that had inhabited their location.

Departure through Solving the Generation Conflict

In Chapter 5, I discussed Glaspell's contribution to a common preoccupation in the heart of American theater, the animosity amongst generations. As Chaudhuri points out, family as pathology is particularly a burden highly difficult to overcome in realistic drama (2000: 110). In some of her plays, Glaspell, however, solves this animosity, turning the resolution of this conflict into a dramatic device to soften the negative conditions of place, making it more hospitable. As an early critic said, comparing Glaspell's *Inheritors* to Chekhov's *The Cherry Orchard*, one aim that both playwrights endeavor to achieve is to "investigat[e] the ordinary, homely phases of life in their respective countries" ("Tchehov and Susan Glaspell" 1929: np). That is, Glaspell, as Chekhov, investigates the different generations, with "a tremendous hope in the generations to come. No matter how pessimistic to day [*sic*] may appear, the vision for the future seems to become ever more distinct. They both believe that the suffering of those living in the present will be the happiness of the future" (1929: np). In terms of dramatic geopathology and its possible solutions as principles of departure, these negotiations between generations can be dramatically used to either turn place into a peaceful one, once the conflict is solved, or to eventually force the geopathic character to leave their location.

As argued earlier, in *Alison's House*, the agreement on setting Alison free by publishing her poems passes through the understanding among the members of the Stanhope family and their own solution to the generational conflict. Glaspell materializes this solution proxemically when at the end of the play Stanhope gives the poems to Elsa. This act also implies the reconciliation between father and daughter, as he understands that Elsa's love for Bill is right, and that she does not deserve to be as lonely as Alison was obliged to be by her family in particular and by society in general. Regarding this issue, Laughlin has affirmed that "while the balance of power does seem to be tipping in favor of the younger generation as the play closes, Glaspell cannot envision 'a revision of the family unit so complete that patriarchy would be unacceptable'" (1995: 229). Nevertheless, in the final act the audience has discovered a secret part of Stanhope, a side of him that disables him as a patriarch in the most traditional sense. And, above all, negotiation with younger ones is not part of the roles of a patriarch, and less with the daughter that had disgraced the family. In this manner, Glaspell does not support patriarchy at the end of the play, but the agreement among generations that will liberate the family from their entrapment in society.

In *Inheritors*, Glaspell also suggests that the past can help to mend the present. Madeline takes the corn image from his ancestors, and, by leaving the house, Madeline is the most rightful heiress. Unable to come to terms with the members of the older and younger generations she lives with, Madeline prefers meeting symbolically her dead ancestors. As Mary Papke has said, "Madeline chooses to honor that long line of pioneers in her quest for a better world by adjuring safety and personal luxury to do battle for the disenfranchised, for those denied the freedom of self and collective expression" (2006: 28). This explains why Madeline chooses the outside instead of staying inside the farmhouse, the family, and society. Glaspell reworks the idea of the physicality of home and extends it beyond the walls of the house.[11] Home for Madeline is not the farm, where her father, a victim of the burden of the land, is trapped because of his heritage, nor is it the college, where her ancestors' ideas have been misappropriated. Madeline's home is outside, even if in prison, where she can be herself and defend the ideas her ancestors really defended.

Furthermore, Glaspell constitutes in Madeline's evolution into a New Woman, in the moments close to her departure, a visual echo of the movements her ancestors performed. In the opening act, the pioneers' love and respect for nature was shown in the way they kept the door and windows open to look through them. In Act III, Madeline acts in this way, too. She *"turns and through the open door looks out at the hill, sitting where her GRAND-FATHER MORTON sat when he looked out at the hill"* (214). Equally important is the fact that Madeline also repeats her pioneer ancestors' movements when she goes to the closet and takes the box to find the piece of chalk. Both the piece of chalk and Silas's deed were kept in the same box, and both props denote the moments when these characters enact their most important commitments. Silas's deed embodied this pioneer's will to come to terms with the Native Americans and to do what his heart told him was right. Madeline's piece of chalk is used to draw Fred Jordan's cell on the farm floor, showing her serious commitment to her beliefs and that she is also aware that she has to do what is right. When Madeline repeats her grandfather's movements, the link with a useable past is established. Glaspell makes this point more obvious as Madeline imagines her grandfather joining her crusade against how the farm, a microcosm of the outside world's isolation, has betrayed what it was meant to be. Madeline imagines that Silas visits Fred's cell with her:

> Grandfather Morton, big and — oh, terrible. He was here. And we went to that walled-up hole in the ground [*Rising and pointing down at the chalked cell.*] where they keep Fred Jordan on bread and water because he couldn't be part of nations of men killing each other — and Silas Morton — only he was all that is back of us, tore open that cell — it was his voice tore it open — his voice cried, "God damn you, this is America!" [*Sitting down, as if rallying from a tremendous experience*] [222].

In his granddaughter's imagination, Silas Morton joins Madeline to defend the other unfairly imprisoned characters. Moreover, Madeline imagines Silas opening up the image of the prison to include the whole America. Through what she thinks Silas would say, Madeline articulates her thought that, America, besides its real prison buildings, has become a metaphorical prison for all those who want to keep close to the pioneers' ideals and to fight for democracy and rights. Through Madeline, Glaspell proposes a return to the genuine pioneers' values to escape geopathology, to values that keep on alive and moving. As Silas said: "God damn us if we sit here rich and fat and forget man's in the makin'" (193), a similar line to that the Native-born in *Free Laughter* asserts firmly, "a land satisfied with what it has is *a dying land*" (121, emphasis in original).

In the simplistic *Close the Book*, Glaspell had already revealed that the conflict of generations is not built upon a mere opposition to the immediate previous generation, and less upon a simple appraisal of the present generation. Neither the older nor the younger generations are to be unanimously applauded in Glaspell's plays. She builds a bridge between generations which could be meaningful to solve the problem of place. Although Peyton apparently despises the immediately previous generation, for instance, his uncle and Senator Byrd, he does go back to his past when it suits him. He relates the paper on free speech which he and Jhansi are writing to the Declaration of Independence, explicitly establishing a link to a past generation that he admires: "I suppose that's an inherited tendency. You know, one of my ancestors signed a paper on free speech. It had a high falutin' name: 'The Declaration of Independence'" (41). The way the play ends, with Grandmother demanding to close the book, constitutes a similar image. It has been argued that Grandmother's demand is a proof of her dubious Midwestern morality, describing her as "snobbish small-town matron who hides her family's black sheep within a closed book on genealogy" (Waterman 1966: 69). Nevertheless, a negative reading of this pioneer female character contradicts the long-established privilege that Glaspell grants to this kind of character. With her command to close the book, Grandmother is telling future generations to stop looking into those former generations that did not behave right, as Peyton and Jhansi are doing, and to take the model of those ancestors with good values, as Madeline does in *Inheritors*. It must be noted that the original title for *Close the Book* was *Family Pride*. This change from a noun phrase to an order is enlightening. Taking into account Glaspell's attitude towards the past in this play, family pride must not be a petrified bastion to back up the acts we perform in the present. There must be a rightful selection of the past one can be proud of, hence the demand to close the book. Family pride in Glaspell's plays is a useful tool to make characters come to terms with the space they inhabit, as long as the pride in the past they make use of is truly worthy.

While in *Close the Book* the resolution is a command, in *Springs Eternal* Glaspell argues onstage the power of debate. Although its ending can hardly be praised from a dramatic point of view, the thematic consistency of *Springs Eternal* deserves attention. Glaspell resolves the conflict of *Springs Eternal* with a negotiation between generations embodied in the toast which closes the play. It could be said that the character of Stewie summarizes the reason why the world is inhospitable with his assertion: "We *forget* so much. Forget what we were going to be" (387, emphasis in original). In Glaspell's discourse, the world is a mess partly because older generations failed both their own heritage and the promise of a better future for their offspring. The toast to the "Brave Old World" at the end of the play, significantly suggested by the younger characters, brings both generations together in their work for the future. Although Gainor has observed that *Springs Eternal* was rejected for production because theater-goers "would want to look to the future" (2001: 246), I believe that Glaspell's ending is a call to the audience to look and work for that future, but taking the past as a starting point, too. As Bill and Dotty are making up the toast, Jumbo reflects upon it:

> Wait please! I'm sure it's very nice if they were brave, but I shall put up my mind on what they *felt*—long gone, but alive then. [*Suddenly lighted with happy surprise.*] Alive now! [*Exaltedly.*] You know something? Feeling doesn't go. It stays on —*in* things — in people who weren't even born when it was born [405, emphasis in original].

It is not only important if in the past they were brave or not, but their ideals, their feelings, and their hopes also count. The feelings that have passed unnoticed from generation to generation, as the seeds blowing from mind to mind in *Inheritors*, are also essential. The final reconciliation reaches its climax when Owen and Stewie ask for forgiveness for having failed the younger generation and thank them for the new opportunity to join them in saving the world from war. Owen will put his mind on a new book that will help "to fix it so there won't be any more wars" (400). Bill utters the final line in the play: "Swell! We're off! Put your minds on the Brave Old World!" (405). In her clear reference to Shakespeare's "Brave New World," which was indeed an alternative title for *Springs Eternal*,[12] Glaspell asks the audience to take advantage of the good things from the past and not to forget that we are obliged to work for a better future. The real world outside, which Glaspell's geopathic dramatic places represent, can only be pacified if we, the people, as her characters, commit to act.

Afterword

Art only becomes useful to man and society if it contains within it an urge to action [Brook 1989: 235].

Having analyzed the geography of Susan Glaspell's plays, I can affirm that the experience has proved stirring in many ways. One of my original goals, to dive into the consistency between Glaspell's characters and their location as a device to develop characters' identities and to set in motion the dramatic development of her plays, has demonstrated the rich imagery that nurtures dramatic geopathology. And I can conclude that Glaspell's technique relies heavily on these relationships. The present research has discussed the different means Glaspell employs to show her characters' victimage of location. Starting from those images, themes, and tropes that Una Chaudhuri had proposed in *Staging Place*, not only have we witnessed that Glaspell's work fits into Chaudhuri's pattern quite closely, as for instance, in her revision of the American Myth of Mobility, the dichotomist coding of her dramatic worlds, or the image of the buried child. But also, by focusing on the physical configuration of Glaspell's settings as well as on her spatial imagery, I have shown that Glaspell's plays offer a greater range of "geopathic" images and devices. With the solid background that feminist geographers, literary critics and women writers provide, other different means Glaspell uses to suggest geopathology on the part of her female characters have also emerged. In this manner, the more general American Myth of Mobility that Chaudhuri proposed has been more accurately presented regarding the role played by women in this myth, and related to (im)mobility. The role of women in the American Dream and the Pioneer Myth has also been revisited. Dichotomies such as representations of home as shelter vs. representations of home as prison, or inside vs. outside, are always changing in Glaspell's plays, suggesting the way we code the world subjectively and the fact that our identities are in continuous change. Other figures Chaudhuri proposed, such as the homecoming, the immigrant character, or family as a problem, have also been discussed in this study, in addition to other figures alien to Chaudhuri's theory, such as isolation, the spatial representation of the past, and images of death as origins of victimage of location. Chaudhuri's model has been left aside almost completely in the final chapter, as her "heroism of departure" has been modified into "principles of departure" accounting for the many ways Glaspell offers to her characters as a way out from their victimage of location; such as nature, art, or women's coalition. The issues treated in this book lead me to reaffirm that the close relationship between Glaspell's onstage places and her characters, which she emphasizes as a bidirectional relationship where place affects identity as much as the other way around, is more modernist than realist. Glaspell's fictional places are not decorative backgrounds to support a character's identity, as happens in realistic theater, but an entity she makes her characters engage with in a verbal and kinesic dialectic. The images and dramatic devices discussed here cannot but make me assert that geopathology is indeed central to Glaspell's plays, and that her drama is the drama of place.

The present study, rather than ending here, has opened several lines of further research. The concept of geopathology can also be applied to Glaspell's fiction. Her plays, novels, and short stories often treat similar topics, and victimage of location seems to be a central issue. All of Glaspell's novels and many of her short stories usually have a female protagonist trapped in a place from where she wants to escape, at the same time that this female protagonist yearns for an identity of her own. For instance, in "Out There" (1912) Glaspell suggests, as she does in many of her plays, that the American Dream is not made for girls. Her female protagonist is a victim of location because she has to leave her beloved hometown to go to work in Chicago. Trying to find a place for herself, she rejoices in the pictures of mountains she sees displayed in a window. A victim of her geopathology, and unable to fulfill her homecoming, the girl dies in front of this window. Glaspell's male protagonists in her short stories can also be analyzed regarding geopathology. In this book I have tried to highlight those few instances in Glaspell's plays where her male characters also experience victimage of location. Given that in many of her short stories and novels, Glaspell portrays male characters more fully than she does in her plays, there appears the opportunity to analyze her male characters' victimage of location. In "The Manager of Crystal Sulphur Springs" (1915), for instance, Bert Groves has created an imaginary world where the sanatorium he and his family had built still exists. In Bert, Glaspell depicts a character unable to live in the reality where the Groves have lost their place and where he is a dweller in a poorhouse. Glaspell even presents euthanasia as Bert's principle of departure.

Two of the features that, at least theoretically, marked the difference between the Provincetown Players and other little theatres were their work system and their collaborative spirit. Thus, it is also interesting to see if, given the collaboration they promoted, the plays of other women of the Provincetown Players follow the pattern of dramatic geopathology. Plays such as Neith Boyce's *Winter's Night* (1916) seem to do so. In *Winter's Night*, a play which has indeed many parallels with *Trifles*, Rachel Westcott lives on an enclosing Midwest farm. Released from her imprisonment when the play opens, as her husband has died and she can move out now, Rachel must struggle against victimage of location as her brother-in-law desperately wants to marry her, insisting that Rachel stay on the farm. In this play several of the key images seen in this book appear: isolation, coldness, death, violence, inside vs. outside, the buried child, and home as prison. Besides analyzing geopathology *per se*, I also find interesting a possible analysis of the similarities and differences in the portrayal of victimage of location and principles of departure in the plays of the women of the Provincetown Players, in order to assess to what extent these women artists collaborated or inspired one another. Similarly, a comparison could be established among the plays of Glaspell and her female counterparts with the works of their male colleagues of the Provincetown Players.

The method of analysis and the findings of my discussion might also be applied to more contemporary playwrights. According to Helen Krich Chinoy, Glaspell, among other women dramatists, is the settler of the "subjects and the structures now widely used by today's women playwrights" (1987: 131). In the 20th and 21st centuries, as much as at the time Glaspell wrote her plays, we still worry about having a room of one's own, a room where our identity can be projected and supported. Theater, as a mirror of the problems society faces, still offers its stage to make the audience think about this issue, urging us to take action. An appealing research unfolds as the factors leading to victimage of location that have been identified in this book are detected in the works of playwrights such as Maria Irene Fornes, Suzan-Lori Parks, Paula Vogel, or Marsha Norman. For instance, in Norman's *'Night, Mother* (1983) dramatic geopathology appears in the representation of the house as prison for a woman who considers herself an unsuccessful mother and wife, in the depiction of the broken family, in the generation conflict between mother and daughter, in addictions, and in the imagery of death. This kind of analysis of dramatic geopathology, establishing a comparison between Glaspell's work and more contemporary plays, could help reveal whether Elaine Showalter's claim that there is "an imaginary continuum, the recurrence of certain patterns, themes, problems, and images from generation to generation" (1977: 12) is true or not in terms of contemporary North American women playwrights.

The different tropes, images, and dichotomies presented in this book might also be useful in analyzing dramatic geopathology in the works of non–North American playwrights. There is one thing Glaspell did not wholly respect regarding the manifesto of the Provincetown Players. One of their aims was to create "native" drama, but Glaspell transcended frontiers. It is true that some of the themes seen in this book, above all those related to American myths, are mainly native in the sense that they relate to the United States. However, Glaspell's emphasis on the place that women deserve to have, on women's struggle to create an identity of their own, and on assumed hierarchies of power geometry which usually leave women in unfavorable positions, are universal topics. This may explain Glaspell's success in the United Kingdom, not only while she was alive, but also more recently. The Orange Tree Theatre in Richmond (London) produced *The Verge* in 1996, *Inheritors* in 1997, *Chains of Dew*, *The Outside*, *Trifles*, and *Suppressed Desires* in 2008, and *Alison's House* in 2009. *The Verge* was also produced at the University of Glasgow in 1996. *Trifles* has been produced recently at Suzhou University in China. *Trifles* has also been translated into Spanish,[1] and together with *The Outside*, *The Verge*, *Alison's House,* and *Bernice*, into Portuguese.[2] And the Susan Glaspell Society, founded in 2003,[3] is little by little increasing numbers outside the United States. Definitely, Glaspell's appeal is not restricted to the United States or to her own times. Susan Glaspell has been a victim of location for too long, trapped in the obscure corner of oblivion, in the closet where so many other female playwrights still are. Released from such entrapment some decades ago, Glaspell's departure still needs to be heard more strongly. Further studies of her work, together with research on the influence which she has exerted upon many other writers, will help to maintain Glaspell in the very special room of her own that she deserves in the great house of literary history.

Chapter Notes

Introduction

1. It must be noted that Glaspell won a Pulitzer Prize for drama in 1931 for *Alison's House*, a prize that, as critics agreed, she received not only for this play, but for her theater career.

2. The first comprehensive work on Glaspell's novels is Martha C. Carpentier's *The Major Novels of Susan Glaspell* (2001).

3. In *Strange Bedfellows: The First American Avant-Garde* (1991), Steven Watson accounts for the different exchanges that took place among European and American modernists in the early decades of the 20th century. See part "Before 1913. Cradles of Modernism," pp. 12–96 for detailed information about this topic.

4. These clubs were not merely literary clubs, but they were also interested in discussing and promoting new ideas about politics, feminism, or social care, among other issues. For more information see, for instance, Judith Schwarz's *Radical Feminists of Heterodoxy: Greenwich Village, 1912–1940* (1986) and Christine Stansell's *American Moderns: Bohemian New York and the Creation of a New Century* (2000).

5. For more information about the organization of the Armory Show, see Milton Brown's "The Armory Show and Its Aftermath," pp. 165–166.

6. For more details about John Quinn, see Steven Watson's *Strange Bedfellows: The First American Avant-Garde*, pp. 174–175.

7. According to O'Neill's biographers, Arthur and Barbara Gelb, O'Neill admitted several times that he had not learned much from Baker's course, but "O'Neill did acknowledge it was from Baker that he grasped the essential technical procedure of writing a scenario before attempting any actual dialogue — a rule he followed with only rare exceptions throughout his career" [2000: 466].

8. Robert Károly Sarlós corrects the dimensions of the wharf shed. He states that the wharf was between twenty-four and twenty-six feet wide, thirty-four to thirty-six feet long, and twenty-four to twenty-six feet high [1982: Appendix C].

9. Ben-Zvi states that "the stage was 14-by-10½ feet" [2005: 180].

10. Marcia Noe briefly comments on the metaphorical use of space in these plays in her article "Region as a Metaphor in the Plays of Susan Glaspell." Alkalay-Gut discusses the men's outside world vs. the women's kitchen world in *Trifles* in her article "Jury of Her Peers: The Importance of *Trifles*." In "Feminism in Motion: Pushing the 'Wild Zone' Thesis into the Fourth Dimension," John Kanthack asserts that in *Trifles* "a wild zone takes vivid form and shapes the outcome of the play" [2003: 150].

11. See Klaus Schwank's "Die dramatischen Experimente Susan Glaspells: *The Outside* und *The Verge*," pp. 413–417.

12. Citations from Glaspell's plays are taken from *Susan Glaspell: The Complete Plays* (2010). Further references will be given in numbers parenthetically.

13. The dates given correspond to their first production, except in the cases of *Free Laughter*, which Linda Ben-Zvi and J. Ellen Gainor date in 1919, and *Springs Eternal*, never produced, and dated accordingly to its typescript. It must be noted that though *Chains of Dew* was first produced in 1922, which led scholars to think that Glaspell had written it after *The Verge*, Ozieblo discovered that this play was indeed written earlier, in 1920 [2000: 155]. Regarding the plays written in collaboration, *Suppressed Desires* and *The Comic Artist*, though it is impossible to state for sure which parts correspond to Glaspell and which ones to her collaborators, the consistency in the dramatic language and certain set of images compared to other works Glaspell wrote on her own, has led me to consider these plays righteous members in the present analysis of geopathology in Susan Glaspell's plays.

Chapter 1

1. See Michel McKinnie's "The State of This Place: Convictions, the Courthouse, and the Geography of Performance in Belfast," pp. 80–81, for his brief and concise summary of these approaches.

2. Linda Ben-Zvi quotes this fragment in *Susan Glaspell: Her Plays and Times,* p. 146, and gives the following reference: Undated fragment "On Home," "Notes to go into plays." Susan Glaspell Papers, BCNYPL. I thank The Henry W. and Albert A. Berg Collection of English and American Literature, The New York Public Library, Astor, Lenox and Tilden Foundation for their permission to reproduce this material.

3. Elaine Aston succinctly defines this term: "Materialist feminism has now widely been adopted as the nomenclature for the theoretical position which in the 1970s was labelled as Marxist or socialist feminism. This position critiques the historical and material conditions of class, race, and gender oppression, and demands the radical transformation of social structures" [1995: 8–9].

4. In *The Women of Provincetown, 1915–1922* Cheryl Black affirms, "The women of Provincetown were pursuing a formidable objective: to revolutionize all human relationships — to create a new world. Their every aspiration, including their desire to create an experimental theatre company, can best be understood as part of that objective" [2002: 31]. Black develops and discusses this affirmation throughout her book.

5. See, for instance, Catherine Belsey's "Constructing the Subject/ Deconstructing the Text," pp. 51–56; Sue-Ellen Case's *Feminism and Theatre*, p.124; Jill Dolan's *The Feminist Spectator as Critic*, pp. 84–87; and Jeanie Forte's "Realism, Narrative, and the Feminist Playwright — A Problem of Reception," p. 116.

6. Elin Diamond's "Mimesis, Mimicry, and the 'True-Real'" is usually quoted as a defense of the feminist possibilities of Realism. For Judith Barlow, if women had not adopted apparently realistic forms, "feminist drama would scarcely have appealed to the powerful male producers and conventional audiences" [1994: xiii]. Similarly, in "The Provincetown Players' Experiments with Realism," J. Ellen Gainor argues that these playwrights subverted the conventions of realism "without completely transgressing its generic parameters" [1996: 62].

Chapter 2

1. During the Second Feminist Wave, many books on women's history came out. After Nancy Cott published her *Root of Bitterness: Documents of the Social History of American Women* (1972), other feminist scholars followed her path and endeavored to make the effort of pioneer women known. Rosalyn Baxandall, Linda Gordon and Susan Reverby edited *America's Working Women. A Documentary History — 1600 to the Present* (1976), Anette Kolodny published *The Land Before Her: Fantasy and Experience of the American Frontiers, 1630–1860* (1984), and Glenna Matthews presented her research in *The Rise of the Public Woman: Woman's Power and Woman's Place in the United States 1630–1970* (1992). Glenda Riley focused more exclusively on the Midwest pioneer woman in her brilliant *Frontierswomen: The Iowa Experience* (1981).

2. For more information about the relationship between chairs and hierarchy within the family, see Daphne Spain's *Gendered Spaces*, p. 126.

3. Glaspell scholarship has extensively analyzed the significance of quilting in *Trifles*. See, for instance, Ben-Zvi's "Murder, She Wrote: The Genesis of Susan Glaspell's *Trifles*," p.153; C.W.E. Bigsby's *A Critical Introduction to Twentieth-Century American Drama. Volume One, 1900–1940*, p. 25; Elaine Hedges's "Small Things Reconsidered: 'A Jury of Her Peers,'" pp. 61–62; Veronica Makowsky's "Susan Glaspell and Modernism," p. 53; Carme Manuel's "Susan Glaspell's *Trifles* (1916): Women's Conspiracy of Silence Beyond the Melodrama of Beset Womanhood," p. 62; Elaine Showalter's *Sister's Choice. Tradition and Change in American Women's Writing*, p. 145; Beverly Smith's "Women's Work — *Trifles*? The Skill and Insights of Playwright Susan Glaspell," pp. 175–176; and Karen Stein's "The Women's World of Glaspell's *Trifles*," p. 254.

4. See Caroline Violet Fletcher's "'Rules of the Institution': Susan Glaspell and Sisterhood," pp. 252–253. I am not endorsing here the idea that Glaspell might not have supported the feminist agenda of Heterodoxy, which, as Ben-Zvi says, was enormously "significant for her theatre work" [2005: 127]. I am considering instead what Glaspell's commitment to the other women of the group really was. It must not be forgotten that, for instance, her Heterodite friend and member of the Provincetown Players, Ida Rauh, had a sexual relation with Glaspell's husband.

5. Barbara Ozieblo provides this detail in *Susan Glaspell. A Critical Biography*, p. 140.

6. In the version published in the *Metropolitan*, there is "a divan" [1917: 19], and in a typescript held at the University of Virginia, this is "a divan with leopard's skin" [1].

(Eugene O'Neill Papers, MSS 6448-b, Clifton Waller Barrett Library of American Literature, Special Collections, University of Virginia Library.)

7. Bachelard defines the felicitous space also as "the space we love," and "eulogized space" [1994: xxxv]. For Bachelard's definition of topophilia and its importance for the poetics of space, see *The Poetics of Space*, pp. xxxv–xxxvi.

8. There is another reference to African Americans in Glaspell's *Close the Book* [40]. In this case, Glaspell brings to the front the issue of interracial marriages and mulatto offspring, to suggest the prosecution these racially different American born individuals had to bear. Given that there is only one comment about this issue in the play, the relationship it may have with dramatic geopathology is not developed here.

9. Reviewers of *Inheritors* acknowledged the links between both plays. For instance, in 1926, N. G. Royde-Smith wrote an article for *The Outlook* in which the author pinpointed the parallels between both plays. Royde-Smith claims that both plays share common purposes, such as that both playwrights wanted to show that "our forefathers made steps towards the brotherhood of man — they smoked the pipe of peace with the Indian brave whose land they conquered," that is, that some white men and some Native Americans attempted to live peacefully, smoking the pipe of peace [1926: 25].

Chapter 3

1. "Trifles," typewritten draft, undated. Susan Glaspell Papers. I thank The Henry W. and Albert A. Berg Collection of English and American Literature, The New York Public Library, Astor, Lenox and Tilden Foundation for their permission to reproduce this material.

2. It is very probable that Glaspell had read this letter, given that *The Masses* was the New York-based journal in which most of the Greenwich Village radicals participated. Several of Glaspell's acquaintances and friends used to write for it. Max Eastman was its editor, and Floyd Dell and Jack Reed were among its regulars.

3. Linda Ben-Zvi has suggested other models for Fred Jordan. Ben-Zvi comments on the case of Fred Robinson, suggesting that this conscientious objector is behind Glaspell's character because of the name Fred. Ben-Zvi also points to the well-known case of Philip Grosser, who spent thirty-five years in Alcatraz, "where he was often chained to his cell door and kept in solitary confinement in the hole for long periods of time" [2006: 289].

4. See, for instance, Karen Alkalay-Gut's "Murder and Marriage: Another Look at *Trifles*," p. 74; C.W.E. Bigsby's "Introduction," p. 11; Elaine Hedges's "Small Things Reconsidered: 'A Jury of Her Peers,'" p. 59; Veronica Makowsky's "Susan Glaspell and Modernism," p. 52; and Carme Manuel's "Susan Glaspell's *Trifles* (1916): Women's Conspiracy of Silence Beyond the Melodrama of Beset Womanhood," p. 61.

5. In "Women's Work — *Trifles*? The Skill and Insights of Playwright Susan Glaspell," Beverly Bronson Smith affirms that "Minnie does fit, at least in some respects, the psychological/social pattern of the battered wife" [1982: 179]. Smith includes in her analysis aspects such as the isolated farm, Minnie's detachment from friends — which Smith sees as an indicator of the fact that Minnie did not want to be seen with a black eye, and John as the prototypical possessive battering husband. See pp. 179–180.

6. Marcia Noe, in "The New Woman in the Plays of Susan Glaspell," briefly notes that "the audience views Claire alone 'as if shut into the tower' through the huge convex window that separates them from the proscenium. In this way, Glaspell foregrounds the convention of the invisible fourth wall through which the audience can see the actors with a set that works expressionistically and experimentally against convention even as it suggests one of the conventions of realism." See pp. 160–161.

7. In "The Verge: *L'Écriture Fémenine* at the Provincetown," Marcia Noe points out that "through setting, lighting, action, and dialogue, Glaspell sets up a number of binary oppositions that emphasize the symbolic system Claire sets out to destroy" [1995: 133]. See also J. Ellen Gainor's "A Stage of Her Own: Susan Glaspell's *The Verge* and Women's Dramaturgy," pp. 83–84.

Chapter 4

1. "It is very sad a great..." Undated play fragment. Susan Glaspell Papers. I thank The Henry W. and Albert A. Berg Collection of English and American Literature, The New York Public Library, Astor, Lenox and Tilden Foundation for their permission to reproduce this material.

2. It is interesting to notice that in *The Road to the Temple* Glaspell comments on Cook's delight in drawing genealogy charts, and on his finding entertainment in his ancestors. Cook even found his connection with Benjamin Franklin: "He was my father's mother's mother's father's father's father's father's son's son" [Cook qtd. in Glaspell 2005: 34]. It seems possible that Glaspell found inspiration for *Close the Book* in one of her husband's hobbies.

3. In *Susan Glaspell in Context*, J. Ellen Gainor affirms, "The second phase of [Glaspell's] dramatic career, which included the creation of *The Comic Artist*, *Alison's House*, and *Springs Eternal*, is marked by its focus on the family" [2001: 235].

Chapter 5

1. In her article titled "Silenced Mothers and Questing Daughters in Susan Glaspell's Mature Novels," Barbara Ozieblo focuses on the "unwanted, dead, illegitimate or adopted children that recur in Susan Glaspell's novels," which "indicate a certain preoccupation or even obsession with motherhood" [2006a: 137]. In this article, Ozieblo provides several details that may explain Glaspell's "thwarted maternal wish" [2006a: 141].

2. For more information about the real case, see Patricia L. Bryan and Thomas Wolf's *Midnight Assassin: A Murder in America's Heartland*.

3. For an extended analysis of the birth control movement in Greenwich Village, see Christine Stansell's *American Moderns: Bohemian New York and the Creation of a New Century*, pp. 225–272. Hutchins Hapgood's position about this movement appears in his autobiography *A Victorian in the Modern World*, pp. 239–240, 280; and for Floyd Dell's support of feminist movements, see his *Homecoming: An Autobiography*, pp. 247, 261, 283. Judith Barlow notes in "Susan's Sisters: The 'Other' Women Writers of the Provincetown Players": "Yet Hapgood, like

such fellow Provincetowners as Harry Kemp, Max Eastman, and Floyd Dell, *apparently saw themselves as feminists*" [1995: 278, emphasis added]. Lois Rudnick makes a similar criticism in "The New Woman": "The male feminists of Greenwich Village whose idealistic rhetoric was often undermined by what they actually wanted from the real women in their lives. ...[What] they most often sought in their own personal relationships and celebrated in their fiction and poetry were women who were joyful and exciting companions, willing to subordinate home, community, and their own desires to men's needs.... Seeking a New Woman who would give them the best of all possible worlds, they wanted a lover who was always available to fulfill their sexual needs; a mother to provide them with the emotional security they lost when they abandoned their middle-class roots; and a muse to inspire them to world-transforming political and aesthetic feats" [1991: 78]. In "Una imagen propia: La innovación protagonizada por dramaturgas norteamericanas de principios de siglo" Barbara Ozieblo even labels Glaspell's male mates "machoist feminists" ["feministas machistas] [2002: 33–34].

4. "Inheritors," typescript. Susan Glaspell Papers. I thank The Henry W. and Albert A. Berg Collection of English and American Literature, The New York Public Library, Astor, Lenox and Tilden Foundation for their permission to reproduce this material.

5. In *Susan Glaspell in Context*, J. Ellen Gainor observes that Glaspell's treatment of conscientious objection also reveals her interventionist position: "Fred Jordan, the conscientious objector who is the absent center in *Inheritors*, is made a martyr figure for his beliefs, but in the later play Freddie, a soldier, is the idealized individual, and not Harold" [2001: 256]. Indeed, unlike Fred Jordan in *Inheritors*, Harold's/Jumbo's choice is devoid of any heroism as he is not in a prison cell on bread and water, but apparently being fairly treated in the Civilian Public Service camps. As Gainor says, "There is no evidence in this play of his mistreatment or details involving any other objectors" [2001: 257].

6. Sandra M. Gilbert and Susan Gubar develop this idea in *No Man's Land: The Place of the Woman Writer in the Twentieth Century*. Vol. 1: *The War of Words* (1988).

7. See J. Ellen Gainor's *Susan Glaspell in Context*, p. 230, and Kristina Hinz-Bode's *Susan Glaspell and the Anxiety of Expression. Language and Isolation in the Plays*, p. 200.

Chapter 6

1. See, for instance, Cheryl Black's "Making Queer New Things: Queer Identities in the Life and Dramaturgy of Susan Glaspell," p. 56

2. A typewritten carbon version of this different ending is held at the Berg Collection, New York Public Library. "The Comic Artist with ms. stage directions in unknown hands with another typewritten (carbon) version of the ending." Susan Glaspell Papers.

3. See, for instance, Gerhard Bach's "Susan Glaspell: Mapping the Domains of Critical Revision," p. 254; Christine Dymkowski's "On the Edge: The Plays of Susan Glaspell," p. 101; J. Ellen Gainor's "A Stage of Her Own: Susan Glaspell's *The Verge* and Women's Dramaturgy," p. 96; Kristina Hinz-Bode's *Susan Glaspell and the Anxiety of Expression. Language and Isolation in the Plays*, p. 162; Kecia Driver McBride's "Silence and the Struggle for Representational Space in the Art of Susan Glaspell," p. 166; Nancy L. Nester's "The Agoraphobic Imagination: The Protagonist Who Murders and the Critics Who Praise Her," p. 3; Margit Sichert's "Claire Archer: A 'Nietzscheana' in Susan Glaspell's *The Verge*," p. 295; and Arthur Waterman's "Susan Glaspell's *The Verge*: An Experiment in Feminism," p. 22.

4. See, for instance, Karen Alkalay-Gut's "Murder and Marriage: Another Look at *Trifles*," p. 80; Patricia L. Bryan's "Stories in Fiction and in Fact: Susan Glaspell's 'A Jury of Her Peers' and the 1901 Murder Trial of Margaret Hossack," p. 1309; Sherri Hallgreen's "'The Law Is the Law and a Bad Stove Is a Bad Stove': Subversive Justice and Layers of Collusion in 'A Jury of Her Peers,'" pp. 212–213; Elaine Showalter's *Sister's Choice: Tradition and Change in American Women's Writing*, p. 146, and Cynthia Sutherland's "American Women Playwrights as Mediators of the 'Woman Problem,'" p. 323.

5. In "Feminist Encounters: Locating the Politics of Experience," Chandra Talpede Mohanty

discusses and compares the works of different feminist scholars that define various kinds of female bonding. Like Mohanty, I agree that Beverley Reagon is right to prime survival over shared oppression as the ground for coalition. Borrowing Reagon's words: "You don't go into coalition because you like it. The only reason you would consider trying to team up with somebody who could possibly kill you, is because that's the only way you can figure you can stay alive" [1983: 357]. See Mohanty 1997.

6. In her analysis of Glaspell's "The Rules of the Institution," Caroline Violet Fletcher asserts that this short story "portrays most clearly what Glaspell seems to have seen as the alarming side of sisterhood, a code of prescriptive behavior that punishes expressions of individuality and harms eccentric hearts" [2006: 241]. See also Chapter 2, n. 4.

7. In *Susan Glaspell and the Anxiety of Expression*, Kristina Hinz-Bode affirms that this ending "seems to condemn [Henrietta's] move into the (male) realm of public discourse," and Steve "has regained control over the situation, and — as he has the final word in the play — he has successfully wrestled the floor from his wife" [2006b: 232]. On a similar note, Brenda Murphy has affirmed, "It is Steve who takes control of the house, reestablishing the power hierarchy that had been undermined by Henrietta's intrusion of psychoanalysis into their relations" [2005: 72].

8. See, for instance, Barbara Ozieblo's *Susan Glaspell: A Critical Biography*, pp. 9–10.

9. For brief analyses of the influence of Transcendentalism on Susan Glaspell, see Linda Ben-Zvi's *Susan Glaspell: Her Life and Times*, pp. 82–84; Kristina Hinz-Bode's "Susan Glaspell and the Epistemological Crisis of Modernity: Truth, Knowledge, and Art in Selected Novels," p. 93; Veronica Makowsky's *Susan Glaspell's Century of American Women: A Critical Interpretation of Her Work*, p. 4. Mary Papke provides a longer analysis in "Susan Glaspell's Naturalist Scenarios of Determinism and Blind Faith," pp. 25–28.

10. It is interesting to note that, for Glaspell, the image of the yellow corn had such a symbolic aura that it was Ann Harding's blonde hair that earned her the role as Madeline. As Edna Kenton recalls, "Susan wanted the 'just right' actress for Madeline in this play of yellow corn and yellow pollen and revolutionary spirit gone 'yellow.' One after another had read the part.... One morning, while casting was still going on, a pretty young thing came into the playhouse and asked for a part. Jasper Deeter, directing the play, gave her a glance and said, 'She might do for one of the giggling girls.' But Ida [Rauh], catching a glimpse of something corn-yellow about an ear, said, 'Take off your hat.' When the swirl of pale gold hair appeared, Susan called to her, had her read, and in a few minutes Ann Harding had her first part. Her stage career had begun" [1997: 135–136].

11. In "Antigone Redux: Female Voice and the State in Susan Glaspell's *Inheritors*," which explores the influence of classical scholarship on *Inheritors*, especially Sophocles' *Antigone*, Marie Molnar asserts, "[Madeline's] willingness, not only to speak, but to act for [the Hindu students] and suffer arrest along with them signals Madeline's extension of the family (her *oikos*) beyond the walls of the home in which she grew up" [2006: 41].

12. A draft typescript with this title is held at the Berg Collection, Susan Glaspell Papers, in the New York Public Library.

Afterword

1. See Alberola, Nieves and Yvonne Shafer (eds.) 2007. *Nimiedades para la eternidad*. Castellón: Ellago Ediciones.

2. See Sander, Lucia V. (ed.) 2002. *O Teatro de Susan Glaspell: Cinco peças*. Trans. Lucia V. Sander. Brazil: United States Embassy in Brazil.

3. For more information about the Susan Glaspell Society, see its web site: https://www.susanglaspell.org.

Bibliography

1926. *The Road to the Temple*. London: Bern Stern. (2005. Ed. Linda Ben-Zvi. Jefferson, NC: McFarland.)

Drama

1917. *Suppressed Desires* (with George Cram Cook). *Metropolitan* 45 (January 1): 19–20, 57–59. (1991. *Suppressed Desires. 1915. The Cultural Moment. The New Politics, the New Woman, the New Psychology, the New Art, and the New Theater in America*. Eds. Adele Heller and Lois Rudnick. New Brunswick, New Jersey: Rutgers University Press. 281–291; and 1994. *Suppressed Desires. The Provincetown Players. A Choice of the Shorter Works*. Ed. Barbara Ozieblo. Sheffield: Sheffield Academic Press. 34–51.)

1920. *Plays*. Boston: Small, Maynard. (*Trifles, Suppressed Desires, The People, Close the Book, The Outside, Woman's Honor, Bernice, Tickless Time*.)

1920. *Chains of Dew*. Typescript, Library of Congress, Washington D.C.

1927. *The Comic Artist* (with Norman Matson). London: Ernest Benn.

1930. *Alison's House*. New York: Samuel French. Reprinted in 1935, *The Pulitzer Prize Plays, 1918–1934*. Ed. Kathryn Coe and William H. Cordell. New York: Random House. 649–691.

1943. *Springs Eternal*. Typescript, Susan Glaspell Papers, Berg Collection, New York Public Library.

1987. *Plays by Susan Glaspell*. Ed. C. W. E. Bigsby. Cambridge: Cambridge University Press. (*Trifles, The Outside, The Verge, Inheritors*.)

2010. *Susan Glaspell: The Complete Plays*. Eds. Linda Ben-Zvi and J. Ellen Gainor. Jefferson, NC: McFarland.

Fiction

Novels

1909. *The Glory of the Conquered: The Story of a Great Love*. New York: Frederik A. Stokes.

1911. *The Visioning*. New York: Frederik A. Stokes.

1915. *Fidelity*. London: Jarrods.

1928. *Brook Evans*. New York: Frederik A. Stokes.

1929. *Fugitive's Return*. New York: Frederik A. Stokes.

1931. *Ambrose Holt and Family*. New York: Frederik A. Stokes.

1939. *The Morning Is Near Us*. New York: Frederik A. Stokes.

1940. *Cherished and Shared of Old*. New York: Julian Messner.

1942. *Norma Ashe*. Philadelphia: J. B. Lippincott.

1945. *Judd Rankin's Daughter*. Philadelphia: J. B. Lippincott. (Also published as *Prodigal Giver*. London: Victor Gollancz, 1946)

Short Stories

1896. "Tom and Towser." *Davenport Weekly Outlook* (December 26): 8.
1898. "His Literary Training." *The Delphic* 13: 83–85.
"The Philosophy of War." *The Delphic* 15 (October): 24.
"The Tragedy of Mind." *The Delphic* 14 (February): 98–102.
1900. "The Unprofessional Crime." *The Delphic*: 109–112.
1902. "On the Second Down." *Author's Magazine* 3.1: 2–11.
1903. "The Girl from Downtown." *Youth's Companion* 77 (April 2): 160–161.
"In the Face of His Constituents." *Harper's Monthly Magazine* 107 (October): 757–762.
1904. "The Intrusion of the Personal." *Frank Leslie's Monthly* 57 (November 1903–April 1904): 629–632.
"The Man of Flesh and Blood." *Harper's Monthly Magazine* 108 (May): 957.
"Contrary to Precedent." *Booklovers* 3 (January–June): 235–256.
"Freckles M'Grath." *Munsey's* 31 (July): 481.
"The Work of the Unloved Libby." *Black Cat* (August): np.
1905. "The Return of Rhoda." *Youth's Companion* 79 (January 26): 40.
"For Tomorrow. The Story of an Easter Sermon." *The Booklovers Magazine* 5 (March): 559–570.
"For Love of the Hills." *Black Cat* 11 (October): 1–11.
"From the Pen of Failures." *Quax*: 215–218.
1906."The Boycott on Caroline." *The Youth's Companion* 80.12 (March 22): 137–138.
"How the Prince Saw America." *The American Magazine* 62: 274.
1907. "At the Turn of the Road. (A Christmas Story.)" *The Speaker* 2.4 (September 1907): 359–361.
1909. "From A-Z." *American* 65 (October): 543.
1910. "The Rekindling." *Designer* (October): 325, 384–385.
1911. "According to his Lights." *The American Magazine* 72 (June): 153–162.
1912. "A Boarder of Art." *Ladies' Home Journal* 29 (October): 11, 92–93.
"At the Source." *Woman's Home Companion* 39 (May): 5–6.
"Out There." *The Delineator* (July): 15–17.
"The Anarchist: His Dog." *The American Magazine* 74 (June): 145–154.
1913. "The Resurrection and the Life." *Smart Set* (September): 65–68.
"Whom Mince Pie Hath Joined Together: The Story of a Starving Girl and a Thanksgiving Dinner in Paris." *Ladies' Home Journal* 30 (November): 10, 71–73.
1914. "The Rules of the Institution." *Harper's Monthly Magazine* 128 (Dec 1913–May 1914): 198–208.
"Looking After Clara: What Happened to Mr. Stephen Blatchford When He Decided to Marry." *Ladies' Home Journal* 31 (August): 9, 35–37.
1915. "The Manager of Crystal Sulphur Springs." *Harper's Monthly Magazine* 131 (June–November): 176–184.
"Agnes of Cape's End. A Complete Novel in Miniature." *The American Magazine* 80.3 (September): 6–7, 67–72.
1916. "Unveiling Brenda." *Harper's Monthly Magazine* 133 (June): 14–16.
"'Finality' in Freeport." *Pictorial Review* 17 (July): 14–15, 32.
"Her Heritage of Ideals." *The Canadian Magazine* 48.1 (November): 63–68. (Also published as "The Lie God Forgave" in an unidentified magazine, pp. 14–23, Susan Glaspell Papers, Berg Collection, New York Public Library.)
"Miss Jessie's Trip Abroad." *Woman's Home Companion* 48 (November): 9–10, 79.

1917. "The Hearing Ear." *Harper's Monthly Magazine* 134 (December 1916–May 1917): 233–241.

"A Jury of Her Peers." *Everyweek* (March 5): np.

"Everything You Want to Plant." *Magazine Selection* (August 12): 5–7, 15.

"A Matter of Gesture." *McClure's Magazine* 49 (August): 36, 38, 65–67.

1918. "Poor Ed." *Liberator* 1 (March): 24–29.

"Beloved Husband." *Harper's Monthly Magazine* 136 (December 1917–May 1918): 675–679.

"Good Luck." *Good Housekeeping* 67: 44–46, 122–126.

"The Busy Duck." *Harper's Monthly Magazine* 137 (June–November): 828–836.

1919. "Pollen." *Harper's Monthly Magazine* 138 (December 1918–May 1919): 446–451.

1920. "The Escape." *Harper's Monthly Magazine* 140 (December 1919–May 1920): 29–38.

"The Nervous Pig." *Harper's Monthly Magazine* 140 (December 1919–May 1920): 309–320.

1921. "His Smile." *Pictorial Review* (January): 15–16, 91.

1923. "Dwellers on Parnassos." *The New Republic* (January 17): 198–200.

1926. "The Faithless Shepherd." *Cornhill* 60 (January): 51–71.

1927. "A Rose in the Sand. The Salvation of a Lonely Soul." *Pall Mall Magazine*: 45–51.

1945. Glaspell, Susan. "Cleo." Typescript (incomplete) of short story, dated Oct 26, Nov 27, 1945. Susan Glaspell Papers. Berg Collection. New York Public Library. 21 pages.

1946. "Government Goat." (1919). *Social Insight through Short Stories.* Ed. Josephine Strode. 43–61.

1993. *Lifted Masks and Other Works* (1912) ("At Twilight," "Freckles McGrawth," "From A to Z," "His America," "For the Love of the Hills," "How the Prince Saw America," "One of Those Impossible Americans," "Out There," "The Anarchist," "The Last Sixty Minutes," "The Man of Flesh and Blood," "The Plea," and "The Preposterous Motive.") Ed. Eric S. Rabkin. Ann Arbor: University of Michigan Press.

2010. *Her America: "A Jury of Her Peers" and Other Stories by Susan Glaspell.* ("Looking After Clara," "The Manager of Crystal Sulphur Springs," "Unveiling Brenda," "A Jury of Her Peers," "A Matter of Gesture," "Poor Ed," "Beloved Husband," "The Busy Duck," "Pollen," "Government Goat," "The Nervous Pig," "A Rose in the Sand.") Eds. Patricia L. Bryan and Martha C. Carpenter. Iowa City: University of Iowa Press.

Undated Short Stories

"An Approximation." *The Smart Set.* 85–91.

"Are We Birds? Are We Fishes?" Typescript of short story. Susan Glaspell Papers, Berg Collection, New York Public Library.

"Bastards I Have Known." Unpublished typescript (incomplete) of short story. Susan Glaspell Papers, Berg Collection, New York Public Library. 4 pages.

"Bound." pp. 107–113. Source unknown. Susan Glaspell Papers, Berg Collection, New York Public Library.

"Coming Years." Unpublished typescript. Susan Glaspell Papers, Berg Collection, New York Public Library. 12 pages.

"Faint Trails." Unpublished typescript. Susan Glaspell Papers, Berg Collection, New York Public Library. 21 pages.

"First Aid Teacher." Unpublished typescript. Susan Glaspell Papers, Berg Collection, New York Public Library. 16 pages.

"His Grandmother's Funeral." *Metropolitan Magazine*: 737–743.

"Linda." Unpublished typescript. Susan Glaspell Papers, Berg Collection, New York Public Library. 6 pages.

Essays and Miscellanea

1925. "Last Days in Greece." *Greek Coins.* New York: George Doran. 31–49.

1942b. "Susan Glaspell Says We Need Books Today as Never Before." *Chicago Sunday Tribune.* 6 December 1942. np.

"Stones That Once Were [a Temple.]" Typescript of poem. Undated. Susan Glaspell Papers, Berg Collection, New York Public Library.

Susan Glaspell's comments on "My Life in Art" by Stanislavski. Holograph and typewritten notes, unsigned and undated. Susan Glaspell Papers, Berg Collection, New York Public Library. 4 pages.

"The Busy Duck." Typescript of poem. Undated. Susan Glaspell Papers, Berg Collection, New York Public Library.

Secondary Sources

A Jury of Her Peers. 1981. Dir. Sally Heckel. Perf. Diane de Lorian, Dorothy Lancaster. Texture Films.

Aarons, Victoria. 1986. "A Community of Women: Surviving Marriage in the Wilderness." *Rendezvous. Idaho State University Journal of Arts and Letters* 22.2: 3–11.

Alberola, Nieves, and Yvonne Shafer, eds. 2007. *Nimiedades para la eternidad.* Castellón, Spain: Ellago Ediciones.

Alkalay-Gut, Karen. 1984. "Jury of Her Peers: The Importance of *Trifles.*" *Studies in Short Fiction* 21.1: 1–9.

_____ 1995. "Murder and Marriage: Another Look at *Trifles.*" *Susan Glaspell: Essays on Her Theater and Fiction.* Ed. Linda Ben-Zvi. Ann Arbor: University of Michigan Press. 71–81.

Ammons, Elizabeth. 1991. "The New Woman as Cultural Symbol and Social Reality. Six Women Writers' Perspectives." *1915: The Cultural Moment: The New Politics, the New Woman, the New Psychology, the New Art, and the New Theater in America.* Eds. Adele Heller and Lois Rudnick. New Brunswick, New Jersey: Rutgers University Press. 82–97.

Ardener, Shirley, ed. 1975. *Perceiving Women.* London: Malaby Press.

Aston, Elaine. 1995. *An Introduction to Feminism and Theatre.* London and New York: Routledge.

Bablet, Denis. 1981. *The Theatre of Edward Gordon Craig.* London: Methuen.

Bach, Gerhard. 1978. "Susan Glaspell — Provincetown Player." *Great Lakes Review* 4.2: 31–43.

_____ 1995. "Susan Glaspell: Mapping the Domains of Critical Revision." *Susan Glaspell: Essays on Her Theater and Fiction.* Ed. Linda Ben-Zvi. Ann Arbor: University of Michigan Press. 239–258.

Bachelard, Gaston. 1994. *The Poetics of Space.* Trans. Maria Jolas. Boston: Beacon Press. (1958. *La Poetique de L'espace.* Paris: Presses Universitaires.)

Barlow, Judith E. 1994 (1985). "Introduction." *Plays by American Women 1900–1930.* Ed. Judith Barlow. New York: Applause. ix–xxxiii.

_____ 1995. "Susan's Sisters: The 'Other' Women Writers of the Provincetown Players." *Susan Glaspell: Essays on Her Theater and Fiction.* Ed. Linda Ben-Zvi. Ann Arbor: University of Michigan Press. 259–300.

Barrett, Michèle. 1985. "Ideology and the Cultural Production of Gender." *Feminist Criticism and Social Change. Sex, Class, and Race in Literature and Culture.* Eds. Judith Newton and Deborah Rosenfelt. London and New York: Methuen. 65–85.

Baxandall, Rosalyn, Linda Gordon and Susan Reverby, eds. 1976. *America's Working Women. A Documentary History–1600 to the Present.* New York: Vintage Books.

Beard, Rick, and Leslie Cohen Berlowitz, eds. 1993. *Greenwich Village: Culture and Counterculture.* New Brunswick, NJ: Rutgers University Press.

Belsey, Catherine. 1985. "Constructing the Subject/ Deconstructing the Text." *Feminist Criticism and Social Change: Sex, Class, and Race in Literature and Culture.* Eds. Judith Newton and Deborah Rosenfelt. London and New York: Methuen. 45–64.

Ben-Zvi, Linda. 1982. "Susan Glaspell and Eugene O'Neill." *The Eugene O'Neill Newsletter* 6.2: 21–29.

_____ 1986. "Susan Glaspell and Eugene O'Neill: The Imagery of Gender." *The Eugene O'Neill Newsletter* 10.1: 22–27.

_____ 1989. "'Home Sweet Home': Deconstructing the Masculine Myth of the Frontier in Modern American Drama." *The Frontier Experience and the American Dream: Essays on American Literature.* Eds. David Mogen, Mark Busby and Paul Bryant. Texas: Texas A & M University Press. 217–225.

_____ 1992. "Murder, She Wrote: The Genesis of Susan Glaspell's *Trifles.*" *Theatre Journal* 44: 141–162.

_____ 1995a. "O'Neill's Cape(d) Compatriot." *The Eugene O'Neill Review* 19.1–2: 129–137.

_____ (ed.) 1995b. *Susan Glaspell: Essays on Her Theater and Fiction.* Ann Arbor: University of Michigan Press.

_____ 2005. *Susan Glaspell: Her Life and Times.* Oxford and New York: Oxford University Press.

_____ 2006. "The Political as Personal in the Writing of Susan Glaspell." *Disclosing Intertextualities: The Stories, Plays, and Novels of Susan Glaspell.* Eds. Martha C. Carpentier and Barbara Ozieblo. Amsterdam and New York: Rodopi. 275–294.

Bigsby, C. W. E. 1983 (1982). *A Critical Introduction to Twentieth-Century American Drama. Volume One, 1900–1940.* Cambridge: Cambridge University Press.

_____ 1987. "Introduction." *Plays by Susan Glaspell.* Ed. C. W. E. Bigsby. Cambridge: Cambridge University Press. 1–31.

Björkman, Edwin. 1920. "Miss Glaspell's Plays." *The Freeman.* August 11: 518–520.

Black, Cheryl. 2002. *The Women of Provincetown, 1915–1922.* Tuscaloosa, AL, and London: University of Alabama Press.

_____ 2005. "Making Queer New Things: Queer Identities in the Life and Dramaturgy of Susan Glaspell." *Journal of Dramatic Theory and Criticism* 20.1 (Fall): 49–64.

Bondi, Liz. 1993. "Locating Identity Politics." *Place and the Politics of Identity.* Eds. Michael Keith and Steve Pile. London and New York: Routledge. 84–101.

Bottoms, Stephen J. 1998. "Building on the Abyss: Susan Glaspell's *The Verge* in Production." *Theatre Topics* 8.2 (September): 127–147.

Boyce, Neith. 1929. *Winter's Night* (1916). *Fifty More Contemporary One-Act Plays.* Ed. Frank Shay. New York: Appleton. 40–46.

Brecht, Bertolt. 1997 (1964). "Short Description of a New Way of Acting which Produces an Alienation Effect" (1940). *Brecht on Theatre: The Development of an Aesthetic.* Ed. and trans. John Willett. London: Metheun. 136–147.

Brockett, Oscar G. 1995 (1968). *History of the Theatre.* Boston: Allyn and Bacon.

Brook, Peter. 1972 (1968). *The Empty Space.* London: Penguin.

_____ 1989 (1987). *The Shifting Point: Forty Years of Theatrical Exploration, 1946–87.* London: Methuen.

Brown, Milton W. 1991. "The Armory Show and Its Aftermath." *1915. The Cultural Moment: The New Politics, the New Woman, the New Psychology, the New Art, and the New Theater in America.* Eds. Adele Heller and Lois Rudnick. New Brunswick, NJ: Rutgers University Press. 164–184.

Bryan, Patricia L. 1997. "Stories in Fiction and in Fact: Susan Glaspell's 'A Jury of Her Peers' and the 1901 Murder Trial of Margaret Hossack." *Stanford Law Review* 49.6: 1293–1363.

_____ 2006. "Foreshadowing 'A Jury of Her Peers': Susan Glaspell's 'The Plea' and the Case of John Wesley Elkins." *Susan Glaspell: New Directions in Critical Inquiry.* Ed. Martha C. Carpentier. Cambridge: Cambridge Scholars Press. 45–65.

Bryan, Patricia L., and Thomas Wolf. 2005. *Midnight Assassin: A Murder in America's Heartland*. Chapel Hill, NC: Algonquin Books.

Bürger, Peter. 1992 (1984). *Theory of the Avant-Garde*. Trans. Michael Shaw. Minneapolis: University of Minnesota Press. (1974. *Theorie der Avantgarde*. Frankfurt a. M.: Suhrkamp.)

Burke, Sally. 1996. *American Feminist Playwrights: A Critical History*. New York: Twayne Publishers.

Busby, Mark, and David Morgen, and Paul Bryant. 1989. "Introduction: Frontier Writing as a 'Great Tradition' of American Literature." *The Frontier Experience and the American Dream: Essays on American Literature*. Eds. David Mogen, Mark Busby and Paul Bryant. Texas: Texas A & M University Press. 3–12.

Butler, Judith. 1993. *Bodies That Matter: On the Discursive Limits of Sex*. New York and London: Routledge.

_____ 1999 (1990). *Gender Trouble: Feminism and the Subversion of Identity*. London and New York: Routledge.

Capo, Beth Widmaier. 2004. "Can this Woman Be Saved? Birth Control and Marriage in Modern American Literature." *Modern Language Studies* 34.1–2: 29–41.

Carlson, Marvin. 2004 (1996). *Performance: A Critical Introduction*. New York and London: Routledge.

Carpentier, Martha C. 2001. *The Major Novels of Susan Glaspell*. Gainesville: University Press of Florida.

_____ 2006a. "Apollonian Form and Dionysian Excess in Susan Glaspell's Drama and Fiction." *Disclosing Intertextualities: The Stories, Plays, and Novels of Susan Glaspell*. Eds. Martha C. Carpentier and Barbara Ozieblo. Amsterdam and New York: Rodopi. 35–50.

_____ (ed.) 2006b. *Susan Glaspell: New Directions in Critical Inquiry*. Cambridge: Cambridge Scholars Press.

Carpentier, Martha C., and Barbara Ozieblo, eds. 2006. *Disclosing Intertextualities: The Stories, Plays, and Novels of Susan Glaspell*. Amsterdam and New York: Rodopi.

Case, Sue-Ellen. 1988. *Feminism and Theatre*. London: Macmillan.

Chaudhuri, Una. 2000 (1995). *Staging Place: The Geography of Modern Drama*. Ann Arbor: University of Michigan Press.

Chávez-Candelaria, Cordelia. 1997. "The 'Wild-Zone' Thesis as Gloss in Chicana Literary Study" (1993). *Feminisms: An Anthology of Literary Theory and Criticism*. Eds. Robyn R. Warhol and Diane Price Herndl. Houndmills, Basingstoke, Hampshire: Macmillan. 248–256.

Chinoy, Helen Krich. 1987. "Where Are the Women Playwrights?" *Women in American Theatre*. Eds. Helen Krich Chinoy and Linda Walsh Jenkins. New York: Theatre Communications Group. 129–131.

Chinoy, Helen Krich, and Linda Walsh Jenkins, eds. 1987. *Women in American Theatre*. New York: Theatre Communications Group.

Collins, J. H. 1917. Letter. *The Masses*, 9.10 74 (August): 30.

Conzen, Michael P., ed. 1994. *The Making of the American Landscape*. London and New York: Routledge.

Corbin, John. 1919. "Susan Glaspell's *Bernice*." *The New York Times*: np.

Cott, Nancy. 1987. *The Grounding of Modern Feminism*. New Haven: Yale University Press.

Cott, Nancy, and Jeanne Boydston, Ann Braude, Lori Ginzberg and Molly Lad-Taylor, eds. 1972. *Root of Bitterness: Documents of the Social History of American Women*. Boston: Northeastern University Press.

Craig, Edward Gordon. 1983. *Craig on Theatre*. Ed. J. Michael Walton. London: Methuen.

Czerepinski, Jackie. 1995. "Beyond *The Verge*: Absent Heroines in the Plays of Susan Glaspell." *Susan Glaspell: Essays on Her Theater and Fiction*. Ed. Linda Ben-Zvi. Ann Arbor: University of Michigan Press. 145–154.

Dell, Floyd. 1969 (1933). *Homecoming: An Autobiography*. Dallas: Kennikat Press.

Demastes, William. 1996. "Preface: American Dramatic Realisms, Viable Ways of Thought." *Realism and the American Tradition*. Ed. William Demastes. Tuscaloosa: University of Alabama Press. ix–xvii.

Deutsch, Helen, and Stella Hanau. 1972 (1931). *The Provincetown: A Story of the Theatre*. New York: Russell and Russell.

Diamond, Elin. 1988. "Brechtian Theory/ Feminist Theory: Toward a *Gestic* Feminist Criticism." *The Drama Review* 32: 82–94.

_____ 1989. "Mimesis, Mimicry, and the 'True-Real.'" *Modern Drama* 32.1: 58–72.

_____ 1995. "The Garden is a Mess." *The Theatrical Gamut. Notes for a Post-Beckettian Stage*. Ed. Enoch Brater. Ann Arbor: University of Michigan Press. 121–139.

_____ 1997. *Unmaking Mimesis: Essays on Feminism and Theater*. London and New York: Routledge.

Dickey, Jerry, and J. Ellen Gainor. 2005. "Susan Glaspell and Sophie Treadwell: Staging Feminism and Modernism, 1915–1941." *A Companion to Twentieth-Century American Drama*. Ed. David Krasner. Oxford: Blackwell. 34–52.

Dolan, Jill. 1988. *The Feminist Spectator as Critic*. Ann Arbor: University of Michigan Press.

Duneer, Anita. 2006. "On the Verge of a Breakthrough: Projections of Escape from the Attic and the Thwarted Tower in Charlotte Perkins Gilman's 'The Yellow Wallpaper' and Susan Glaspell's *The Verge*." *The Journal of American Drama and Theatre* 18.1: 34–53.

Dymkowski, Christine. 1988. "On the Edge: The Plays of Susan Glaspell." *Modern Drama* 31.1 (March): 91–105.

Egan, Leonora Rust. 1994. *Provincetown as a Stage: Provincetown, the Provincetown Players, and the Discovery of Eugene O'Neill*. Orleans, MA: Parnassus Imprints.

Eisenhauer, Drew. 2006. "She and She: Rachel Crothers and Susan Glaspell's Turn to Playwriting." *Disclosing Intertextualities: The Stories, Plays, and Novels of Susan Glaspell*. Eds. Martha C. Carpentier and Barbara Ozieblo. Amsterdam and New York: Rodopi. 115–135.

Elam, Keir. 2001 (1980). *The Semiotics of Theater and Drama*. London: Methuen.

Esslin, Martin. 1988 (1987). *The Field of Drama: How the Signs of Drama Create Meaning on Stage and Screen*. London: Methuen.

Farjeon, Herbert. 1925. "Susan Glaspell's Play." *The Weekly Westminster*. April 11: 708.

Fernández Morales, Marta. 2002. "The Two Spheres in Susan Glaspell's *Trifles* and *The Verge*." *Staging a Cultural Paradigm: The Political and the Personal in American Drama*. Eds. Barbara Ozieblo and Miriam López-Rodríguez. Bruxelles, Bern, Berlin, Frankfurt, New York, Oxford, Wien: Peter Lang. 163–176.

Ferris, Lesley. 1989. *Acting Women: Images of Women in Theatre*. New York: New York University Press.

Fetterley, Judith. 1986. "Reading about Reading: 'A Jury of Her Peers,' 'The Murders of the Rue Morgue,' and 'The Yellow Wallpaper." *Gender and Reading: Essays on Readers, Texts and Contexts*. Ed. Elizabeth A. Flynn. Baltimore: John Hopkins Press. 147–164.

Fischer, Jerilyn. 2003. "Women Righting Wrongs: Morality and Justice in Susan Glaspell's *Trifles* (1916)." *Women in Literature: Reading through the Lens of Gender*. Eds. Jerilyn Fischer and Ellen S. Silber. Westport, CT: Greenwood Press. 289–292.

Fischer-Lichte, Erika. 1992. *The Semiotics of Theater*. Trans. Jeremy Gaines and Doris L. Jones. Indianapolis: Indiana University Press. (1983. *Semiotik des Theaters*. Tübingen: Narr.)

Fletcher, Caroline Violet. 2006. "'Rules of the Institution': Susan Glaspell and Sisterhood." *Disclosing Intertextualities: The Stories, Plays, and Novels of Susan Glaspell*. Eds. Martha C. Carpentier and Barbara Ozieblo. Amsterdam and New York: Rodopi. 239–256.

Forte, Jeanie. 1989. "Realism, Narrative, and the Feminist Playwright — A Problem of Reception." *Modern Drama* 32.1: 115–128.

Foucault, Michel. 1988. *Power/Knowledge: Selected Interviews and Other Writings 1972–1977*. Ed. Colin Gordon. Suffolk: Harvester Press. 63–77.

Fowler, Dorothy Heald. 1928. "I Remember the Young Susan." Newspaper Clipping, edited by Helen Cowles Lecron: np. Susan Glaspell Papers, Berg Collection, New York Public Library.

France, Rachel. 1987. "Apropos of Women and the Folk Play." *Women in American Theatre.* Eds. Helen Krich Chinoy and Linda Walsh Jenkins. New York: Theatre Communications Group. 145–152.

Frank, Steve. 2003. "On 'The Verge' of a New Form: *The Cabinet of Dr. Caligari* and Susan Glaspell's Experiments in *The Verge.*" *Experimenters, Rebels, and Disparate Voices: The Theatre of the 1920s Celebrates American Diversity.* Eds. Arthur Gewirtz and James J. Kolb. Wesport, CT, and London: Praeger. 119–129.

Freedman, Estelle B. 1983. "The New Woman: Changing Views of Women in the 1920s." *Decades of Discontent: The Women's Movement, 1920–1940.* Eds. Lois Scharf and Joan M. Jensen. Westport, CT, and London: Greenwood Press. 21–42.

Friedman, Sharon. 1984. "Feminism as Theme in Twentieth-Century American Drama." *American Studies* 25: 69–89.

_____ 2006. "Honor or Virtue Unrewarded: Susan Glaspell's Parodic Challenge to Ideologies of Sexual Conduct and the Discourse of Intimacy." *New England Theatre Journal* 17: 35–58.

Fuchs, Eleanor, and Una Chaudhuri, eds. 2002. *Land/Scape/Theater.* Ann Arbor: University of Michigan Press.

Fuller, Margaret. 1999. *Woman in the Nineteenth Century* (1845). Ed. Joslyn T. Pine. Dover thrift editions. Mineola, NY: Dover.

Gainor, J. Ellen. 1989. "A Stage of Her Own: Susan Glaspell's *The Verge* and Women's Dramaturgy." *Journal of American Drama and Theatre* 1.1 (Spring): 79–99.

_____ 1995. "*Chains of Dew* and the Drama of Birth Control." *Susan Glaspell: Essays on Her Theater and Fiction.* Ed. Linda Ben-Zvi. Ann Arbor: University of Michigan Press. 165–193.

_____ 1996. "The Provincetown Players' Experiments with Realism." *Realism and the American Tradition.* Ed. William Demastes. Tuscaloosa: University of Alabama Press. 53–70.

_____ 2001. *Susan Glaspell in Context: American Theatre, Culture, and Politics, 1915–1948.* Ann Arbor: University of Michigan Press.

Galbus, Julia. 2000. "Susan Glaspell's *The Verge*: A Socratic Quest to Reinvent Form and Escape Plato's Cave." *Journal of Dramatic Theory and Criticism* 15.1: 81–95.

Gardiner, Karen H. 2006. "Reaching for 'Out There': Susan Glaspell's Rhetoric of the Female Artist." *Disclosing Intertextualities: The Stories, Plays, and Novels of Susan Glaspell.* Eds. Martha C. Carpentier and Barbara Ozieblo. Amsterdam and New York: Rodopi. 183–200.

Garner, Staton B. Jr. 1994. *Bodied Spaces: Phenomenology and Performance in Contemporary Drama.* Ithaca, NY: Cornell University Press.

Gelb, Arthur, and Barbara Geld. 2000. *O'Neill: Life with Monte Cristo.* New York and London: Applause.

George, Rosemary Marangoly. 1999 (1996). *The Politics of Home: Postcolonial Relocations and Twentieth-Century Fiction.* Berkeley: University of California Press.

Gilbert, Sandra M., and Susan Gubar. 1979. *The Madwoman in the Attic: The Woman Writer and the Nineteenth-Century Literary Imagination.* New Haven and London: Yale University Press.

_____ 1988. *No Man's Land: The Place of the Woman Writer in the Twentieth Century.* Vol. 1: *The War of Words.* New Haven: Yale University Press.

Goldberg, Isaac. 1922. "Susan Glaspell." *The Drama of Transition: Native and Exotic Playcraft.* Cincinnati: Stewart Kidd Co. 472–481.

Hallgreen, Sherri. 1995. "'The Law Is the Law and a Bad Stove Is a Bad Stove': Subversive Justice and Layers of Collusion in 'A Jury of Her Peers.'" *Violence, Silence, and Anger: Women's Writing as Transgression.* Ed. Deidre Lashgari. Charlottesville: University Press of Virginia. 203–218.

Hapgood, Hutchins. 1939. *A Victorian in the Modern World*. New York: Harcourt, Brace and Company.

Harvey, David. 1993. "Class Relations, Social Justice and the Politics of Difference." *Place and the Politics of Identity*. Eds. Michael Keith and Steve Pile. London and New York: Routledge. 41–66.

Hedges, Elaine. 1995. "Small Things Reconsidered: 'A Jury of Her Peers.'" *Susan Glaspell: Essays on Her Theater and Fiction*. Ed. Linda Ben-Zvi. Ann Arbor: University of Michigan Press. 49–70.

Hedges, M. H. 1923. "Miss Glaspell's Vision of Life." *The Nation*, April 4: 393.

Heller, Adele, and Lois Rudnick, eds. 1991. *1915. The Cultural Moment: The New Politics, the New Woman, the New Psychology, the New Art, and the New Theater in America*. New Brunswick, NJ: Rutgers University Press.

Hinz-Bode, Kristina. 2006a. "Social Rebels? Male Characters in Susan Glaspell's Writings." *Disclosing Intertextualities. The Stories, Plays, and Novels of Susan Glaspell*. Eds. Martha C. Carpentier and Barbara Ozieblo. Amsterdam and New York: Rodopi. 201–222.

_____ 2006b. *Susan Glaspell and the Anxiety of Expression. Language and Isolation in the Plays*. Jefferson, NC: McFarland.

_____ 2006c. "Susan Glaspell and the Epistemological Crisis of Modernity: Truth, Knowledge, and Art in Selected Novels." *Susan Glaspell: New Directions in Critical Inquiry*. Ed. Martha C. Carpentier. Cambridge: Cambridge Scholars Press. 89–108.

Holstein, Suzy Clarkson. 2003. "Silent Justice in a Different Key: Glaspell's *Trifles*." *Midwest Quarterly: A Journal of Contemporary Thought*. Spring 44.3: 282–290.

Jacobson, Doranne. 1995. *Presidents and First Ladies of the United States*. New York: Todtri.

Jones, Ann. 1980. *Women Who Kill*. New York: Holt, Rinehart and Winston.

Jones, Robert Edmond. 1985 (1941). *The Dramatic Imagination: Reflections and Speculations on the Art of Theatre*. New York: Theatre Arts Books.

Kanthak, John F. 2003. "Feminism in Motion: Pushing the 'Wild Zone' Thesis into the Fourth Dimension." *Literature Interpretation Theory* 14: 149–163.

Keith, Michael, and Steve Pile. 1993. "Conclusion: Towards New Radical Geographies." *Place and the Politics of Identity*. Eds. Michael Keith and Steve Pile. London and New York: Routledge. 220–226.

Kenton, Edna. 1997. "The Provincetown Players and the Playwrights' Theatre, 1915–1922." *The Eugene O'Neill Review* 21.1–2 (Spring–Fall): 15–160.

Kern, Stephen. 1983. *The Culture of Time and Space, 1880–1910*. Cambridge: Harvard University Press.

Kirby, Andrew. 1982. *The Politics of Location: An Introduction*. London and New York: Methuen.

Kolb, Deborah S. 1975. "The Rise and Fall of the New Woman in American Drama." *Educational Theatre Journal* 27.2: 149–160.

Kolin, Philip C. 1988. "Therapists in Susan Glaspell's *Suppressed Desires* and David Rabe's *In the Boom Boom Room*." *Notes on Contemporary Literature*. 18.5 (November): 2–3.

Kolodny, Annette. 1984. *The Land Before Her: Fantasy and Experience of the American Frontiers, 1630–1860*. Chapel Hill and London: University of North Carolina Press.

_____ 1986. "A Map for Rereading. Gender and the Interpretation of Literary Texts." *The New Feminist Criticism: Essays on Women, Literature, and Theory*. Ed. Elaine Showalter. New York: Pantheon Books. 46–62.

Koprince, Susan. 2006. "The Narrow House: Glaspell's *Trifles* and Wharton's *Ethan Frome*." *Disclosing Intertextualities: The Stories, Plays, and Novels of Susan Glaspell*. Eds. Martha C. Carpentier and Barbara Ozieblo. Amsterdam and New York: Rodopi. 63–78.

Larabee, Ann E. 1990. "'Meeting the Outside Face to Face': Susan Glaspell, Djuna Barnes, and O'Neill's *The Emperor Jones*." *Modern American Drama: The Female Canon*. Ed. June Schlueter. Rutherford, NJ: Farleigh Dickinson University Press. 77–85.

Laughlin, Karen. 1995. "Conflict of Interest: The Ideology of Authorship in *Alison's House.*" *Susan Glaspell: Essays on Her Theater and Fiction.* Ed. Linda Ben-Zvi. Ann Arbor: University of Michigan Press. 219–235.

Lefèbvre, Henri. 1991. *The Production of Space.* Trans. Donald Nicholson-Smith. London: Basil Blackwell. (1974. *La production de l'espace.* Paris: Gallimard, Collection Idées.)

Leslie, D. A. 1997. "Femininity, Post-Fordism, and the 'New Traditionalism'" (1993). *Space, Gender, Knowledge: Feminist Readings.* Eds. Linda McDowell and Joanne P. Sharp. London: Arnold. 300–317.

Leuchtenberg, William E. 1958. *The Perils of Prosperity, 1914–32.* Chicago and London: University of Chicago Press.

Lewis, Peirce F. 1979. "Axioms for Reading the Landscapes. Some Guides to the American Scene." *The Interpretation of Ordinary Landscapes: Geographical Essays.* Ed. D. W. Meinig. New York: Oxford University Press. 11–32.

Lewisohn, Ludwig. 1922. "Susan Glaspell." *The Drama and the Stage.* New York: Harcourt, Brace and Company. 102–110.

Lincoln, Abraham. 1989. "First Inaugural Address" (1861). *Speeches and Writings: 1859–1865. Speeches, Letters, and Miscellaneous Writings. Presidential Messages and Proclamations.* Ed. Don E. Fehrenbacher. United States of America: The Library of America. 215–224.

Loraux, Nicole. 1991. *Tragic Ways of Killing a Woman.* Trans. Anthony Foster. Cambridge: Harvard University Press. (1985. *Façons tragiques de tuer une femme.* Paris: Hachette.)

Makowsky, Veronica. 1993. *Susan Glaspell's Century of American Women: A Critical Interpretation of Her Work.* New York and Oxford: Oxford University Press.

_____ 1999. "Susan Glaspell and Modernism." *The Cambridge Companion to American Women Playwrights.* Ed. Brenda Murphy. Cambridge: Cambridge University Press. 49–65.

Malpede, Karen. 1995. "Reflections on *The Verge.*" *Susan Glaspell: Essays on Her Theater and Fiction.* Ed. Linda Ben-Zvi. Ann Arbor: University of Michigan Press. 123–127.

Manuel, Carme. 2000. "Susan Glaspell's *Trifles* (1916): Women's Conspiracy of Silence Beyond the Melodrama of Beset Womanhood." *Revista de Estudios Norteamericanos* 7: 55–65.

Mason, Jeffrey D., and J. Ellen Gainor, eds. 1999. *Performing America: Cultural Nationalism in American Theater.* Ann Arbor: University of Michigan Press.

Massey, Doreen. 1995. "Places and Their Pasts." *History Workshop Journal* 39 (Spring): 182–191.

_____ 1998 (1994). *Space, Place, and Gender.* Cambridge: Polite Press.

Matthews, Glenna. 1992. *The Rise of the Public Woman: Woman's Power and Woman's Place in the United States, 1630–1970.* New York and Oxford: Oxford University Press.

May, Henry F. 1960. *The End of American Innocence: A Study of the First Years of Our Own Time, 1912–1917.* London: Jonathan Cape.

McAuley, Gay. 2000 (1999). *Space in Performance: Making Meaning in the Theatre.* Ann Arbor: University of Michigan Press.

McBride, Kecia Driver. 2006. "Silence and the Struggle for Representational Space in the Art of Susan Glaspell." *Disclosing Intertextualities: The Stories, Plays, and Novels of Susan Glaspell.* Eds. Martha C. Carpentier and Barbara Ozieblo. Amsterdam and New York: Rodopi. 159–181.

McDowell, Linda, and Joanne P. Sharp. 1997. "Introduction to Section Five: Gendering Everyday Spaces." *Space, Gender, Knowledge: Feminist Readings.* Eds. Linda McDowell and Joanne P. Sharp. London: Arnold. 263–268.

McKinnie, Michael. 2003. "The State of This Place: Convictions, the Courthouse, and the Geography of Performance in Belfast." *Modern Drama* 46.4. Special Issue "Space and the Geographies of the Theatre." Ed. Joanne Tompkins: 580–597.

McKnight, Jeannie. 1980. "American Dream, Nightmare Underside: Diaries, Letters, and Fiction of Women on the American Frontier." *Women, Women Writers, and The West.* Eds. L. L. Lee and Merrill Lewis. Troy, NY: Whinston Publishing. 25–44.

Meinig, D. W. 1979. "Introduction." *The Interpretation of Ordinary Landscapes: Geographical Essays.* Ed. D. W. Meinig. New York: Oxford University Press. 1–10.

Mohanty, Chandra Talpede. 1997. "Feminist Encounters: Locating the Politics of Experience" (1992). *Space, Gender, Knowledge: Feminist Readings.* Eds. Linda McDowell and Joanne P. Sharp. London: Arnold. 82–97.

Molnar, Marie. 2006. "Antigone Redux: Female Voice and the State in Susan Glaspell's *Inheritors.*" *Susan Glaspell: New Directions in Critical Inquiry.* Ed. Martha C. Carpentier. Cambridge: Cambridge Scholars Press. 37–44.

Morris, Jan. 2000 (1999). *Lincoln. A Foreigner's Quest.* London: Penguin Books.

Moy, James S. 1995. "Asian American Visibility: Touring Fierce Racial Geographies." *Staging Difference: Cultural Pluralism in American Theatre and Drama.* Ed. Marc Maufort. Bruxelles, Bern, Berlin, Frankfurt, New York, Oxford, Wien: Peter Lang. 191–200.

Murphy, Brenda. 1987. *American Realism and America Drama, 1880–1940.* Cambridge: Cambridge University Press.

_____ 2005. *The Provincetown Players and the Culture of Modernity.* Cambridge: Cambridge University Press.

Mustazza, Leonard. 1989. "Generic Translation and Thematic Shift in Susan Glaspell's 'Trifles' and "A Jury of Her Peers." *Studies in Short Fiction* 26.4 (Fall): 489–496.

Nelligan, Liza Maeve. 1995. "The Haunting Beauty from the Life We've Left: A Contextual Reading of *Trifles* and *The Verge.*" *Susan Glaspell: Essays on Her Theater and Fiction.* Ed. Linda Ben-Zvi. Ann Arbor: University of Michigan Press. 85–104.

Nester, Nancy L. 1997. "The Agoraphobic Imagination: The Protagonist Who Murders and the Critics Who Praise Her." *American Drama* Spring 6.2: 1–24.

Noe, Marcia. 1981. "Region as a Metaphor in the Plays of Susan Glaspell." *Western Illinois Regional Studies* 4.1: 77–85.

_____ 1983. *Susan Glaspell: Voice from the Heartland.* Western Illinois Monograph Series. Macomb: Western Illinois University Press.

_____ 1995. "The Verge: *L'Écriture Fémenine* at the Provincetown." *Susan Glaspell: Essays on Her Theater and Fiction.* Ed. Linda Ben-Zvi. Ann Arbor: University of Michigan Press. 129–142.

_____ 2002. "The New Woman in the Plays of Susan Glaspell." *Staging a Cultural Paradigm. The Political and the Personal in American Drama.* Eds. Barbara Ozieblo and Miriam López-Rodríguez. Bruxelles, Bern, Berlin, Frankfurt, New York, Oxford, Wien: Peter Lang. 149–162.

Noe, Marcia, and Robert Lloyd Marlowe. 2005. "*Suppressed Desires* and *Tickless Time*: An Intertextual Critique of Modernity." *American Drama* 14.1: 1–14.

Ozieblo, Barbara. 1990. "Rebellion and Rejection: The Plays of Susan Glaspell." *Modern American Drama: The Female Canon.* Ed. June Schlueter. Rutherford, NJ: Farleigh Dickinson University Press. 66–76.

_____ 1994a. "Love and Envy in Provincetown: Susan Glaspell, George Cram Cook, and Eugene O'Neill." *Amor, odio y violencia en la literatura norteamericana.* Alcalá de Henares, Spain: Servicio de Publicaciones de la Universidad de Alcalá de Henares. 215–233.

_____ (ed.) 1994b. *The Provincetown Players: A Choice of the Shorter Works.* Sheffield: Sheffield Academic Press.

_____ 1995. "Suppression and Society in Susan Glaspell's Theater." *Susan Glaspell: Essays on Her Theater and Fiction.* Ed. Linda Ben-Zvi. Ann Arbor: University of Michigan Press. 105–122.

_____ 1998. "Radical Feminist or Handmaiden? Fact and Fiction in Susan Glaspell's Life." *Writing Lives: American Biography and Autobiography.* Eds. Hans Bak and Hans Krabbendam. Amsterdam: VU University Press. 192–200.

_____ 2000. *Susan Glaspell: A Critical Biography.* Chapel Hill and London: University of North Carolina Press.

_____ 2002. "Una imagen propia: La innovación protagonizada por dramaturgas norteamericanas de principios de siglo." *Voces e imágenes de mujeres en el teatro del siglo XXI*. Eds.
Rosa García Rayego and Eulalia Piñero Gil. Madrid: Editorial Complutense. 15–44.

_____ 2006a. "Silenced Mothers and Questing Daughters in Susan Glaspell's Mature Novels."
Disclosing Intertextualities: The Stories, Plays, and Novels of Susan Glaspell. Eds. Martha C.
Carpentier and Barbara Ozieblo. Amsterdam and New York: Rodopi. 137–157.

_____ 2006b. "Susan Glaspell and the Modernist Experiment of *Chains of Dew*." *Susan
Glaspell: New Directions in Critical Inquiry*. Ed. Martha C. Carpentier. Cambridge: Cambridge Scholars Press. 7–24.

Ozieblo, Barbara, and Jerry Dickey. 2008. *Susan Glaspell and Sophie Treadwell*. Routledge
Modern and Contemporary Dramatists. London: Routledge.

Papke, Mary E. 1993. *Susan Glaspell: A Research and Production Sourcebook*. Modern
Dramatists Research and Production Sourcebooks 4. Westport, CT: Greenwood Press.

_____ 2006. "Susan Glaspell's Naturalist Scenarios of Determinism and Blind Faith."
Disclosing Intertextualities: The Stories, Plays, and Novels of Susan Glaspell. Eds. Martha C.
Carpentier and Barbara Ozieblo. Amsterdam and New York: Rodopi. 19–34.

Pfefferkorn, Kristin. 1991. "Searching for Home in O'Neill's America." *Eugene O'Neill's
Century. Centennial Views on America's Foremost Tragic Dramatist*. Ed. Richard F. Mortoon.
London: Greenwood Press. 119–143.

Rathburn, Stephen. 1921. "'It's up to You' Will Have Postponed Opening on Next Monday
Evening. Miss Anglen's Production of 'Joan of Arc' Will Be Seen To-morrow. The Province-
town Players Present Susan Glaspell's 'Inheritors.'" np. Newspaper clipping, Susan Glaspell
Papers, Berg Collection, New York Public Library.

Reagon, Beverly Johnson. 1983. "Coalition Politics: Turning the Century." *Home Girls: A
Black Feminist Anthology*. Ed. Barbara Smith. New York: Kitchen Table, Women of Color
Press. 356–368.

Revill, George. 1993. "Reading *Rosehill*. Community, Identity and Inner-city Derby." *Place
and the Politics of Identity*. Eds. Michael Keith and Steve Pile. London and New York:
Routledge. 117–140.

Rich, Adrienne. 1986. "Notes Towards a Politics of Location" (1984). *Blood, Bread, and Poetry:
Selected Prose 1979–1985*. New York: Norton. 210–231.

Riley, Glenda. 1981. *Frontierswomen: The Iowa Experience*. Ames: University of Iowa Press.

Rohe, Alice. 1921. "The Story of Susan Glaspell." *New York Morning Telegraph*, December
18: 18.

Rose, Gillian. 1993. *Feminism and Geography: The Limits of Geographical Knowledge*. Cambridge: Polity Press.

Royde-Smith, N. G. 1926. "The Drama. The American Play. 'Inheritors.'" *The Outlook*.
January 9: 25.

Rudnick, Lois. 1991. "The New Woman." *1915. The Cultural Moment: The New Politics, the
New Woman, the New Psychology, the New Art, and the New Theater in America*. Eds. Adele
Heller and Lois Rudnick. New Brunswick, NJ: Rutgers University Press. 69–
81.

Russell, Judith K. 1997. "Glaspell's *Trifles*." *Explicator* 55.2: 88–90.

Sander, Lucia V. (ed.) 2002. *O Teatro de Susan Glaspell: Cinco peças*. Trans. Lucia V. Sander.
Brazil: United States Embassy in Brazil.

Sarlós, Robert Károly. 1982. *Jig Cook and the Provincetown Players: Theatre in Ferment*.
Amherst: University of Massachusetts Press.

_____ 1991. "Jig Cook and Susan Glaspell. Rule Makers and Rule Breakers." *1915. The Cultural
Moment: The New Politics, the New Woman, the New Psychology, the New Art, and the New
Theater in America*. Eds. Adele Heller and Lois Rudnick. New Brunswick, NJ: Rutgers
University Press. 250–259.

Shafer, Yvonne. 1988. "Susan Glaspell: German Influence, American Playwright." *A Quarterly of Language, Literature and Culture (Zeitschrift für Anglistik und Amerikanistik)* 36.4: 333–338.

Schroeder, Patricia. 1989. *The Presence of the Past in Modern American Drama.* Rutherford, NJ: Farleigh Dickinson University Press.

_____ 1996. *The Feminist Possibilities of Dramatic Realism.* Madison, NJ: Farleigh Dickinson University Press, London Associated University Press.

Schwank, Klaus. 1989. "Die dramatischen Experimente Susan Glaspells: *The Outside* und *The Verge.*" *Amerikastudien/American Studies* 34.4: 413–421.

Schwarz, Judith. 1986 (1982). *Radical Feminists of Heterodoxy: Greenwich Village, 1912–1940.* Revised edition. Lebanon, NH: New Victoria Publishers.

Shafer, Yvonne. 1997 (1995). *American Women Playwrights. 1900–1950.* Bruxelles, Bern, Berlin, Frankfurt, New York, Oxford, Wien: Peter Lang.

Showalter, Elaine. 1977. *A Literature of Their Own. British Women Novelists from Brontë to Lessing.* Princeton, New Jersey: Princeton University Press.

_____ 1991. *Sister's Choice: Tradition and Change in American Women's Writing.* Oxford and New York: Oxford University Press.

Sichert, Margit. 1997. "Claire Archer: A 'Nietzscheana' in Susan Glaspell's *The Verge.*" *The Yearbook of Research in English and American Literature* 13: 271–297.

Sievers, David W. 1955. *Freud on Broadway: A History of Psychoanalysis and the American Drama.* New York: Hermitage House.

Smith, Beverly A. 1982. "Women's Work — *Trifles*? The Skill and Insights of Playwright Susan Glaspell." *International Journal of Women's Studies* 5.29: 172–184.

Smith, Beverly Bronson. 2003. "They Knew What They Wanted: American Theatre's Use of Nonverbal Communication Codes to Marginalize Non-Native Characters in the 1920s." *Experimenters, Rebels, and Disparate Voices: The Theatre of the 1920s Celebrates American Diversity.* Eds. Arthur Gewirtz and James J. Kolb. Westport, CT, and London: Praeger. 131–138.

Sochen, June. 1972. *The New Woman: Feminism in Greenwich Village 1910–1920.* New York: Quadrangle.

Soja, Edward. 1980. "The Socio-spatial Dialectics." *Association of American Geographers Annals* 70.2: 207–225.

Soja, Edward, and Barbara Hooper. 1993. "The Spaces that Difference Makes. Some Notes on the Geographical Margins of the New Cultural Politics." *Place and the Politics of Identity.* Eds. Michael Keith and Steve Pile. London and New York: Routledge. 183–205.

Solow, Eugene. 1930. "America's Great Woman Dramatist: Susan Glaspell. A Few Words About Her and Her Plays." *The World.* February 9: np.

Spain, Daphne. 1992. *Gendered Spaces.* Chapel Hill: University of North Carolina Press.

Stansell, Christine. 2000. *American Moderns: Bohemian New York and the Creation of a New Century.* New York: Henry Holt and Company.

States, Bert O. 1985. *Great Reckonings in Little Rooms: An Essay on the Phenomenology of Theater.* Berkeley and Los Angeles: University of California Press.

Stein, Karen F. 1987. "The Women's World of Glaspell's *Trifles.*" *Women in American Theatre.* Eds. Helen Krich Chinoy and Linda Walsh Jenkins. New York: Theatre Communications Group. 253–256.

Stephens, Judith L. 1990. "Gender Ideology and Dramatic Convention in Progressive Era Plays, 1890–1920." *Performing Feminisms: Feminist Critical Theory and Theatre.* Ed. Sue-Ellen Case. Baltimore and London: John Hopkins University Pres. 283–293.

Stretch, Cynthia. 2006. "Socialist Housekeeping: *The Visioning*, Sisterhood, and Cross-Class Alliance." *Disclosing Intertextualities: The Stories, Plays, and Novels of Susan Glaspell.* Eds. Martha C. Carpentier and Barbara Ozieblo. Amsterdam and New York: Rodopi. 223–238.

Stufft, Monica. 2006. "Flowers by Design: Susan Glaspell's Re-vision of Strindberg's *A Dream Play.*" *Disclosing Intertextualities: The Stories, Plays, and Novels of Susan Glaspell.* Eds. Martha C. Carpentier and Barbara Ozieblo. Amsterdam and New York: Rodopi. 79–91.

"Susan Glaspell's 'Chains of Dew' Is Sharp Satire. Provincetown Players' Production Attacks Bobbed Hair and Birth Control." *New York Herald*, 28 April 1922: 10.

Sutherland, Cynthia. 1978. "American Women Playwrights as Mediators of the 'Woman Problem." *Modern Drama* 21.3: 319–336.

"Tchehov and Susan Glaspell. A Comparison of the Work of Two Dramatists of the Soil, Both Now Represented at the Civic Repertory Theatre." *New York Evening Post*, 16 November 1929: np.

Tompkins, Joanne. 2003. "Space and the Geographies of Theatre: Introduction." *Modern Drama* 46. 4. Special Issue "Space and the Geographies of the Theatre." Ed. Joanne Tompkins: 537–541.

Ubersfeld, Anne. 1999. *Reading Theatre*. Trans. Frank Collins. Toronto: University of Toronto Press. (1977. *Lire le théâtre*. Paris: Éditions Sociales.)

_____ 1981. *L'école du spectateur. Lire le théâtre II*. Paris: Éditions Sociales.

Valgemae, Mardi. 1972. *Accelerated Grimace: Expressionism in the American Drama of the 1920s*. Carbondale: Southern University Press.

_____ 1973. "Expressionism in the American Theater." *Expressionism as an International Literary Phenomenon*. Ed. Ulrich Weisstein. Paris: Didier, and Budapest: Akadémiai Kiadó. 193–203.

Velázquez Valoria, Isabel. 1995. "Alojarse, vivir, construir desde los dos géneros." *El espacio según el género. ¿Un uso diferencial?* Eds. Constanza Tobío and Concha Denche. Madrid: Dirección General de la Mujer. 119–129.

Villegas-López, Sonia, and Beatriz Domínguez-García. 2004. "Foreword." *Literature, Gender, Space*. Eds. Sonia Villegas-López and Beatriz Domínguez-García. Huelva, Spain: Servicio de Publicaciones de la Universidad de Huelva. 11–13.

Vorse, Mary Heaton. 1991. *Time and the Town. A Provincetown Chronicle* (1942). Ed. Adele Heller. New Brunswick, NJ: Rutgers University Press.

Wainscott, Ronald H. 1997. *The Emergence of Modern American Theater, 1914 -1929*. New Haven and London: Yale University Press.

Waterman, Arthur. 1966. *Susan Glaspell*. Twayne's United States Authors Series 101. Ed. Sylvia E. Bowman. New York: Twayne Publishers.

_____ 1979. "Susan Glaspell's *The Verge*: An Experiment in Feminism." *Great Lakes Review* 6.1: 17–23.

Watson, Steven 1991. *Strange Bedfellows: The First American Avant-Garde*. New York: Abbeville Press.

Weisstein, Ulrich, ed. 1973. *Expressionism as an International Literary Phenomenon*. Paris: Didier, and Budapest: Akadémiai Kiadó.

Wheeler, Kenneth W., and Virginia Lee Lussier, eds. 1982. *Women, the Arts, and the 1920s in Paris and New York*. New Brunswick, NJ, and London: Transaction Books.

Wilcox, Dean. 2003. "Ambient Space in the Twentieth-century Theatre: The Space of Silence." *Modern Drama* 46.4. Special Issue "Space and the Geographies of the Theatre." Ed. Joanne Tompkins: 542–557.

Wilmer, S. E. 2002. *Theatre, Society and the Nation: Staging American Identities*. Cambridge: Cambridge University Press.

Wilmeth, Don B., and Christopher Bigsby, eds. 1999. *The Cambridge History of American Theatre*. Cambridge: Cambridge University Press. 289–341.

Wolff, Jane. 1990. *Feminine Sentences: Essays on Women and Culture*. Berkeley: University of California Press.

Wolff, Tamsen. 2003. "Eugenics and the Experimental Breeding Ground of Susan Glaspell's *The Verge*." *Evolution and Eugenics in American Literature and Culture, 1880–1940: Essays on Ideological Conflict and Complicity*. Eds. Lois A. Cuddy and Claire M. Roche. Lewisburg, PA: Bucknell University Press. 203–219.

Wood, Sharon E. 1998. "Susan Glaspell and the Politics of Sexuality." *Red Badges of Courage:*

Wars and Conflicts in American Culture. Rivista di Studi Anglo-Americani 9.11. Eds. Biancamaria Pisapia, Ugo Rubeo and Anna Scacchi. Roma: Bulzoni. 315–320.

Woolf, Virginia. 2000. *A Room of One's Own.* In *A Room of One's Own. Three Guineas* (1929). London: Penguin Books. 1–112.

Worthen, W. B. 1992. "Invisible Women: Problem Drama, 1890–1920." *Modern Drama and the Rhetoric of Theater.* Berkeley: University of California Press. 29–53.

Wright, Stobbs Janet. 2002. "Law, Justice, and Female Revenge in 'Kerfol,' by Edith Wharton, and *Trifles* and 'A Jury of Her Peers,' by Susan Glaspell." *Atlantis* 24.1: 225–244.

Index

Numbers in **bold italics** indicate pages with photographs

Judd Rankin's Daughter 125
"A Jury of Her Peers" 60, 136, 181*c*2*n*3, 182*n*4, 183*c*6*n*4

Kenton, Edna 3, 5, 6, 7, 8, 25, 184*n*1
King, Pendleton 18
Kolodny, Annette 2, 180*c*2*n*1

Lefèbvre, Henri 11, 12, 13, 21, 85, 156
Liberal Club 3, 48, 49, 122, 157
Lincoln, Abraham 54, 56, 95

MacDougal Street 7–8
Maeterlinck, Maurice 1
Makowsky, Veronica 2, 153, 162
male gaze 26–27
"The Manager of Crystal Sulphur Springs" 176
The Masses 64, 181*c*3*n*2
Massey, Doreen 12, 13, 22, 25, 28, 32, 91
materialist feminism 25, 180 n.3
Matson, Norman 10, 29; *see also The Comic Artist*
McAuley, Gay 14, 15; and taxonomy of spatial functions in theater 15–17
Metropolitan Playhouse (NYC) 2; *see also Inheritors*
Midwest in Glaspell's plays 34, 44, 45, 70, 120, 128, 160, 177
Millay, Edna St. Vincent 6
Miller, Arthur 29, 31
Mulvey, Laura 26
Murphy, Brenda 5, 18, 184*n*7

native drama *see* Provincetown Players, native drama
New England in Glaspell's plays 61–62, 93, 98
New Stagecraft 5
New Woman 39, 106; fall of 107–108; Glaspell's definition of 106; kinds of 107; vs. True Woman in Glaspell's works 106–107; *see also separate entries for individual works*
New York in Glaspell's plays 34, 35, 38, 39, 44–45, 46–47, 61, 67, 99–100, 103, 111, 129, 157, 161
New York Herald 123
Nineteenth Amendment 106, 107
Noe, Marcia 2; and Glaspell's use of space 9, 60, 179*n*10, 182*n*7
Norma Ashe 33
Norman, Marsha 177

O'Neill, Eugene 1; *Bound East for Cardiff* 6; *The Emperor Jones* 6, 8; *The Hairy Ape* 5; *Long Day's Journey into Night* 29
Orange Tree Theatre (Richmond, London) 2, 178; *see also Alison's House; Chains of Dew; The Outside; Suppressed Desires; Trifles*

"Out There" 176
The Outside 9, 10; American Myth of Mobility 39–40; body language 74, 116, 169; departure though nature 168–170; home as grave 115–117; home as shelter 73–75; invasion 74; isolation 61, 62; Orange Tree Theatre *116*; and women's coalition 169
Ozieblo, Barbara 2

Papke, Mary 75, 87, 171
Parks, Suzan-Lori 177
Paterson Strike Pageant 5–6
patriarchy 21, 98, 112, 151–152, 160, 162, 163, 171
The People 10, 166–167
Performance Lab 115 (NYC) 2; *see also The Verge*
performance space 16
Pinter, Harold 28
place: definitions of 12; and identity of the past 91–92; and ideology 12–13; and power 13; and social relations 12–13; in theater and drama 13–17
power geometry 32, 151–152
powerlessness 153
presentational space 16
Provincetown, MA, in Glaspell's plays 10, 39, 40, 61
Provincetown Players 1, 3, 4, 176–177; and birth control 122; decline of 8–9; dome 8–9; and dramatic forms 6; female participation 8; founding of 5; and native drama 3; and their theaters 6–8
Pulitzer Prize 179*n*1

Rauh, Ida 108, 181*n*4, 184*n*10
Realism 23–24; and feminist criticism 25–27
Red Scare 58
The Road to the Temple 4, 7, 29, 30, 33, 56, 94
Rodman, Henrietta 108
Rohe, Alice 1, 3, 25, 33

Sanger, Margaret 122
Sarlós, Robert Károly 19, 179*n*8
scenic place 14
Schechner, Richard 17
Second World War *see* World War II
Sedition Act 65, 129
Shaw, George Bernard 1
Shepard, Sam 29, 30, 31, 119
Sistine Madonna 99, 119, 123–124, 158, 161
Smith, Rita Creighton 6
Soja, Edward 12, 22
space: and chorologists 12; definitions of 11–12; and ideology 12–13; and Newtonians 11–12; and power 13; and social relations